Female Child Soldiering, Gender Violence, and Feminist Theologies

"This courageous and interdisciplinary book disturbs and provokes the readers by putting the plight of female child soldiers at the center of theological, ethical, and pastoral inquires. The atrocities inflicted on girls because of war, violence, rape, poverty, and global racism are discussed with cultural sensitivity and astute moral insights. This book issues a clarion call for action, commitment, and solidarity. I highly recommend it."

—Kwok Pui-lan, *author of* Postcolonial Imagination and Feminist Theology *(2005)*

"This unusual volume helps us understand the way that child soldiers who are girls and young women are exploited in war, on one hand, and resist and exercise agency through their soldiering, on the other. These well-written essays will leave the reader both sobered and surprised—and with much to ponder! I commend this book to anyone concerned about the role of children in violence and peace."

—Pamela D. Couture, *Jane and Geoffrey Martin Chair in Church and Community, Emmanuel College of Victoria University in the University of Toronto*

"An excellent showcase of transnational feminist collaborative scholarship! Through multilayered, multidisciplinary and multi-context-based analyses of female child soldiering, the book educates readers on the complexity of the issue which requires transnational feminist interrogation and hidden militarization policies of the US, a critical blind spot in many North American feminist theologies. The book advances current feminist theories of power and resistance to an embodied ethical and moral engagement of solidarity."

—Boyung Lee, *Professor of Practical Theology, Iliff School of Theology, USA*

"This collection of essays is a timely and urgent wakeup call. It draws attention to a neglected moral outrage and scandal of our times: the militarization and even weaponization of children. The essays call all of us to identify and address root causes, such as hegemonic toxic sexualities. They are also a call to action for soul searching to discern and acknowledge how we may be complicit in our denial, hypocrisy and misplaced justification of the violence through our actions of omission and of commission. They summon us to pull the enduring scandal of violence against women from the margins to the center of our ethical discernment and action. The book is a must read for all who care about children's rights, the duty to protect those rights and the duty to ensure an environment where children, both male and female, can flourish with dignity."

—Teresia Hinga, *Associate Professor of Religious Studies/African Christianity, Santa Clara University and founding member of the Circle of Concerned African Women Theologians*

"This book challenges the reader to not only listen to the horrors of what being a child soldier entails, but it also opens one's eyes to the resistance and resilience inbuilt in each story. Furthermore, the authors challenge the reader to be part of a strong definitive voice that elevates these girls'/women's resistance, healing and their peace-building approaches to take a stand in contributing to the process of unpacking moral, religious and political commitments which help to dismantle the ongoing recruitment and deployment of child soldiers. For persons committed to ensuring that all live life in abundance with gender justice and peace without sexual, gender-based violence, this book is a must read."

—Fulata Lusungu Moyo, *World Council of Churches*

Susan Willhauck
Editor

Female Child Soldiering, Gender Violence, and Feminist Theologies

palgrave
macmillan

Editor
Susan Willhauck
Atlantic School of Theology
Halifax, NS, Canada

ISBN 978-3-030-21981-9   ISBN 978-3-030-21982-6   (eBook)
https://doi.org/10.1007/978-3-030-21982-6

Cover illustration: Junichi Ota / EyeEm, Getty Images

This Palgrave Macmillan imprint is published by the registered company Springer Nature Switzerland AG.
The registered company address is: Gewerbestrasse 11, 6330 Cham, Switzerland

ACKNOWLEDGMENTS

This book would not exist without the encouragement and support of friends, family, colleagues, and editors. Many thanks to Amy Invernizzi at Palgrave Macmillan for recognizing its worth and for her guidance throughout the project. I have valued her wisdom, expertise, and graciousness. I am grateful to the Women and Religion Unit of the American Academy of Religion for first giving space to this topic and generating critical review. With all my heart and soul, I thank the contributors to this volume for stepping up to the challenge to write on this topic, and for their bold and provocative ideas. My hope is that these chapters will expand knowledge, discussion, and action toward restoring the lives and well-being of children everywhere and further the resistance and resilience of girls and women in the wake of violence.

I deeply appreciate the administration, faculty, and students of the Atlantic School of Theology (AST), where I teach. I have great respect for my colleagues there—quintessential dialogue partners and superb scholars. Thank you to the administration for supporting and promoting faculty scholarship. Robert Martel and Brad Murray in the AST library were an enormous help. I also wish to acknowledge the Pine Hill Foundation at AST (and Brenda Munro) for providing me with the Leni Groeneveld Research Grant. And a special thank you to Cynthia O'Connell, my research assistant at AST, candidate for ministry in the United Church of Canada and "citation machine," for her intensive labor and dedication to this project.

I have felt the weight of this material as those who read it likely will as well. Until that time when violence is heard in the land no more, may we lay our trust in the bosom of God.

Susan Willhauck

CONTENTS

NOTES ON CONTRIBUTORS

Débora B. A. Junker, PhD, is Assistant Professor of Christian Education at Garrett-Evangelical Theological Seminary in Evanston, IL, where she directs the Hispanic-Latinx Center. She is the founder and director of the *Cátedra* Paulo Freire and the author of several books in Portuguese and the forthcoming *Religious Education for Global Citizenship: Embracing Compassion and Solidarity*.

Georgette I. Mulunda Ledgister, PhD, is a scholar of social ethics, whose research interests focus on the intersection of religion, conflict, and gender. Ledgister is the executive director of Fearless Dialogues, a non-profit organization based in Atlanta, Georgia, and is a visiting instructor at Agnes Scott College.

Marjorie Lewis, PhD, was the first woman to be appointed President of the United Theological College of the West Indies. She is a minister of the United Church in Jamaica and the Cayman Islands and a member of the Caribbean Women Theologians for Transformation.

Mazvita Machinga, PhD, is a psychotherapist with Pastoral Care and Counselling Services, Mutare, Zimbabwe, and dean of student affairs at Africa University.

Dianne McIntosh, M.Phil, is Permanent Secretary of the Ministry of National Security, Kingston, Jamaica. Her work experiences have evolved around areas such as human security, sociology, project management, and public administration within international, public, and private organizations.

Beverly Eileen Mitchell, PhD, is Professor of Historical Theology, Wesley Theological Seminary, Washington, DC. She is the author of *Plantations and Death Camps: Religion, Ideology and Human Dignity* (2009).

Mary Nyangweso, PhD, is the J. Woolard and Helen Peel distinguished professor in Religious Studies at East Carolina University (Greenville, North Carolina). She has written extensively on matters related to domestic violence, female genital cutting, and HIV/AIDS. She is author of two books: *Female Genital Cutting: Mutilation or Cultural Right?* (2014) and *Female Circumcision: The Interplay between Religion, Gender and Culture in Kenya* (2007).

Keun-Joo Christine Pae, PhD, is Associate Professor of Religious Studies at Denison University in Ohio. As a Christian feminist ethicist, her academic interests include feminist peacemaking and interfaith spiritual activism, transnationalized militarism with a focus on the intersection between gender and race, transnational feminist ethics, and Asian/Asian-American perspectives on post-colonial racial relations.

Evelyn L. Parker, PhD, is Associate Dean for Academic Affairs and the Susanna Wesley Centennial Professor of Practical Theology, Perkins School of Theology, Southern Methodist University, Dallas, TX. She edited the volume *The Sacred Selves of Adolescent Girls: Hard Stories of Race, Class, and Gender* (2010).

Anna Kasafi Perkins, PhD, is a Roman Catholic ethicist moonlighting as a quality assurance professional at the University of the West Indies, Regional Headquarters, Jamaica. A former dean of studies/lecturer at St Michael's Theological College and graduate of Cambridge University and Boston College, she has an eclectic set of research interests centering around Christianity, ethics, and popular culture in the Jamaican/Caribbean context with a particular focus on Dancehall.

Traci C. West, PhD, is Professor of Christian Ethics and African American Studies, Drew University Theological School, Madison, NJ. She is the author of *Solidarity and Defiant Spirituality: Africana Lessons on Racism, Religion, and Ending Gender Violence* (2019), *Disruptive Christian Ethics: When Racism and Women's Lives Matter* (2006) and *Wounds of the Spirit: Black Women, Violence, and Resistance Ethics* (1999).

Shelly Whitman, PhD, is Executive Director of The Roméo Dallaire Child Soldiers Initiative and Professor of International Studies, Dalhousie

University, Halifax, Nova Scotia. She leads an international team based in Canada, Somalia, and South Sudan. She helped to write two UN Security Council Resolutions: UNSC RES 2143 on *Children and Armed Conflict* and 2151 on *International Peace and Security and Security Sector Reform.*

Susan Willhauck, PhD, is Associate Professor of Pastoral Theology at Atlantic School of Theology in Halifax, Nova Scotia. She is the co-author of *Qualitative Research in Theological Education: Pedagogy in Practice* (2018) and the author of *Back Talk: Women Leaders Changing the Church* (2005).

CHAPTER 1

Violence, Power, Resistance and Resilience: An Introduction

Susan Willhauck

A student of mine from Sierra Leone told me that she spent most of her teenage years living in daily terror, as two of her close relatives had been snatched (or "taken up" in her words) by roving militia and never returned. In our class on feminist theology, she voiced frustration at the lack of responsiveness on the part of feminists, theologians and people of faith. She pleaded for feminists to stand with girls and women everywhere against this violence and abuse. The student returned to humanitarian work in Sierra Leone and we corresponded until her death from cancer last year. As a long-time child advocate and practical theologian, I felt compelled to bring together scholar activists to examine and speak out on this moral issue through the lens of feminist theology. While I acknowledge my own inadequacy to interpret this complex issue and my social position of privilege, at the same time I seek to learn more in order to not leave to others to do what I can do. For me, it is more than an academic exercise to gather strong definitive voices to elevate women's resistance, healing and peace-building. I have learned that we need to really listen to the first-

S. Willhauck (✉)
Atlantic School of Theology, Halifax, NS, Canada
e-mail: swillhauck@astheology.ns.ca

© The Author(s) 2019

S. Willhauck (ed.), *Female Child Soldiering, Gender Violence, and Feminist Theologies*, https://doi.org/10.1007/978-3-030-21982-6_1

1

person accounts and critical discourse contained in these pages. At a time when the US political leadership engages in belligerent and divisive denigration of certain countries and of heightened awareness of sexual exploitation, and when women who disclose it are publicly ridiculed, we are overdue for critical examination of ideologies, policies and practices that lead to gender violence, genocide and the forced militarization of girls and women. Girls' experiences of war have accounted for "the smallest percentage of scholarly and popular work on social and political violence" (Nordstrom 1997, 5). This volume is an interdisciplinary work that brings together feminist voices, including Latina, Korean, Womanist, Caribbean and Africana perspectives, to help rectify the void. I looked to the resources of the Circle of Concerned African Women Theologians and the Caribbean Women Theologians for Transformation as well as other Womanist and feminist scholars to engage their various disciplines of ethics, education, sociology and pastoral care.

There are approximately 300,000 child soldiers worldwide and about 40 percent of them are female.[1] Many armed groups and some government forces operating in regions of conflict have actively sought out underage female recruits. Girls are often subjected to sexual slavery, receive weapons training and are deployed in combat. The phenomenon of child soldiers has been discussed in an expanding body of literature and popular media and non-profit organizations have been mobilized to respond to the crisis.[2] Child soldiering is not a new phenomenon. Consider the *Hitlerjugend* of World War II, and in Chap. 4 of this book, Traci C. West discusses the use of children in the Civil Rights movement, but of late, the number of child combatants has risen dramatically. Children in armed conflict is a complex issue and several studies have examined the root causes and explanations.[3] Myriam Denov, in *Girls in Fighting Forces: Moving Beyond Victimhood* (2007), notes how in certain war-torn regions

---

[1] According to the United Nations and the Council of Foreign Relations. It is impossible to pinpoint exact numbers due to underreporting. https://childrenandarmedconflict.un.org/effects-of-conflict/six-grave-violations/child-soldiers/.

[2] Such as Global Network of Religions for Children; Roméo Dallaire Child Soldiers Initiative https://www.childsoldiers.org/ and Isis: Women's International Cross Cultural Exchange http://isis.or.ug/. See the Appendix for a list.

[3] Such as Shepler, Susan. 2004. *The Social and Cultural Context of Child Soldiering in Sierra Leone*. Oslo: PRIO; Wessells, Michael. 2006. *Child Soldiers: From Violence to Protection*. Cambridge, MA: Harvard University Press; Denov, Myriam. 2007. *Girls in Fighting Forces: Moving Beyond Victimhood*. Canadian International Development Agency, 2007.

of Africa, girls are particularly valued because "they are perceived as highly obedient and easily manipulated, they can swell the ranks if there is a shortage of adults, and ensure a constant pool of forced and compliant labor" (2007, 4). Mostly, girls enter into armed groups after being forcibly abducted and torn apart from their families. However, some girls have been known to voluntarily join militias, sometimes motivated by ideology. In other circumstances, girls hope armed groups will provide protection from poverty, sexual abuse, forced marriages, and state- or rebel-inflicted violence.

Violence has itself been a means of resistance at times, and that girls and women would heed its call as a means of survival or to better their circumstances is no surprise. One would not want to downplay the historic role of women in struggles for liberation. I would not want to suggest that girls and women are less violent or ought to be than men because of their nature—a growing phenomenon of "girls with guns" does not bear out that notion. Some feminists themselves have applauded images of the strong female warrior that permeates culture (including children's programming). Of course, boys are also forced into combat and abused. Girls and women, however, face unique challenges, according to scholars Emeline Ndossi (2010, 133) and Therese Tinkasiimire (2010, 165, 167) as well as Beverly Mitchell and Mary Nyangweso in this volume, because of the inferior status projected onto them by culture, their vulnerability and increased stigmatization in their communities. Because females are abducted, sexually violated and forced into combat in an extreme form of oppression with a particular sense of urgency, this work explores what feminist theology could provide that would witness against such atrocity. While child soldiering takes place in many countries across the globe, I have found African feminist theologies to be a hopeful resource. Many African feminist theologians, however, articulate western Christianity as one of the sources of their oppression. Essays in this volume provide important critique of some assumptions of liberal Christian feminism. To bring ideas born of white western privilege to bear on child soldiering, as in "I know what is good for you," smacks of colonialism. I have had to examine and re-think my own assumptions during this project. In the diversity of African cultures, African Christian feminists localize their concerns to inculcate their experiences into doing theology (Kasomo and Maseno 2011). Yet African feminists in my experience welcome alliance with others seeking similar reformation. We need to ask what can white women and women of color say and do to address the problem, as several of the contributors here attest that race is at the heart of the matter. I am cognizant of the glaring racism of the "white savior" trope, yet identity politics around who is allowed to speak about what only serve to divide us further. This book represents the reflections of a diverse group of feminist theologians and researchers in search of understanding the complexities of sexual violence in conflict and the militarization of girls and women. It confronts privileged detachment and the "danger of a single story" (Adichie 2009). To begin the conversation, I will present here some ways that feminist theory and epistemology have conceived power and the role of power in resisting sexual violence, and elaborate on how the authors in this volume take on specific aspects of the issue to point out what could provide a way forward in understanding and dismantling another form of gender injustice.

Christian Feminist Theory and Power

Serene Jones has written that feminist theory has the goal of the liberation of women (2000, 3). One could expect that includes the liberation of female child soldiers. In her groundbreaking work, *Wounds of the Spirit: Black Women, Violence, and Resistance Ethics*, Christian ethicist Traci C. West asserts that "at the core of Christian tradition is a call to morally engage this world by demonstrating opposition to social injustice and human suffering" (1999, 1). Jones claims that feminist theory offers an opportunity to consciously analyze oppression and the possibility of imagining and training for a different future. It allows the opportunity to deconstruct understandings of power and unjust power relations that give rise to oppression (2000, 5). Christian feminist theology, Womanist and Latina theology bring feminist theory to bear on many theological concepts, moral questions and practices.

Despite these claims, Christian feminist scholarship has been curiously muted on the issue of female child soldiering, being occupied with gender study, equality, critique of patriarchy, ordination rights and so on, issues that could be perceived as residing in white privilege (work that I myself have done). Also, awareness of Christianity's flawed history of colonialism causes feminists to tread lightly at best or render us paralyzed at worst. We may tend to suspend thinking about it because we perceive it to be distanced from our concerns and we are reluctant to get into somebody else's business. Yet the suffering of girls and women in this way affects all Christians and calls for resistance. I suggest that feminist resistance theory with its analysis and reconstruction of unjust power relations offers a basis for such moral engagement and preventative actions.

Amy Allen in *The Power of Feminist Theory* writes that it is the work of feminists to critique, challenge, subvert and aim to overthrow the "multiple axes of stratification affecting women in contemporary western societies" (1999, 1–2). But what about non-western societies? As feminist theory impacts Christian theology, feminist theology and praxis have always gone together. It is not enough for feminist theologians to talk about changing the world; they are usually directly involved in attempts to change it. Feminist theologians work in many different arenas of advocacy, some directly focused on gender and some emphasizing other issues with a feminist critique. The authors in this volume consider how the power of feminist theology unleashes in women the audacity to resist the violence.

Allen offers a critique of some understandings of power that I think is helpful to this work. She rejects understanding power as a resource because it assumes that it is something that can be possessed, distributed and re-distributed, and if we just re-distribute power in certain places, all will be well. It seems to assume a power-over relationship—that someone always has power over another (master/slave) and must give/share that power that the other would not have (1999, 3, 11, 18). Power viewed as a relation of domination and subordination assumes that power must be dismantled. Gender difference is described as men have power and women do not. The goal of feminists in this view would be to eliminate male domination and binary conceptions of gender. This understanding of power does not take into account other differences of class, economics, race or culture. Another conception of power as empowerment contends that there are feminine traits or qualities or practices that have been de-valued in misogynist cultures, but that allow the ability to empower and transform systems of domination. Yet empowerment theory can reinforce old stereotypes of women. But if you reject the category of women altogether, you lose the basis on which to have any common experience or cause (104). According to Serene Jones, differences among women make it difficult (some believe impossible) to speak of ourselves as any identifiable group, and while we should not generalize across racial and ethnic boundaries, feminists generally do claim some kind of unity among women (2000, 7). To deal with this conundrum, Amy Allen re-posits Foucault's analysis of power to argue that resistance is an act of power. While resistance can take the form of exercising power over others, it does not have to. We are all both subjects which are dominated and self-determining agents who can resist. One's location and culture surely may influence the balance or imbalance of these. Rather than insisting that power is a strategic means of controlling others, she affirms the power generated through collective social action and solidarity (1999, 53, 55–56). For Allen resistance and empowerment cannot be understood best as instances of "power over." Though resistance and empowerment can use power in this way, it is not best understood as domination but as a "power to"—the ability of individuals to attain an end. Subordinated groups retain the power to act despite their subordination (125–126). Yet it is important to note that she respects Judith Butler's critique of the sisterhood model of solidarity ("power with") which does not take into consideration different experiences among women of color and for assuming a common oppression of all women (103–105). But Allen argues for solidarity, not as thinking alike, but as a power itself that emerges out of concerted action that binds members of feminist movements together and links them to social struggles against domination, racism and heterosexism. It is not a sister feeling, and group cohesiveness does not need to rest on a shared identity. In the wake of charges that mainstream feminists have marginalized women of color, lesbians and working-class women, feminists must be able to think about the kind of power that a diverse group of women can exercise collectively to define and strive to achieve feminist aims—a collective power that can form alliances to bridge the diversity of individuals to challenge, subvert and ultimately overturn systems of domination (126–127). That goal informs this book as I did not attempt consensus but rather fostered divergent thinking.

Violence and Resistance

The abduction of girls and young women in order to co-opt them into rebel forces and to use them for sexual favors is a horrific oppression and part of a systemic and far-reaching reality of violence against women. Violence against girls and women is a problem that society has helped create and sustain. As Serene Jones has written, cultural and institutionalized beliefs and practices globally have created a climate where such violence is tolerated or assumed to be unpreventable. These acts are not just the criminal acts of disturbed men (2000, 89–90). It is legitimated military activity. Anna T. Höglund has claimed that rape is not the result of single or small groups of soldiers who have "lost control," but is a systematic weapon of war (2003, 347). African feminist Eve Ayiera has exposed the lack of legal accountability for sexual violence in conflict. She argued that the helplessness to stop sexual violence is due to the way the problem is conceptualized. The awareness and dialogue raised by the United Nations and non-governmental organizations on sexual violence in combat should have mitigated the high incidence of the criminal activity. The reality is bleaker, as it has become more complex and seemingly intractable. Applying legal and policy measures to deter it has not worked. The problem, she writes, is the normalization of violence against women in general. It is simply accepted, particularly as an inherent part of war and armed conflict. The binary construction of gender affirms a patriarchal social order and assumes male power over women. Yet assuming that violence against women only takes place in war fails to recognize the normativity of sexual violence in domestic and peaceful environments. Yet militarism and its pervasiveness are significant obstacles to democratization and gender justice (2010, 8, 12). Phraseology that perhaps seeks to call attention to the problem, like "the worst humanitarian crisis in the world" inadvertently may glorify the violence. Reasoned scholarship such as is found in this volume is needed to dispel the hype and hysteria to move beyond the "ain't it awful" approach. Without addressing the systems, political, social and cultural through which sexual violence is feminized and "disseminated as an inevitable part of social relations" even the peak concentration of efforts will not succeed in stemming the problem (14). Nozizwe Madlala-Routledge says, "[W]e need an international campaign to resist androcentric, militarized neo-colonial masculinities" (2008, 85).

Beverly Mitchell begins the dialogue herein to examine human dignity as a theological construct and its violation through child soldiering and addresses the challenges of reintegration specific to female child soldiers. Anytime children are caught up in war violence it confronts our failures in sustaining human rights and dignity and religious claims about children, childhood and theological anthropology. Some of us have images of the killing of children in Vietnam etched in our memory. Mitchell calls us to live up to our theological claims. Shelly Whitman, the Executive Director of the Roméo Dallaire Child Soldiers Initiative, contributes with a wide-angle view of sexual violence during and after conflicts toward understanding the experience of child soldiers and relates long-term implications of child soldering observed through her work in South Sudan.

Theological underpinnings of resistance run deep from the experience of the exile to the message of Jesus. In order to resist, we must ask what brokenness creates conditions which turns one to violence. Christian theology may use the language of sin in regards to the systemic structures and forces that lead to such violence because it defies God's divine purpose for the flourishing of all God's people. Traci C. West has said that we must "unravel the elements that keep male violence secured within the social fabric of our culture" (1999, 2). She uses the term "victim-survivor" for those girls and women in order to avoid diminishing the experiences of the girls/women as well as their own agency and actions in surviving. This avoids pitting notions of victimization against those of agency as an "either/or" (5). She notes how the androcentric Christian tradition's notion of female sexuality as something evil, as temptation for men, can perpetuate feelings of shame and self-blame for victim-survivors (74). In her chapter in this volume, *Confronting U.S. Moral Hypocrisy on Child Soldiers, Inventing Antiracist Solidarity*, West suggests that Euro-Christian expressions sanctioned racism that allows whites to view sexual violence toward African and black women as their problem or a factor of their race and culture. This affirms that the attitude of "that is their problem over there" is inherently racist and confirms and reinforces a disconnectedness and denial of the fact that we have not "taken care of" the problem of violence in our western cultures. West asserts that any sign of dissent is resisting. Surviving is resistance and whatever one has to do to survive can be an act of resistance and can open up possibilities for a degree of healing to take place. Resistance work does not belong solely to victim-survivors. There are forms of resistance that "unleash a woman-preserving spiritual force" (1999, 170). One form of resistance is theological and scholarly discourse. The Circle of Concerned African Women Theologians has been engaging in this and other forms of resistance to genocide, child sex trafficking, gender violence, among other unjust structures and practices. Mercy Amba Oduyoye, often called the mother of African feminist theology, has drawn upon the wisdom of indigenous religious traditions and called for an indigenized Christianity, respecting the traditions and localized cultures to address issues of sexual violence among others (Roncolato 2016). "Women-defined theology" that seeks to free women from marginalization and oppression to assert women's rightful dignity permeates this volume, and Oduyoye's work is specifically discussed in the final chapter. Women-defined theology with women speaking for and of themselves emphasizes inclusiveness to rebuild and restore. A 2010 issue of *Feminist Africa* on "Rethinking Gender and Violence" attends to the diverse dynamics of creative responses and resistance that have emerged in postcolonial Africa and delves into problematic and demeaning western images of the victimized African woman, ravaged by war, to be pitied and developed, which serves to reinforce stereotypes of helplessness. Being a soldier, being actively involved in fighting for a cause, has empowered women. For example, I learned about Kurdish female fighters. In Kurdistan 30–40 percent of combatants are women, many of whom joined up as teenagers to battle jihadists and are followers of the Kurdistan Worker's Party that champions women's freedom and rights (Lazarus 2019). Yet at the same time it is important to share stories of women whose lives have been radically violated by conflict and war-mongers. This conundrum is played out in Georgette Ilunga Mulunda Ledgister's chapter on an ethnographic account of a female Mai-Mai fighter in the Congo that challenges the application of western liberal feminist constraints on African women, particularly in contexts of conflict. Ledgister claims the lived experience of a female warrior calls for a reimagining of gender, and a turn toward cultural epistemologies that honor personhood, agency and hope.

In her 2017 book *Reset the Heart: Unlearning Violence, Relearning Hope*, Mai-Anh Le Tran catalogs the myriad ways violence is normalized in culture. Because violence is learned behavior, it is correct to say that it is also taught. And she indicts the Christian Church for its role in a pedagogy of violence and for its inertia and "cultural captivity" (9, 21–22). In that vein Débora Junker offers here a foundation for educational practices utilizing Paulo Freire's emancipatory pedagogy that attempts to counter "disimagination" toward resistance and healing. Christine Pae's chapter analyzes other experiences of the militarization of girls and women and militarized sexual slavery and prostitution as a result of necropolitics, or sovereignty as the right to kill, in Korea that is challenged by a Christian feminist ethics of peace. And three Caribbean women theologians collaborate to examine girl gangs and female gangsters in Jamaica for similarities with female soldiers in war or armed conflict elsewhere. They review the rise of female membership in gangs and explore gender dynamics at work in gang activity and violence. They suggest theological and ethical insights and the potential of religion to contribute to expanding community self-advocacy. A sociologist of religion and noted authority on religion and gender in Africa, Mary Nyangweso, looks at the challenges of being female in Africa. Her chapter describes how gender-based violence is socially constructed and legitimized and shows how such legitimation enables gender-based violence during conflict situations.

Documenting the experience of women victim-survivors is based on the conviction that women's stories matter and lead to ways to organize leadership. Participatory action research (PAR) can also empower resistance. Emerging out of the praxis intervention work of Paulo Freire, researchers in partnership with NGOs in Liberia, Sierra Leone and Uganda, including African academics, use local knowledge and situate the participants as the experts to identify problems they face in their communities (Worthen et al. 2010, 150–152). The Isis (female goddess of creativity) Women's International Cross Cultural Exchange promotes women's human rights by documenting women's realities and providing skills training (Liebling-Kalifani et al. 2011). An Appendix to this volume provides a list of activist organizations. Of course, ethnographic and field research on former child soldiers raises important ethical considerations. Consent, freedom, power relationships come into play.[4] This does not mean that it cannot be done or have a positive impact to empower girls and women in their communities as the research is being used as a tool for advocacy.

REINTEGRATION, RESILIENCE AND THE CHURCH

The reintegration of child soldiers back into society represents tremendous cultural challenges. Needless to say, girls exposed to the horrors of war are traumatized with long-lasting effects. Girls formerly associated with armed groups, in particular those "girl mothers" who return with children born while they were away from their villages, have been identified as extremely vulnerable, facing social rejection (Shanahan and Veale 2010, 115). Culturally appropriate interventions, crisis responses to trauma are critical. A psychotherapist from Zimbabwe, Mazvita Machinga, has contributed a chapter that identifies components of pastoral care in situations of trauma from gender violence, including that which occurs in armed conflict and pastoral concerns for reintegration.

Theology calls for the church to reflect on its witness and practice to measure how it is faithful to the mandate of the Gospel. How might the church, informed by feminist, African feminist and Latina theologies, or the *ekklesia* of women challenge power structures that contribute to violence and stigma to aid in reintegration and empower resilience? The Church in countries where forced female soldering takes place and else-

---

[4] See for example the qualitative research of Pamela Couture. 2016. *We Are Not All Victims: Local Peacebuilding in the DRC.* Lit Verlag; and Todd D. Whitmore 2019. *Imitating Christ in Magwi: An Anthropological Theology.* London: T & T Clark.

where can actively seek to alleviate the situation. In the important work, *Culture, Religion, and the Reintegration of Female Child Soldiers in Northern Uganda*, Emeline Ndossi related how the Christian Churches in Northern Uganda work to educate the Acholi people with sensitization programs and others against stigmatization and serve as caring centers and receptive sanctuaries (2010, 139, 141–143). Yet economic resources are limited. Strategies for peaceful protection, the interruption of community narratives of stigma and shame and ritualization are important means of healing. Practical theologian Evelyn L. Parker closes this volume with an examination of divine fortitude in girl soldiers as an expression of the incarnation. She describes that fortitude in the smart sassiness of young African girls which bookends well with Beverly Mitchell's chapter that calls upon theologies of childhood. We have work to do to heed the stern revelations to de-normalize male violence and to deconstruct systems that propagate the perpetration of violence. It is the hope of this volume to energize collective alliances to unleash intelligent solidarities with the power to act.

REFERENCES

Adichie, Chimamanda Ngozi. 2009. The Danger of a Single Story. *Ted Global.* https://www.ted.com/talks/chimamanda_adichie_the_danger_of_a_single_story.

Allen, Amy. 1999. *The Power of Feminist Theory: Domination, Resistance, Solidarity.* Boulder, CO: Westview Press.

Ayiera, Eve. 2010. Sexual Violence in Conflict: A Problematic International Discourse. *Feminist Africa* 14: 7–20.

Denov, Myriam. 2007. *Girls in Fighting Forces: Moving Beyond Victimhood.* Canadian International Development Agency.

Höglund, Anna T. 2003. Justice for Women in War? Feminist Ethics and Human Rights for Women. *Feminist Theology* 11 (3): 346–361.

Jones, Serene. 2000. *Feminist Theory and Christian Theology: Cartographies of Grace.* Minneapolis, MN: Fortress Press.

Kasomo, Daniel, and Loreen Iminza Maseno. 2011. A Critical Appraisal of African Feminist Theology. *International Journal of Current Research* 2 (1): 154–162.

Lazarus, Sarah. 2019. Women. Life. Freedom: Female Fighters of Kurdistan. *Cable News Network.* https://www.cnn.com/2019/01/27/homepage2/kurdish-female-fighters/index.html.

Liebling-Kalifani, Helen, Victoria Mwaka, and Ruth Ojiambo-Ochieng. 2011. A Situational Analysis of the Women Survivors of the 1989–2003 Armed Conflict in Liberia. *Journal of International Women's Studies* 12 (1): 1–21.

Madlala-Routledge, Nozizwe. 2008. We Need an International Campaign to Resist Androcentric Militarized Neo-Colonial Masculinities! *Feminist Africa* 10: 85–90.

Maeland, Bard, ed. 2010. *Culture, Religion, and the Reintegration of Female Child Soldiers in Northern Uganda.* New York: Peter Lang.

Ndossi, Emeline. 2010. Stigma As Encountered by Female Returnees and the Role of the Church in Northern Uganda. In *Culture, Religion and the Reintegration of Female Child Soldiers in Northern Uganda,* ed. Bard Maeland, 133–148. New York: Peter Lang.

Nordstrom, Carolyn. 1997. *Girls and Warzones: Troubling Questions.* Uppsala: Life and Peace Institute.

Roncolato, Carolyn. 2016. Meet the Mother of African Feminist Theology. *Sojourners.* https://sojo.net/articles/sheroes-faith/meet-mother-african-feminist-theology.

Shanahan, Fiona, and Angela Veale. 2010. 'The Girl Is the Core of Life' Social Reintegration, Communal Violence and the Sacred in Northern Uganda. In *Culture, Religion and the Reintegration of Female Child Soldiers in Northern Uganda,* ed. Bard Maeland, 115–131. New York: Peter Lang.

Shepler, Susan. 2004. *The Social and Cultural Context of Child Soldiering in Sierra Leone.* Oslo: PRIO.

Tinkasiimire, Therese. 2010. Women and War in Northern Uganda: A Theological Reflection on the Dignity of Women in the Reintegration Process. In *Culture, Religion, and the Reintegration of Female Child Soldiers in Northern Uganda,* ed. Bard Maeland, 165–178. New York: Peter Lang.

Tran, Mai-Anh Le. 2017. *Reset the Heart: Unlearning Violence, Relearning Hope.* Nashville: Abingdon Press.

Wessells, Michael. 2006. *Child Soldiers: From Violence to Protection.* Cambridge, MA: Harvard University Press.

West, Traci C. 1999. *Wounds of the Spirit: Black Women, Violence, and Resistance Ethics.* New York: New York University Press.

Worthen, Miranda, Susan McKay, Angela Veale, and Wessells Michael. 2010. 'I Had No Idea You Cared About Me' Empowerment of Vulnerable Mothers in the Context of Reintegration. In *Culture, Religion and the Reintegration of Female Child Soldiers in Northern Uganda,* ed. Bard Maeland, 149–164. New York: Peter Lang.

CHAPTER 2

Human Rights, Dignity, and Female Child Soldiers: A Theological Approach

Beverly Eileen Mitchell

The use of child soldiers in armed conflict represents a disturbing failure of the global community to safeguard the dignity of children 17 years of age and younger. Even though the United Nations Convention on the Rights of the Child, adopted in 1989 and enforced in 1990, was intended to serve as an international mechanism to ensure the safety and well-being of children all over the world, there were 300,000 child soldiers serving in armed conflicts worldwide as of 2017 (Robison 2018). The US State Department, which monitors the use of child soldiers, published in June 2018 its annual list of countries who engage children in combat. Included in that list were Burma, Democratic Republic of Congo, Iran, Iraq, Mali, Niger, Nigeria, Somalia, South Sudan, Syria, and Yemen (Becker 2018).[1]

---

[1] Although the State Department has documents which reflect that the Afghan National Police and the Afghan Local Police continue to use child soldiers, Afghanistan has still not been restored to this list.

B. E. Mitchell (✉)
Wesley Theological Seminary, Washington, DC, USA
e-mail: bmitchell@wesleyseminary.edu

© The Author(s) 2019
S. Willhauck (ed.), *Female Child Soldiering, Gender Violence, and Feminist Theologies*, https://doi.org/10.1007/978-3-030-21982-6_2

13

There are several reasons for the growing phenomenon of employing children for combat. Poverty plays a role in making children vulnerable to recruitment as child soldiers. Failed nation-states and armed conflicts with radical groups in such states also provide a breeding ground for the use of juvenile warriors in order to replenish the supply of combatants. Additionally, small weapons, such as AK-47s, which are inexpensive, easy to assemble, and ideally made for the actual conditions of war, are weapons of choice for children (Chivers 2010). Moreover, both governments and armed groups employ children in combat situations because their immaturity in psycho-social development makes them good prospects for recruitment and indoctrination. Children tend to be easier to condition to obey without questioning and to kill without undue scruples. Economically, the use of children is appealing because they are inexpensive to support. Psychologically, their ability to assess danger is underdeveloped; thus, they are more willing to take risks and accept difficult assignments that adults or older teenagers would more readily refuse. Children are often more impressionable than adults and, depending on their age and background, their value systems and consciences are not yet fully developed. This makes them much easier to exploit (Steel 2008).

The experiences of children who are kidnapped from their families or who "volunteer" to take up arms are dire. Military commanders use diverse tactics to produce unquestioning obedience in homesick children as they transform them into killers. Often, commanders force new recruits to kill or perpetrate various acts of violence against others; including strangers, escapees, members of their village, and even family members. An added advantage of exploiting these children is that when they are forced to harm or kill others, these youngsters realize that they will not be welcomed back home. This knowledge then discourages them from trying to escape. Some armed groups, through coercion and peer pressure, have forced the young recruits to drink the blood or eat the flesh of their victims. As Michael Wessells is quoted as saying, the motivation in these tactics is designed to "force children to quiet their emotional reactions to seeing people killed and demolish their sense of the sanctity of life and their tendency to show respect for the dead" (Steel 2008). Children are administered drugs to deaden the effects of their consciences. According to Amnesty International (2000), children who refuse the drugs are beaten or killed. Though these tactics of commanders are successful in turning the children into killers, the violence they perpetrate does adversely impact their psychological well-being in the long term (Steel 2008).

Gender differences add a special dimension to the plight of child soldiers. Because of the prevalent perception of child soldiers as males, it is important to highlight the plight of female child soldiers. Even though the tragedy of using boys and girls for armed combat is egregious because they are *children*, the particularity of the experiences of girls is much less well known and needs elucidation.[2]

Girls fight on the front lines, just as boys do, but they also provide domestic labor and serve as "wives." From the age of 13, they are sometimes given to boy soldiers or adult commanders. If they refuse, they are killed or raped. Many of the girls become mothers and have the added responsibility of providing for their children. However, often infants born under these circumstances do not survive. Malnutrition, exhaustion, and abusive treatment exacerbate the situation of these underaged mothers. The actual birthing process itself for these girls can be quite brutal.[3] Dyan Mazurana and Susan McKay have asserted that the Revolutionary United Front's birthing practices in Sierra Leone included "jumping on the abdomens of expectant girls and inserting objects into their vaginas to force labor before they are properly dilated" (Steel 2008). Moreover, repeated sexual assaults against girl soldiers can lead to infection, disease (including HIV/AIDS), deformation of the uterus, vaginal sores, complications of menstruation, sterility, and death. The psychological impact includes "shock, loss of dignity, shame, low self-esteem, poor concentration and memory, persistent nightmares, depression, and other forms of stress effects" (2008).

The litany of complaints of girl soldiers from diverse places has a familiar ring to them. When Child Soldiers International (CSI) interviewed 150 girls from the Democratic Republic of Congo in 2016, the girls gave the interviewers a variety of reasons as to why they were part of armed groups. Two-thirds of the girls were abducted; however, one-third of

[2] The UN Convention on the Rights of the Child defines "child" as "every human being below the age of 18 years." Most child soldiers are between 13 and 18 years of age; although many groups include children aged 12 and under. Both government and non-state forces in developed and developing countries are guilty. Steel notes that even the UK, the US, Australia, Canada, and New Zealand recruit youths as young as 17. See Michelle Steel, "Child Soldiers."

[3] Dyan Mazurana's research focus includes women's and children's rights during armed conflict and post conflict; serious crimes and violations committed during armed conflict and their effects on victims and civilian populations; armed opposition groups; and remedy and reparation. Susan McKay's teaching and research have focused on women, girls, and armed conflict; women and peacebuilding; and feminist issues in peace psychology. See Michelle Steel, "Child Soldiers."

them joined these groups for other reasons. Some of the girls, whose families were experiencing significant financial hardship, were enticed into joining in hopes that they could earn enough money to return to school. Poverty made these girls vulnerable to exploitation and abuse. Others joined to avenge the death of a friend or family member. Still others joined in hopes of protecting themselves from violence, looting, and rape. Not surprisingly, the money for education or protection from harm never materialized for them. The common fate of children and teenagers was physical and sexual abuse, combat, hard labor, and the constant fear of death. One 17-year-old recalled her experience: "I was often drugged. I would wake up and find myself naked. They gave us drugs so that we would not get tired of all of them using us" (Olsson 2017). The Congolese girls spoke of the many hardships once they were released from armed conflict. Reintegration into their former communities compounds their difficulties. Frequently, their experience has been rejection, ostracism, and isolation from their former communities. Other parents view them as unfit to associate with their daughters (Olsson 2017).

Polline Akello, an activist committed to gaining more support for abducted child soldiers, is herself a survivor. Abducted when she was 12, Akello was raped and bore a child who did not survive. She spent seven years in the bush in Uganda, before she escaped. While a forced participant in the Lord's Resistance Army, she saw her best friend killed right in front of her. She was also given to a rebel commander to be his "wife." She described her harrowing experience as a child soldier:

> In the camp girls are there to be used whenever the men want. Soldiers are not allowed to fall in love. If one is caught charming a girl, he is killed. I became pregnant when I was 16. During labor I was forced to walk for miles as the rebels tried to evade the Ugandan army. My son died before he was born and I had to have an operation to remove him without anesthetic. (Akello 2016)

The physical and psychological effects of participating in the armed groups as children exacerbate the difficulties of both girls and boys who return to their former communities. Theresa Betancourt has conducted the first prospective study following male and female child soldiers after the 11-year civil war in Sierra Leone. She has found that former child soldiers in Sierra Leone (and elsewhere) suffer nightmares, intense sadness, intrusive thoughts, and recurring violent images. Those of them who committed extreme acts of violence, or were victims of it, tend to suffer the most persistent mental health problems and need very intensive care. Their relationships within their former communities are difficult. The former child soldiers experience guilt and shame. They are viewed as untrustworthy by others. They are blamed for having destroyed lives, homes, property, society. Socially isolated, they are vulnerable to addictions and abusive relationships (Drexler 2011). The experience of female child soldiers is compounded. They are more likely to experience depression, anxiety, and post-traumatic stress disorder than boys. If they return to their home communities after having had unwanted pregnancies during their time with rebels, they are *doubly* stigmatized: for their participation in the violence and for their perceived lack of sexual purity (2011).

Given the nature of what happens to children who are recruited or "volunteer" in armed conflict situations, the question arises as to what extent we can conclude that child soldiering constitutes a violation of their dignity as human beings. There is something incongruent about the idea of children in their early teens or younger participating in armed conflict. Our images of children focus upon their immaturity of development, physically, emotionally, intellectually, and psychologically. We view them as vulnerable and dependent; in need of guidance, nurturing, monitoring, and protection. We view them as undeveloped or less developed. We view it as our responsibility to protect them from harm and danger. Our default view of children is one of innocence, incapable of committing acts that can lead to injury or death of others. We view them as impressionable and easily led astray because they have not developed the requisite ability to exercise criminal intent. The transformation of children into killers strikes us as an egregious distortion of what it means to be a child. The physical, psychological, and long-term emotional harm done to condition children to participate in armed conflicts constitutes an acute violation of their dignity and rights as human beings.

My definition of human dignity is based upon the divine assertion found in the biblical book of Genesis, chapter 1, verse 27, which says, "Let us make humankind in our image, according to our likeness" (Mitchell 2009). By this divine assertion, the creative deed was done! There are important theological implications for what it means to be human based upon this divine deed—namely, the creation of the human in the image of the divine. The first implication is that a measure of "glory," which signifies value and worth that warrants that each person be treated with respect, arises out of this imprint of the divine on every human creature. It is this "glory" that I define as "human dignity." Second, because this imprint comes from God, human dignity is a gift. As such, it is an aspect of who we are as human beings which cannot be taken away from us by other human beings, for human beings do not have the power to give or take away divine grace. (Even when we attempt to deny the presence of dignity in another, we *violate* but do not *destroy* that dignity.) The inner cry of protest to this violation, whether we can hear it or not, testifies to the continuing presence of that dignity when the value and worth of another is threatened or denied. Third, because of the gifted nature of human dignity and the human inability to destroy it, this dignity is present in every human being, regardless of race/ethnicity, gender, age, sexual identity, religion, national origin, class, physical or mental impairment, or other features of diversity which we use to discriminate against others. This dignity remains, regardless of our abilities, capabilities, or disabilities. It is present at the beginning of life and remains at the end. If this theological baseline is used to establish the value and worth of every human being, then we have an imperative to protect human dignity whenever it is in jeopardy and our decisions on economic, social, and political realities must be informed by this theological assertion.

There are five things we conclude from this definition of human dignity. Human dignity is constitutive, a gift, universal, indestructible, and binds us to each other, theologically. To say that human dignity is constitutive is to say that this dignity is part of what it means to be human. Part of being defined as human is that human beings bear the image of God in them. To speak of human dignity as a gift is to affirm that *God* gives us this dignity because God has made us in the divine image. Human dignity is not something we earn or is granted to us by others. To speak of human dignity as universal is to recognize that all humans are endowed with this sacred worth, regardless of what we have or do not have. Sacred worth is never mitigated because of our age or stage of development. To speak of human dignity as indestructible is to affirm that it cannot be destroyed. It can be (and often is) violated, assaulted, or abused. However, violation of that dignity does not annihilate it. Finally, to speak of human dignity as binding us to fellow human beings is to recognize that because each human being bears the divine image, we are theologically bound to each other in a relationship of sibling-hood.

This theological binding to each other as siblings creates a communal dimension of our experience of dignity. Human dignity is not something we experience individualistically, in isolation from each other. There is a social dimension to this dignity. This dimension is marked by the human need to have our personhood acknowledged or affirmed by others. For a sense of well-being, for our internal equilibrium, we must have our dignity acknowledged, even as we acknowledge the dignity of others. This need for reciprocity or mutuality of acknowledgement is so powerful, that when it is denied, it increases our suffering in the experience of humiliation, degradation, and invisibility. This social dimension of dignity is an indication that our humanness is tied to that of every other human being. It means that in some way our humanity is fulfilled in the presence of others who also know our value and worth. When we lose sight of this worth, it becomes ever so easy to treat others as less than human.

To advance this discussion of human dignity in concrete terms, I have drawn inspiration from the work of the late French philosopher Emmanuel Levinas, who maintained that the ethical demand to be viewed, acknowledged, and treated as a full human being can be seen in his concept of "the face" (1998). Levinas asserts that the philosophical task begins with ethics, and ethics begins in the face of the other. Levinas maintains that the face of the Other commands that we not remain indifferent to the death of the Other. It is in the face that we meet the commandment, "Thou shalt not kill" (1998). I contend, that it also meets us with the insight that, "You are connected to me." What happens to you matters to me and vice versa. There is also a sacredness that we must not breach. Because of human sinfulness we frequently fail to honor, support, or promote the dignity of others, including children. The violation of the dignity of others is *defacement.*

To deface someone or a group is to deny them the respect and honor due to them by virtue of their full humanity. It is to fail to see their sacredness. It is to dismiss a person or persons as having no value or worth. It is to challenge their right to exist. The range of acts which can be classified as defacement extends from the humiliating snub of being treated as invisible by a salesclerk to genocide.

Individually or personally we commit defacement when we render people invisible or inconsequential. Defacement can also be corporate or communal. For example, when our communities or societies engage in activities that exclude designated "others" from the advantages of a decent life by denying them access to the benefits of good neighborhoods, decent schools, and living wages. Defacement often becomes codified in legislation and embedded in social policies which make it legal and the "natural order of things" to keep minorities from the opportunity to participate effectively in life. Defacement is most visible when one group in society decides that another group is unfit to live.

So far, this entire discussion of human dignity and the defacement of that dignity provides a solid theological defense for the promotion of the value and worth of every human being and the importance of safeguarding the dignity of all human beings against its defacement for reasons of race/ethnicity, gender, sexual identity, national origin, class, and so on. The question is whether this discussion applies to children. The question of human dignity in relation to children is critical in our assessment of the ongoing challenge of child soldiers. *Do children have dignity that we are theological and ethically bound to respect?* The answer to this question is not self-evident if we note that children are not often at the center of academic theological and ethical discourse. A response to the question will determine the nature of a theological critique of the practice of using child soldiers and the degree to which we can claim that the use of child soldiers constitutes defacement of these boys and girls that we should do everything in our power to resist. To explore the question of the dignity of children, I draw on the work of Karl Rahner and Marcia Bunge, systematic theologians who have written about the dignity of children.

In his essay, "Ideas for a Theology of Childhood," Karl Rahner makes two observations regarding the way in which adults tend to view childhood. The first observation is that we often conceive of childhood as something that "disappears" (1971, 33). It is not thought to be a stage in life that lasts. The implication is that since that aspect of who we are as humans does not last, its overall value is insignificant. The second observation he makes is that Christians tend to place great emphasis on the subordinate role of childhood. Childhood is simply a provisional preparation for bringing our adult life into its fullness. Consequently, what is of greater importance is adulthood. Correlatively, childhood is less significant than adulthood. The logical conclusion is that children, because of their immaturity, are less important than adults. Rahner rejects both notions and articulates why childhood has lasting significance and that children have great theological significance.

He situates childhood in the context of the human being who exists before God (*coram deo*). We live in relation to God, who chooses to be in relation to us as God's creature. This relationship to God is present at each stage in human development and growth, including in childhood (1971, 33). Though we may conceive of childhood as something that "disappears," (34) such thinking is deceptive because we do not really lose childhood in time. Rather, we only become the children whom we were because we bring our past, including our childhood, into our eternity

(36). If Rahner is correct, then who we are at various stages of our existence remains a part of us into the future. Hence, childhood has value and worth because it is part of who we become. Further, "childhood has value in and of itself," even as it contributes to that which is to come (36–37). Christianity affirms reverence for the child because the child is *human* (38, emphasis added).

In her article, "Rediscovering the Dignity and Complexity of Children: Resources from the Christian Tradition," Marcia Bunge also affirms the humanness and the dignity of children, but first articulates the ways in which US society and even the Christian Church manifest inconsistent convictions regarding the value and worth of children. We make noises that we care about children; yet, when it comes to ensuring that children have their basic needs met, they are not a priority in decisions about budget cuts on the state and federal level. This consigns children to inadequate education, poverty, and inadequate health insurance. The Christian Church has been just as inconsistent in its convictions regarding the value and worth of children. Some of the more appalling failures of our churches include the priest abuse scandal; the ways in which our consumerist culture views children as "commodities, consumers, or even economic burdens"; and our overly simplistic views of children (2004). She calls for a broader, more complex view of children and the nature of childhood that strengthens our commitment to safeguarding their intrinsic value and manifests our obligation to protect their dignity (2004). Drawing from the Bible and the history of Christian thought, she identifies six ways of speaking about the nature of children that can broaden our conception of children and strengthen our commitment to them.

The first way of speaking of children comes from texts in the Hebrew Bible, which depict children as gifts of God, who ultimately come from God and belong to God (see Gen. 30:20; I Sam. 1:11, 19; Gen. 30:11; Ps. 127:3). In these texts, they are viewed as sources of joy and pleasure. Whether they are ours biologically or by adoption, they are greater than our own making and will develop in ways that we cannot imagine or control. Moreover, even though they may be perceived as a blessing to their family of origin, they are also a blessing to the entire community. They will play diverse roles over time as they grow and mature; thus, they are neither "property" of their parents nor are they a burden to the community.

Bunge draws the second way of speaking theologically about children from biblical texts and the history of Christian thought. These traditions reveal children as "sinful" creatures and moral agents. These sources maintain that children are sinful insofar as they are born into a "state of sin," that they are born into a world that is not what it ought to be. Children themselves are prone to commit actual sins; as moral agents they will sometimes act in ways that are self-centered and harmful to themselves and others. Though not as sinful as adults because of their immaturity, they have the capacity to engage in harmful actions, and to some degree, they are responsible. They require guidance and nurturing to avoid their falling into egregious, harmful actions. Bunge's discussion seeks to counter a naïve, overly sentimental depiction of children as complete innocents, incapable of committing egregious, harmful acts simply because they are children.

Third, Bunge maintains that because they are developing beings, they need instruction and guidance from adults to mature morally, spiritually, physically, and intellectually. She identifies many biblical texts which encourage adults to provide guidance and nurturance to children. Moreover, she cites writers from the history of Christian thought who have argued for the role adults must play in the development of children.

Fourth, she grounds her conviction that children are fully human and made in the image of God in Genesis 1:27, as I have done. She concurs, as I do, with Karl Rahner's assertion that children have value and dignity in their own right and are fully human from the very beginning. Because of this theological affirmation, adults are bound to respect children from that beginning and need to see them as a "sacred trust" that requires our nurturance and protection at every stage of their lives.

Bunge's fifth component in a comprehensive view of children is that they are both models of faith and sources of revelation. Noting the Gospels, which depict Jesus blessing children, their witness provides insights to adults about the nature of faith and what characteristics we adults need to cultivate as participants in the reign of God. This view of children is a direct contrast to the ways in which children were viewed in the first century. They occupied a low position in society; abandoning them was not seen as a crime; and they were not viewed as models for adults. Her final component, drawn from the biblical witness and from Christian thinkers who were particularly concerned about the plight of poor children, involves viewing orphans, neighbors, and strangers as populations that members of society must treat with justice and compassion.

I believe Bunge's discussion goes a long way toward helping us to develop a more constructive way of viewing children as fully human and, therefore, worthy of the rights afforded to human adults. While it is true that her discussion is focused on a Christian, US context, and the problem of female child soldiers is prevalent in the global south, there are some who might contest a universal application of her insights. However, I maintain that her insights could contribute to the improvement of the way in which members of the global community respond to this human rights crisis. I contend that a theological discussion which affirms the dignity and worth of children must apply to all children, not only our own.

From the discussions of Rahner and Bunge about the dignity and worth of children, we must affirm their full humanity and support their human rights. From this discussion of human dignity, the use of children in armed conflict constitutes their defacement. The adults of the world have been entrusted with the care, nurturing, and support of all its children. Our failure to do so makes us complicit in their defacement.

Although there have been international laws enacted to protect the human rights for children; non-governmental agencies supporting the reintegration of children into their home societies with some success; churches making statements and prophetic denunciations of the practice, the practice continues.[4] Resolving the conflicts that create the context for the use of child soldiers is complicated and the international community (e.g. the United Nations) seems impotent in putting an end to this deface-ment of girls and boys under the age of 18. However, there have been two recent developments that offer a glimmer of hope for incremental improvement.

The first development is the founding of the Roméo Dallaire Child Soldiers Initiative, which is designed to address the use of child soldiers. Because no individual country or regional organization has developed coherent policies or military and police doctrine for dealing with child soldiers during peace operations, the Dallaire Initiative offers an approach that goes beyond child protection. The Initiative works with military, police, and peacekeeping forces, which they believe will be a critical part of interrupting the cycle of recruitment of children by armed groups. The Dallaire Initiative ensures the inclusion of entities which could play an important role in providing the necessary leverage to make the continued use of child soldiering untenable (Dallaire n.d.).

---

[4] With the current sexual abuse scandal involving thousands of children, perpetrated by hundreds of clergy, and the failure of high-level church officials to address this abomination, the church's moral integrity has been seriously compromised.

The second development is the passage of the Women, Peace, and Security Act (WPSA) of 2017. The passage of this act by the US Congress represents an acknowledgment of longitudinal study results, which bear out that the efforts of women involved in peace-building can lead to more lasting efforts. The idea that women can play critical roles not only in the prevention of the recruitment of child soldiers, but also in the security sector as a whole, is not new (Dallaire et al. 2016). The United Nations, which passed United Nations Security Council Resolution 1325 (UNSCR-1325) in October 2000, was a landmark resolution—the first to be made on women, peace, and security. Dallaire et al. indicate that the UN specifically highlights critical reasons for increasing the recruitment of women peacekeepers. Among them are the fact that their recruitment is a way to empower women in the host community; they can address specific needs of female ex-combatants during the process of demobilizing and reintegration into civilian life; they also can help make the peacekeeping force approachable to women in the community; and they are helpful in interacting with societies where women are not permitted to speak to men (Dallaire et al. 2016). The WPSA builds on the policy framework which has developed over the years since the passage of UNSCR-1325 to the adoption of the first US National Action Plan on Women, Peace, and Security in 2011. This action plan was implemented by Executive Order 13595 and updated in 2016 (Vogelstein and Bigio 2017). Although there are countless indications that domestically and internationally many applaud the passage of the WPSA and UNSCR 1325, some women have offered interesting critiques of UNSCR 1325 (see Fryer 2016; O'Connor 2014). Some of the critiques revolve around essentialist notions that women *by nature* are more peaceful and nurturing. Other critiques assert that UNSCR has not been very effective in protecting women in war zones from sexual violence. These critiques bear examination. Further study is needed to assess the degree to which implementation of both acts can help in the tragedy of the use of child soldiers (see Lilleslatten 2017).

Neither these acts nor church statements nor the work of non-governmental organizations *alone* can bring an end to the use of female and male child soldiers. If it takes a village to raise a child, it will take many sectors in the global community to make greater headway toward ending this immoral practice. Progress that involves preventative measures and the healing of those who have been wounded by child soldiering will most likely be incremental. However, it will be critical for those of us committed to upholding the dignity of these and *all* children to keep Shelly Whitman's assertion in mind: "Children are the priority and they need to be protected from joining armed forces and armed groups. We have a duty to humanity to do this" (Power Corporation of Canada n.d.)

References

Akello, Polline. 2016. I Was a Child Soldier. *The Guardian*, February 12. https://www.theguardian.com/commentisfree/2016/feb/12/child-soldier-support-survivors-raped.

Amnesty International. 2000. Hidden Scandal, Secret Shame: Torture and Ill-Treatment of Children. https://www.amnesty.org/download/Documents/132000/act400382000en.pdf.

Becker, Jo. 2018. A Better US List of Countries Using Child Soldiers. *Human Rights Watch*, June 29. https://www.hrw.org/news/2018/06/29/better-us-list-countries-using-child-soldiers.

Bunge, Marcia J. 2004. Rediscovering the Dignity and Complexity of Children: Resources from the Christian Tradition. *Journal of Lutheran Ethics* 4: 1. https://www.elca.org/JLE/Articles/796.

Chivers, C.J. 2010. The AK-47: 'The Gun' That Changed the Battlefield. Author Interview. *Fresh Air*, October 12. https://www.npr.org/templates/story/story.php?storyId=130493013.

Dallaire, Roméo. n.d. What We Do. *Child Soldiers Initiative*, Dalhousie University. https://www.childsoldiers.org/what-we-do.

Dallaire, Roméo, Shelly Whitman, and Sam Holland. 2016. Innovation in the Prevention of the Use of Child Soldiers. *PRISM* 6: 1. https://cco.ndu.edu/PRISM/PRISM-volume-6-no1/Article/684610/innovation-in-the-prevention-of-the-use-of-child-soldiers-women-in-the-security/.

Drexler, Madeline. 2011. Life After Death: Helping Child Soldiers Become Whole Again. *Harvard T.H. Chan School of Public Health Magazine*. https://www.hsph.harvard.edu/news/magazine/child-soldiers-betancourt.

Fryer, Capt. Denna, Australian Army. 2016. Women, Peace, and Security: The Agenda Is Not Women and It Won't Achieve Peace or Security. *Australian Defence Force Journal* 200: 4–14. http://www.defence.gov.au/adc/adfj/Documents/issue_200/Fryer_Nov_2016.pdf.

Levinas, Emmanuel. 1998. *Entre Nous: On Thinking of the Other*. Translated by Michael B. Smith and Barbara Harshav. New York: Columbia University Press.

Lilleslatten, Mari. 2017. A Warning Against Desirable Facts About Women in Peace and Conflict. *KJonnsforskning*, May 11. http://kjonnsforskning.no/en/2017/05/warning-against-desirable-facts-about-women-peace-and-conflict.

Mitchell, Beverly Eileen. 2009. *Plantations and Death Camps, Religion, Ideology, and Human Dignity*. Minneapolis: Fortress Press.

O'Connor, Talitha. 2014. The UNSC & Women: On the Effectiveness of Resolution 1325. *International Affairs*, March 24. https://www.internationalaffairs.org.au/news-item/the-unsc-women-on-the-effectiveness-of-resolution-1325.

Olsson, Sandra. 2017. Hear the Voice of Congo's Girl Child Soldiers. *IRIN*, June 19. https://www.irinnews.org/opinion/2017/06/19/hear-voices-congo%E2%80%99s-girl-child-soldiers.

Power Corporation of Canada. n.d. The Roméo Dallaire Child Soldiers Initiative. https://www.powercorporationcommunity.com/en/projects/community-development/romeo-dallaire-child-soldiers-initiative/.

Rahner, Karl. 1971. Ideas for a Theology of Childhood. In *Theological Investigations*, Vol. 8: Further Theology of the Spiritual Life 2, 33–50. Translated by David Bourke. London: Darton, Longman & Todd.

Robison, McCall. 2018. 10 Shocking Facts About Child Soldiers. *The Blog*, The Borgen Project, January 2. https://borgenproject.org/shocking-facts-about-child-soldiers/.

Steel, Michelle. 2008. Child Soldiers. *Society and Culture*, Fall. http://www.vision.org/visionmedia/social-issues/child-soldiers/6684.aspx.

Vogelstein, Rachel, and Jamille Bigio. 2017. *Three Things to Know: Women, Peace, and Security Act of 2017*. Woman Around the World, Council of Foreign Relations, October 13. https://www.cfr.org/blog/three-things-know-women-peace-and-security-act-2017.

CHAPTER 3

Sexual Violence in Conflict: Understanding the Experience of Child Soldiers

Shelly Whitman

Neither truth or lie serves in war, both have merit when needed.
—Former Child Soldier interviewed in Colombia

INTRODUCTION

There is increasing recognition of the high rates of sexual violence occurring in both active conflicts and in the transitions to peace. This violence occurs during military operations, inside the civilian population, and also within military personnel structures. Young people are highly implicated in these violations as both victims and perpetrators. In particular, children who are recruited and used as soldiers experience exposure to sexual violence in unique and less understood manners. Old assumptions about sexual violence only being a by-product of war are being overturned as more research confirms that sexual violence is often used by armed actors[1]

[1] Actors, in this context, refers to both state and non-state members of national militaries, militias, and gangs.

S. Whitman (✉)
Dalhousie University, Halifax, NS, Canada
e-mail: shelly@childsoldiers.org

© The Author(s) 2019
S. Willhauck (ed.), *Female Child Soldiering, Gender Violence, and Feminist Theologies*, https://doi.org/10.1007/978-3-030-21982-6_3

as a strategic and tactical weapon, and this use particularly targets young people. Case studies in certain countries, such as Sierra Leone, Liberia, and Uganda, have found that girls made up the vast majority of all sexual violence victims. Conflict also increases the prevalence of sexual violence among the civilian population, both during and after conflicts. These factors have led to the call for a better understanding of the experiences of both boys and girls used as child soldiers and their exposure to sexual violence.

What are the long-term implications for peace and security when children and youth are educated in the use of sexual violence as a weapon of war? This chapter will discuss the need to understand the experience of child soldiers with respect to sexual violence as a tactic of war. Child soldiers are exposed to sexual violence as perpetrators and recipients of this violence and the goal includes understanding this reality for both boys and girls.

Sexual Violence in Conflict

While sexual violence in conflict is not a new phenomenon, in the rise of inter-state conflict towards the latter part of the twentieth century, the nature and scale of sexual violence has become an increasingly complex and extreme characteristic of state and (particularly) non-state actors wartime tactics. The complexity of the problem is due to a myriad of factors, some of which include underreporting of sexual violence before, during, and after conflict, which makes it difficult for practitioners to understand the scale of the problem; shifting cultural norms before, during, and after conflict; fear of stigma and shame from the victims' communities and families; and whether sexual violence is used in a way to incite mass atrocity against a particular group of people based on race or religion, for example, as a way to "cleanse" the population. More complicated still, as the United Nations Secretary General's 2018 Report notes: "[I]n several settings … women and girls rarely report sexual violence by members of their own community in times of war, owing to overarching political and ethnic loyalties and pressures" (p. 4).

Sexual violence in conflict is broadly described as either being strategic, tactical, opportunistic, and/or perpetrated as a practice. Strategic and tactical uses are often cited when rape, for example, is known to be used as a weapon of war or to advance military objectives. United Nations Security Council Resolutions 1820 stresses that "sexual violence, when used or commissioned as a tactic of war in order to deliberately target civilians or as part of a widespread or systematic attack … can significantly exacerbate situations of armed conflict and may impede the restoration of international peace and security" (p. 2). Opportunistic sexual violence is typically carried out for personal reasons and not tied to a larger mandate. When sexual violence is understood as a practice, it is violence that is overlooked by commanding officers in military operations. "A practice differs from opportunistic violence in that it may be the product of social interactions, not individual preferences—for example, the combatant's desire to conform to the behaviour of others in the unit. Such social pressures are very strong during military training and combat" (Wood 2014, 471). This is further illustrated in the UNSG's 2018 *Report on Conflict Related Sexual Violence*: "In certain cases, combatants have been permitted to rape with impunity or with the tacit approval of their commanders, who rationalize the practice as a form of compensation." The Report defines the term "conflict-related sexual violence" as "rape, sexual slavery, forced prostitution, forced pregnancy, forced abortion, enforced sterilization, forced marriage and any other form of sexual violence of comparable gravity perpetrated against women, men, girls or boys that is directly or indirectly related to conflict" (p. 2).

The Geneva Conventions also articulate that rape and other forms of sexual violence during armed conflict are prohibited. Child-specific provisions of these treaties specifically forbid sexual violence against children. The United Nations has long recognized the issue, as is demonstrated in the following UN SC Resolutions: 1325, 1820, 1882, 1888, 1960, and 2106. But more significantly, it was addressed in 2008 with the adoption of Security Council Resolution 1820, which recognized and elevated conflict-related sexual violence as a security issue.

> The recognition of the fact that such incidents are not random or isolated but integral to the operations, ideology and economic strategy of a range of State actors and non-State armed groups marked a shift in the classic security paradigm. Wars are still being fought on and over the bodies of women, to control their production and reproduction by force. Across regions, sexual violence has been perpetrated in public or witnessed by loved ones, to terrorize communities and fracture families through the violation of taboos, signifying that nothing is sacred, and no one is safe. (UNSG's 2018 Report, 3–4)

Despite important normative shifts in language and policy, and the widespread adoption of these international policy frameworks, in practice, sexual violence continues to characterize conflicts around the globe, with impunity of the perpetrators exacerbating the problem in post-conflict transition.

CHILD SOLDIERS: RECRUITMENT AND USE

According to the 2018 UN Secretary General's Report on Children in Armed Conflict, there are currently 54 non-state and 7 state armed forces that are known to recruit and use children as soldiers around the globe. The Paris Principles of 2007 defines a child soldier as

> any person below 18 years of age who is or has been recruited or used by an armed force or armed group in any capacity, including but not limited to children, boys and girls, used as fighters, cooks, porters, messengers, spies or for sexual purposes. It does not only refer to a child who is taking or has taken a direct part in hostilities. (7)

Adults recruit and use children for a variety of purposes and tasks. However, the reasons children are vulnerable to recruitment and use are due to a number of factors that range from poverty, unaccompanied children, orphan-hood, being internally displaced or in a refugee camp, lack of access to education, addictions to drugs or alcohol, as a result of being born into an armed group, belonging to a community self-protection militia, forced labour, seeking revenge for loss of loved ones, abduction, human trafficking gangs, or association with a friend who has joined an armed group. It should also be noted that both boys and girls are recruited and used as soldiers. Girls are often tasked with taking on a variety of roles within the armed groups, which includes fighting on the frontlines, being used as suicide bombers, intelligence gatherers, spies, porters, sex slaves, recruiters, messengers, and support functions such as being caregivers to the children of the armed groups, cooks, and domestic servants. Girls are viewed as an incredibly valuable strategic asset to many armed groups because they can help increase troop numbers, give birth to new recruits, can be used to lure other men and boys to the armed group, are often viewed as unassuming, and as rewards to male troops for morale boosting. The roles young women perform in armed insurgency groups in Africa go far beyond being simple "sex slaves" or "camp followers," rather they are essential to the functioning and maintenance of the war system itself (Mazurana and Carlson 2004). Rebel movements in Africa often need women and children to maintain this system and abduct them for this reason.

In 2009, the United Nations Security Council formally identified the Six Grave Violations of Child Rights[2] during armed conflict that affect children disproportionally. These violations are recruitment and use of children; killing or maiming of children; sexual violence against children; attacks on schools or hospitals; abduction of children; and denial of humanitarian access. The persistent issue of the recruitment and use of children into state and non-state armed groups is a cross-cutting violation, as for women, girls, and boys, this often leads to most, if not all, of the other violations. For the purpose of this chapter, the focus is on the third— sexual violence against children—the foundation for which is built upon the special respect and protections against "any form of indecent assault" contained within Article 77 (1) of the Additional Protocol I to the Geneva Conventions.

Children that are used as soldiers often face huge obstacles to returning to their home village and families. Stigma associated with child soldiers is pervasive often due to the horrendous acts they have been forced to carry out or subjected to. Misperceptions by communities about the children's own volition to commit such acts, as well as beliefs that such children are now tainted with evil, often prevail over the reality that the children are coerced, indoctrinated, and subjected to sexual violence, killing of neighbours and loved ones, drug abuse, maiming, torture, and destruction of communities. Armed groups actively find ways to desensitize the children to violence as a means to create loyalty, to cut off ties to families and communities, and to inculcate a sense of shame that prevents the children from being able to leave the armed group.

Children are particularly vulnerable in modern warfare and "function as a commodity that supports the political economy of violence" as Janie L. Leatherman states in her 2011 book. The making of a child into a child soldier involves understanding how military culture and hierarchy functions as well as understanding the unique aspects of children as malleable

---

[2] The Six Grave Violations of Child Rights were formally identified by the UNSC through UN SC Resolution 1612 to improve monitoring and prevention capabilities of violence towards children living in conflict affected areas.

to indoctrination. Adults who control armed groups and benefit from war have unfortunately understood the potential to combine these elements to their own selfish benefit. Indoctrination is the act of imbuing a child with the new worldview of a soldier (Singer 2006). This process involves the use of brutal force, psychological manipulation, fear and intimidation, as well as the severing of ties to one's familial and community connections.

Such acts to indoctrinate children as soldiers often involve the commission of violent acts that include sexual violence tactics. Jill Trenholm describes research with former boy soldiers in the DRC with respect to constructing masculinities. Group pressure to conform combined with the use of sexual violence is powerfully utilized to create a toxic situation for child soldiers as well as the direct victims of the sexual violence.

> Another boy who had witnessed rape, felt a deep sadness but as he explained, 'kept it in his heart' so as to avoid being killed. This participant admitted to witnessing a girl being shot in the vagina and said this, '... I was angry, it really bothered me but I could not show that I didn't agree with them because they would kill me.' (Trenholm 2013)

Unfortunately, rape is often perceived as part of the spoils of war, a normalized process for armed groups to participate in. Through Trenholm's research, it is understood by the former child soldiers that rape was a way of bolstering confidence, quelling anxiety, and restoring their power in times of fear and uncertainty. The commission of rape is often also used as a means to compensate for lack of pay, for vengeance after defeat, or to humiliate the enemy. Participation in gang rape was described as an expectation which cemented group solidarity.

On the one hand, the training and indoctrination of children as soldiers involves the infliction of sexual violence upon the children themselves, but, on the second hand, it often also involves the coercion of committing such acts upon others. Childhood is a time of identity formation. A militarized masculine identity may be viewed as better than no identity at all for boy children who grow up in conflict zones and poverty. As Singer (2006) outlines, childhood is a critical time when interpersonal networks and a child's understanding of their social surroundings is developed. If we consider that this is also extended to their understandings of gender, sexuality, and identity of self, the implications for their commission of brutal violence and rape extend far beyond this period and well into their adulthood. It should also be understood that the extent to which the use of sexual violence is used as both an indoctrination tactic for the child soldier, as well as a form of terror on populations, has lasting effects upon generations to come post conflict.

It should also be noted that boys are not immune, that they too are victims of sexual and gender-based violence in conflict, but that the vast majority of recorded victims are women and girls. In Colombia, girls as young as nine have been recruited into combat, and while they received training to take part in military operations, girls are also subject to sexual abuse from their commanders (Arredondo 2016). The sex trafficking of children is especially common in high tourist areas and areas where there is a large extractive industry. Girls recruited into armed groups are subjected to serious sexual violence in a repeated and systematic manner, including rape, sexual slavery and exploitation, forced pregnancy and abortion, and the passing on of sexually transmitted diseases (UN CRC 2015). Fuerzas Armadas Revolucionarias de Colombia—Ejército del Pueblo (FARC) has reportedly employed a "guerrilla policy" of sexual violence against children which includes acts of rape, forced sterilization, and forced abortion (Human Rights Watch 2016). In Colombia, it is forbidden for the girl soldiers associated with the FARC to have sexual relations with the male soldiers. As a result, if a girl becomes pregnant, she is forced to abort the child. In 2015, the Dallaire Initiative conducted roundtables in Colombia as part of a research project with former child soldiers. Boys in the workshops expressed how the forced abortion of the girls also had a deep impact upon them, for if the unborn child was theirs they too felt the deep loss, yet no one considers their emotions.

Typically, we fail to understand the realities that female fighters are perceived by many local populations as even more brutal and cruel than male fighters. Women who oppose or transgress female stereotypes in war will thus often be regarded as deviant (Barth 2002, Byrne 1996, 35, and Farr 2002 as quoted in Coulter et al. 2008) As an example, many reports about girls in the Lord's Resistance Army (LRA) of Northern Uganda only depict their roles as sex slaves and captive "wives." However, in a study conducted in 2004, 12 percent of the respondents reported that their primary role was as fighters, while 49 percent stated that their secondary role was as fighters (Mckay and Mazurana 2004). Abducted girls were also given as "wives" to LRA commanders. Aside from being fighters in front-line combat, some with command positions, and "wives" to LRA commanders, girls and young women have also carried out supportive tasks such as preparing food, carrying loot, and moving weapons (2004). The prevailing assumption that girls in the Democratic Republic of Congo (DRC) were only used as "wives" and did not serve in active combat roles is incorrect, as stated by Beth Verhey in her book published in 2004 (quoted in Evers et al. 2011). However, although sexual abuse is tragically commonplace in African wars it should nevertheless not be assumed that all female fighters have been sexually exploited (Brett and Specht 2004). Equally important is to understand that not all sexual exploitation experienced by girl soldiers is the same in conflict, as was demonstrated in the case of Colombia.

CASE STUDY: SOUTH SUDAN

The modern history of South Sudan is marked by political instability and insecurity that has spanned over generations. Conflicts in the region have been severe, with numerous grave violations against children, including the recruitment and use of child soldiers and war-based sexual violence. Estimating the numbers of child soldiers in an unstable and conflict environment like South Sudan is a difficult and costly endeavour. According to The United Nations Children's Fund (UNICEF), over 19,000 children have been recruited into armed groups; 3200 children have been abducted; and over 1200 children have been affected by sexual violence, 995 of whom are girls (UNICEF 2017). The Sudan People's Liberation Army, the Sudan People's Liberation Army—In Opposition and the White Army are all listed in the May 2018 Secretary-General's Annual Report on children and armed conflict, for recruiting, using as combatants, killing, maiming, abducting, raping, and sexually exploiting children (UN Security Council 2017). Attempts to end the conflict have repeatedly collapsed over the last five years. A revitalized peace agreement was signed on the 12th of September 2018, at the time of writing this chapter. The recruitment and use of child soldiers is prohibited as part of the peace agreement, as is sexual and gender-based violence (SGBV). Despite concerted efforts to capture and report on the incidents of grave violations being committed against children in ongoing conflicts, current statistics are severely underestimated. Furthermore, when it comes to sexual violence in South Sudan, most available research does not disaggregate violations committed against women versus girls.

In South Sudan, UNICEF's best estimate in 2017 is that more than 19,000 child soldiers were associated with armed forces and armed groups in the country (UNICEF 2017), and less than 1000 have been released since then (UNICEF 2017). The push and pull factors that lead to recruitment, and often re-recruitment, range from social norms and traditions to the false pretence of "safety" associated with organized armed groups. Furthermore, in some regions of South Sudan, children have long been involved in traditional roles as community protectors and cattle raiders. These traditions are accentuated by extreme poverty, in which children often join armed groups seeking basic food and shelter. Children are also involuntarily recruited through abduction, forced marriage, or through impregnation by security sector actors. While the majority of child soldiers in South Sudan are boys, girls are also recruited and face additional dangers related to gender inequality and gender-based violence.

Overall, the rates of violence against women and girls documented in South Sudan are some of the highest in the world. A study in 2017 by the Global Women's Institute and the International Rescue Committee found two-thirds of women and girls in South Sudan have reportedly experienced violence at least once in their lives. While the exact number of people who have been subjected to sexual violence will never be known, the few available statistics are alarming. UNICEF reported that between December 2013 and December 2016, 1130 children were sexually assaulted. A survey conducted in 2015 by the United Nations Population Fund (UNFPA) found that 72 percent of women living in four United Nations Mission in South Sudan Protection of Civilians Sites (PoC) sites in Juba reported having been raped since the conflict broke out.

Militarized sexual violence has been a key facet of the crisis, with the main perpetrators belonging to national security forces or opposition militia. This has resulted in a lack of trust amongst civilians towards the people that are supposed to protect them. According to the UN Secretary-General's 2018 Report on Children and Armed Conflict, as well as a 2017 Report conducted by Amnesty International, all parties to the conflict in South Sudan recruit and use child soldiers and use sexual violence as strategies and tactics of war to terrorize and prolong the instability. In 2017, the United Nations Mission to South Sudan documented 196 cases of conflict-related sexual violence, affecting 128 women and 68 girls. These violations were attributed to the South Sudanese Peoples Defence Forces and Sudanese Peoples Liberation Army-Internal Opposition (SPLA). Violations include rape, gang rape, and abduction for the purposes of sexual assault.

> According to the Commission on Human Rights in South Sudan, appalling acts of rape, mutilation of sexual organs and other forms of sexual violence were perpetrated against women, girls, men and boys, often in front of relatives, in order to humiliate victims, families and entire communities, or as a form of punishment in detention settings. (All Survivors Project 2017)

The proliferation of militias with ready access to arms increased the rate of sexual violence, serving as a driver of displacement. By the end of 2017, there were almost two million civilians displaced in South Sudan, including 209,898 living in sites for the protection of civilians managed by the United Nations Mission in South Sudan (UNMISS). An additional two million civilians had fled across the border, with the risk of sexual violence exacerbated during flight, because elements of the security forces, militias, and roving bands of armed young people were preying upon women and girls. Social stigma and community pressure perpetuate the silence surrounding such crimes, which can result in wives being shunned by their husbands and girls being withdrawn from school.

Amnesty International carried out a comprehensive research study in 2017 to assess the scale and impact of the sexual violence in South Sudan. Researchers interviewed 168 survivors of, and 14 witnesses to, incidents of sexual violence that have occurred since 2013 (2017). In an interview conducted by Amnesty International, a mother by the name of Joy recounts how soldiers abducted her young daughter.

> Then they looked at my elder daughter and they said, 'This girl is going with us'... One of them told me, 'I have been looking for a beautiful Shilluk girl but now I got her, and you are going to be my mother-in-law.' They started laughing at us because we were all crying... They started pulling my daughter because she was refusing to go with them, and I was trying to pull her back, but they warned me that I would die like my father and then they slapped me and I fell down... My daughter cried and told me, 'Mama, let me go with them because if they kill you like my grandfather, my brothers will remain alone in this life. Don't worry, they are taking me as a wife. They will not kill me and if I get a chance where they are taking me, I will come back to you. (2017)

According to the Amnesty Report, sexual violence against men and boys in South Sudan's conflict remains largely invisible, despite indications that it occurs with some frequency.

This is due to common assumptions—and misperceptions—that sexual violence only involves male perpetrators and female victims. In addition to this, in South Sudanese culture and society—where homosexuality is derided and sex between men is a criminal offence—sexual violence against men carries an even deeper stigma for the victim than sexual violence against women. As a result, it is likely that incidents of sexual violence against men and boys in South Sudan are severely underreported. (2017)

Men and boys are particularly at risk of sexual violence while in custody; most of the cases included in this Report occurred during arrests or while in government detention. The acts perpetrated include rape with objects, forced sterilization through castration, and other torture focused on sexual organs. Former child soldier, Emmanuel Jal, recounts in his book how during his time with the SPLA, the boys would place newspaper in their pants at night as a strategy to avoid being sexually violated by their older male commanders. The rustling of the newspaper would alert the other boys to wake up and deter the potential perpetrator (2009).

Other reported examples of sexual violence include the rape and gang rape of women and girls in Koch County, some of whom were later burned alive in their *tukuls*.[3] One survivor stated, "If you look them in the face when they are doing it, they will kill you" (All Survivors Project 2017). The use of brutal forms of sexual violence in South Sudan has had long-reaching consequences that have resulted in the breakdown of familial structures, the spread of sexually transmitted diseases, and the spread of fear, trauma, and distrust amongst many communities.

In South Sudan, a National Gender Policy has been developed to guide the work of the Ministry of Gender, Child and Social Welfare (MOGCSW), as well as gender policy throughout the country. The Child Act sets a legal age of marriage and establishes the punishment for child rape. However, while the legal age of marriage is 18, this is typically not enforced (Kircher 2013). Legally, the Penal Code of 2008 sets a broad definition of rape and heavy punishments, including up to 14 years in prison. However, it denies rape within marriage and does not lay out punishments for domestic violence (Clancy 2012). The constitution also enshrines the importance of the customary legal system at community level. This forms parallel formal and customary legal systems which often reduce violence against women

---

[3] *Tukuls* are a cone-shaped hut traditionally found in Eastern and Northeastern Africa. They are often made of mud and toped with a roof made of straw or a similar material.

and girls to a "second tier" crime that is adjudicated by local chiefs who have limited legal training. While there is no standard codified set of customary laws, overall these laws are seen as supportive of patriarchal norms and biased against survivors seeking justice. For example, unmarried survivors of rape are often made to marry the perpetrator of the rapist under the customary system.

PREVENTION EFFORTS

The United Nations Secretary General's 2018 Report on Conflict Related Sexual Violence (CSRV) notes that "self-reliance, economic empowerment and having a political voice are the most effective forms of protection from sexual violence," and that to alleviate stigma of victims, "engagement with religious and traditional leaders is required to help shift harmful social norms around honour, shame and victim-blaming." In the first instance, how do boys and girls gain better protection, given these measures are considered for adult women?

UNSG's 2018 Report on CRSV notes achievements over the past year: the team of experts in 13 countries and 3 regional bodies; 21 women's protection advisers; successful prosecutions of rape as a war crime and crime against humanity in DRC (Democratic Republic of Congo); specialized police unit for sexual violence in CAR (Central African Republic); strategies developed for investigating and prosecuting sexual violence crimes by ISIL/Da'esh in Iraq; formulation of an action plan with the South Sudanese Armed Forces (now SSPDF); 17 high-ranking military officials indicted in Conakry. "The work of the Team of Experts demonstrates that, with political will and dedicated assistance, Governments can hold perpetrators of conflict-related sexual violence accountable and deliver justice for victims".

These solutions cited in the UNSG's 2018 Report on CRSV are all reactive, back-end solutions and achievements. CRSV continues but is being monitored better and prosecuted better. These are important wins, to be sure, but we cannot celebrate just yet if progress isn't being made on the reduction or elimination of CRSV. It is hoped that deterrence of future crimes occurs as a result of holding perpetrators and high-ranking officials responsible. However, as important as deterrence may be, addressing attitudinal and behavioural change should be the goal.

With respect to children, failure to prevent their exposure to sexual violence, as either perpetrators or victims, is a failure in the fight to end

CRSV. Attitudes and experiences on gender, sexual violence as well as the psycho-social and physical ramifications for children have not been fully explored, researched, or understood. Far too often the debates, research and dialogue are focused purely on the concept of CRSV from an adult perspective, and even more so from the perspective of female victims.

A collective, shared mandate to prevent sexual violence is required. This responsibility must be shared among the United Nations, non-governmental organizations, civil society, and national governments. UNSC 1820 explicitly places the primary responsibility on states and all parties to conflict. UNSG acknowledges in the 2018 Report that "the international community spends far more time and resources responding to crises than preventing them" (p. 7).

Conclusion

Peace and security can only be achieved with the recognition of the protection of children, the prevention of their recruitment and use as soldiers, and the clear links to sexual violence as a tactic of war that must be halted to break cycles of endemic violence.

In South Sudan, there was a clear example of the differences seen in peace processes that engage women and those that do not within the same country/context. In the lead up to the 2005 Comprehensive Peace Agreement, women were almost completely excluded from the negotiations of the Machakos Accords and subsequent peace agreement signed in Naivasha, Kenya. This led to a peace agreement that was completely gender-blind and did not acknowledge that violence against women and girls occurred during the conflict and would continue to affect women as the country transitioned to a post-conflict setting. Comparatively, the process to negotiate the 2013 Agreement on the Resolution of Conflict in the Republic of South Sudan (ARCSS) involved participation of women much more. In fact, women coalesced into a formal "women's bloc" that had a representative formally sign the peace agreement on behalf of the bloc. While this peace agreement has yet to be fully implemented, the existence of these provisions shows that it is possible for women to advocate for the inclusion of these issues in future peace processes in South Sudan and given the current revitalization of the Ceasefire and Peace Agreement as of August 2018, there is renewed hope.

Given the extent of sexual violence, a major problem for young men and women that has been associated with their time in the armed forces is sexually transmitted diseases. However, few are diagnosed and treated unless they go through a rehabilitation or interim care centre where such services are offered or if primary medical care is provided by an NGO, but in war-torn countries there is an almost total absence of sexual and reproductive health services (McKay and Mazurana 2004, 62).

As has been shown, one effect of the social stigma attached to having been a fighter is that many women and girls hide their past and do not come forward to receive the DDR (Disarmament, Demobilization, and Reintegration) benefits they are entitled to (Coulter et al. 2008). Another consequence of having been a female fighter is the difficulty of getting married. It is of great importance in many African societies as marriage is seen as mandatory for women. In Sierra Leone and Uganda, female ex-fighters were worried about their marriage prospects and were reported as saying that, when war was over, men preferred civilian women, women without scars from battle, and women who were sexually "untouched" (2008).

It should be acknowledged that sexual exploitation and abuse are experienced by many boys and girls associated with fighting forces. It is important to understand local concepts of rape and sexual stigma to address these issues adequately on the ground combined with an understanding of the experiences and challenges faced by former child soldiers. Equally critical is to understand the extent to which such experiences and learned behaviour impacts the long-term family structures, sexualized behaviour that perpetuates cycles of violence and abuse.

As Nelson Mandela stated, "There can be no keener revelation of a society's soul than the way in which it treats its children" (Mandela 1995). Understanding how we address these violations of children's basic rights and put the resources towards their prioritization is critical to the future of humanity.

NOTE ON THE ROMÉO DALLAIRE CHILD SOLDIERS INITIATIVE

The Roméo Dallaire Child Soldiers Initiative (Dallaire Initiative) is an international non-profit organization based out of Dalhousie University, Halifax, Canada, with the ultimate goal of progressively ending the recruitment and use of children as soldiers. The Dallaire Initiative takes a multifaceted approach to this issue which includes training security sector actors around the world, leading high-level advocacy with governments and international organizations, and conducting research to help identify critical gaps in knowledge on the issues pertaining to the recruitment and use of child soldiers; which in turn helps the organization make a greater impact on policy development.

The Dallaire Initiative currently works across eight countries, and in 2018 the organization opened its first regional office in South Sudan. The organization was founded by Lt. Gen (Ret'd) Roméo Dallaire and is now lead by Executive Director, Dr. Shelly Whitman. Dr. Whitman has led the Dallaire Initiative since January 2010 and has spearheaded its unique approach around the world to address the prevention of the recruitment and use of children as soldiers. As a result, in 2017, Dr. Whitman assisted the Canadian Government with the creation of the Vancouver Principles on Peacekeeping and the Prevention of the Recruitment and Use of Child Soldiers. To date 70 nations have endorsed the Vancouver Principles. To find out more about the organization, visit their website: www.child-soldiers.org.

REFERENCES

All Survivors Project Foundation. 2017. South Sudan Report. https://allsurvivorsproject.org/wp-content/uploads/2017/08/South-Sudan-1.pdf.
Amnesty International. 2017. South Sudan 'Do Not Remain Silent': Survivors of Sexual Violence in South Sudan Call for Justice and Reparations. July 24. https://www.amnesty.org/en/documents/afr65/6469/2017/en/.
Arredondo, Juan. 2016. Child Soldiers in Colombia. *ICRC*, September 7. https://www.icrc.org/en/document/child-soldiers-colombia-juan-arredondo.
Brett, Rachel, and Irma Specht. 2004. *Young Soldiers: Why They Choose to Fight.* Boulder: Lynne Rienner Publishers.
Clancy, Deidre. 2012. *Falling Through the Cracks: Reflections on Customary Law and the Imprisonment of Women in South Sudan.* A Project of the Strategic Initiative for Women in the Horn of Africa (SIHA). https://www.academia.edu/2642503/Falling_Through_The_Cracks-Refection_on_customary_law_and_the_imprisonment_of_women_in_South_Sudan?auto=download.
Coulter, Chris, Mariam Persson, and Mats Utas. 2008. *Young Female Fighters in African Wars: Conflict and Its Consequences.* Uppsala: The Nordic African Institute.

Evers, Sandra J.T.M., Catrien Notermans, and Erik van Ommering, eds. 2011. *Not Just a Victim: The Child as Catalyst and Witness of Contemporary Africa*, Vol. 20: Afrika-Studiecentrum Series. Boston: Brill.

Human Rights Watch. 2016. *World Report: Colombia*. https://www.hrw.org/world-report/2016/country-chapters/colombia

Jal, Emmanuel. 2009. *War Child: A Child Soldier's Story*. New York: Macmillan.

Kircher, I. 2013. Challenges to Security, Livelihoods, and Gender Justice in South Sudan: The Situation of Dinka Agro-pastoralist Communities in Lakes and Warrap states. http://policypractice.oxfam.org.uk/publications/challenges-to-security-livelihoods-and-gender-justice-in-south-sudan-the-situat-271995.

Leatherman, Janie L. 2011. *Sexual Violence in Armed Conflict*. Cambridge: Polity Press.

Mandela, Nelson. 1995. *Launch of the Nelson Mandela Children's Protection Fund*. Keynote Address at the Launch of NMCPF, Pretoria ZA. http://www.sahistory.org.za/archive/speech-president-nelson-mandela-launch-nelson-mandela-childrens-fund-mahlambandlopfu-pretori.

Mazurana, Dyan, and Khristopher Carlson. 2004. From Combat to Community: Women and Girls of Sierra Leone. *Hunt Alternatives Fund*, December 2018. http://www.peacewomen.org.

McKay, Susan, and Dyan Mazurana. 2004. *Where Are the Girls? Girls in Fighting Forces in Northern Uganda, Sierra Leone, and Mozambique: Their Lives During and After War*. Quebec: International Centre for Human Rights and Democratic Development.

Singer, Peter. 2006. *Children at War*. California: University of California Press.

Trenholm, Jill. 2013. Women Survivors, Lost Children and Traumatized Masculinity. The Phenomena of Rape and War in Eastern Democratic Republic of Congo. Uppsala, SE: Centre for Gender Research, Uppsala University. http://www.diva-portal.org/smash/get/diva2:639033/FULLTEXT01.pdf.

UNICEF. 2017. Childhood Under Attack: The Staggering Impact of South Sudan's Crisis on Children. *UNICEF Briefing Note*, December 15. https://www.unicef.org/southsudan/UNICEF_South_Sudan_Report_Childhood_under_Attack_15Dec_FINAL.pdf.

United Nations Committee on the Rights of the Child. 2015. *United Nations Convention on the Rights of the Child (UNCRC)*, UN Doc. CRC/C/NDL/CO/4, New York, June 8. https://tbinternet.ohchr.org/Treaties/CRC/Shared%20Documents/NLD/INT_CRC_COCNLD_20805_E.pdf.

United Nations Security Council. 2017. *Children and Armed Conflict: Report of the Secretary-General*, UN Doc. S/2017/821, New York, August 24. https://reliefweb.int/sites/reliefweb.int/files/resources/N1726811.pdf.

Wood, Elisabeth Jean. 2014. Conflict-Related Sexual Violence and the Policy Implications for Research. *International Review of the Red Cross* 96 (894, Summer): 457–478.

CHAPTER 4

Confronting US Moral Hypocrisy on Child Soldiers, Inventing Antiracist Solidarity

Traci C. West

The recruitment and deployment of girls as fighters in armed conflict involves a morass of moral issues that must be considered when seeking ideas about ending this practice. But our capacity to generate those ideas may be constrained by racially paternalistic and often hypocritical understandings of the moral issues child soldiering involves. This includes communal moral understandings related to gender norms, sexual violence, childhood, and war. The driving force behind the search for more ideas about the perpetuation of child soldiering should be our concern about the harm to children that can result from their experiences as soldiers. Sometimes the harm includes sexual exploitation by other soldiers. The goal of meaningfully contributing to an approach aimed at stopping this practice demands unflinching scrutiny of our starting assumptions about which basic moral values and religious commitments support child soldiering, and which ones help to dismantle it.

When making a case to oppose the practice, a blanket appeal to a supposedly universal, transnational notion of a child's right to protection seems like an obvious foundational point, but this approach can mislead.

T. C. West (✉)
Drew University Theological School, Madison, NJ, USA
e-mail: twest@drew.edu

© The Author(s) 2019   43
S. Willhauck (ed.), *Female Child Soldiering, Gender Violence, and Feminist Theologies*, https://doi.org/10.1007/978-3-030-21982-6_4

An assumed, broad, moral consensus on child rights fails to appreciate how moral messages about what constitutes virtuousness in societal understandings of gender, sexual violence, childhood, and war can contribute to communal acceptance of the exploitation of girl children as soldiers. The practice of using child soldiers spotlights the presence of conflicting moral understandings that resist easy generalizations about the moral status of children in global conversations. The actions of child soldiers bring into question, for instance, a rigid moral dichotomy juxtaposing childhood as innocence and the right to be defended with soldiering as aggression and the duty to defend. As social anthropologist Alcinda Honwana explains in her study of African child soldiers, "We must go beyond the clear-cut demarcations between child and adult, and between innocence and guilt, to examine the intricate ways in which the condition of child soldier cuts across established categories" (2006, 4).

Another simplistic dichotomy commonly espoused by leaders based in the Americas and Africa distinguishes femaleness from maleness by assuming an innate vulnerability of girls that is not attributed to boys. Such gendered assumptions must not be left unexamined in critiques of child soldiering. Conservative gender narratives tend to be dominant in public rhetoric about moral values that most leaders assume to be shared across differing local communities. These dominant narratives usually associate the femaleness of girls with an intrinsic need for protection and defending. And the need for the protection of girls seems particularly self-evident in the context of war or any endangering community-wide conflict. Even many strands of liberal feminist societal critiques tend to dwell on the association of femaleness with vulnerability to intimate violence, sexual harassment, and sex discrimination that perpetually demands policies of protection and redress. When their actions are seen as marked by some degree of agency, girl child soldiers violate conservative gender narratives and perhaps even liberal ones as well. When opposing this practice one must carefully examine the gendered values to which one appeals. In order to dismantle the practice of child soldiering by girls is it necessary to reinforce some notion of the inherent defenselessness and non-aggression of girls based on the assumption that their femaleness demands that they be relegated to the status of persons fundamentally in need of protection by males and adult females? Or, actually, is it only wealthy white US girls who most authentically occupy the status of inherently defenseless and in need of protection?

Also, the historically influential role of anti-black racism matters when specific atrocities that involve African children as combatants are cited. Child soldiers have been involved in postcolonial civil wars and conflicts during the late twentieth century and early twenty-first century in several settings in Africa such as Sierra Leone, Rwanda, Angola, Mozambique, and the Congo. For US-based interpreters such as myself, caution is in order when specifying the atrocities related to child soldiering that girls suffer in black African contexts that deserve censure. We must critically weigh the long-held, geopolitical notions of US moral exceptionalism and how they may inform the lens of analysis that we bring. Too often US-American judgments about the immoral practices of others in the world emanate from selected, US-American cultural standards or criteria that assume our moral superiority and credibility as a base line, especially in relation to black Africans. Moreover, Christian missionary approaches have played a pivotal role in shaping the expression of moral values within the history of colonialism in Africa as well as current humanitarian NGOs actively responding to the crises spawned by armed conflicts in Africa. There has been courageous and well-intentioned international Christian involvement in responses to African child soldiers. But the nurturing of Christian moral values related to soldiering and sacrifice within the US domestic sphere should be considered as well. Below I consider how endangering communal conflicts within the US context exemplified in the civil rights movement may reveal instances of a black Christian embrace of a certain kind of child soldiering. These examples point to ambiguous societal responses to the use of children in violent national conflicts.

By including illustrations from US-American contexts and recent history in this chapter, I stress the moral grounds for constructing a US-based response to the use of child soldiers, particularly of girls in African contexts. When engaging in transnational moral critiques, I find it imperative to interrogate the vantage point that I bring. I eschew any attempt to obscure the US-American geopolitical perspective in which I am steeped, leaving intact the whiff of long-standing assumptions of cultural superiority rooted in our touted foundational national commitment to democracy, freedom, and equality. There is significant moral content in the global influence of Christianity dominated, US-American politics and culture, as well as the racist legacies of the trans-Atlantic slave trade that permeate them. That anti-black racism infused morality must not be ignored or rendered neutral in the identification of transnational community values related to the rights of children. The crafting of a meaningful response to child soldiering requires an examination of values we bring to the table of shared opposition to certain harms done to African girls in their experiences of child soldiering. An approach that incorporates such self-critical scrutiny helps to clarify the moral issues at stake. But it also enables a more disruptive antiracist conceptualization of which social mores need to change.

A disruptive Africana ethical framework must oppose brutalities suffered by African girls in some of the most egregious and deliberately orchestrated forms of sexual violence, coercion, and humiliation. This ethical framework has to simultaneously confront any racist assumptions of Africans as a barbaric "other" that may lurk in such transnational opposition to the acts of African perpetrators. The confrontation has to begin with an assessment of our relatedness. Racist devaluation may remain an undisturbed component within an ethical response to the harms of child soldiering based on pitying them, revulsion for them, or some other form of critical lens that morally divides them (those with this problem) from us.

OUR VALUES DIFFER FROM THEIRS, OR DO THEY?

In the opening discussion of his study of the daily lives of child soldiers, social psychologist Michael Wessells cites an example of a 15-year-old girl, Fatmata, in 2002 Sierra Leone. She was captured by rebel soldiers, enlisted in their work, and taken as a "wife" by one of her captors. Wessells compellingly recounts this girl's story. He notes the difficulty of comprehending Fatmata's situation that may arise for some of his "western" readers, many of whom are likely US-American. Through a geopolitical analytical starting point, he explains that "when most people in western societies think of their children, they think not of war and horror but of images from their own childhoods of play, outings with their family, summer travels, and going to school" (2006, 2). His framing broadens the moral terrain from the war-torn sociohistorical moment in Sierra Leone to society wide understandings of childhood. The narrative he presents reinforces the need to bridge a perceived cultural gap between Fatmata's society and western societies. But the existence of the gap reassures westerners. In this cultural gap one finds a comforting affirmation of the quality of western societies together with a troubling impression of societies such as Fatmata's. By bringing the gap to the attention of the reader it inculcates a view of dramatic differences between the most common experiences of childhood in each type of society.

But in US-American society, under conditions that do not reflect the war-torn, collapsed state of Sierra Leone in 2002, girls find captivity to sexual violence all too common. Although only a small percentage of child sexual abuse is ever reported, in the late twentieth century it was estimated that one in four US girls would be sexually abused before they turned 18 (Finkelhor et al. 1990). Statistics for the first decade of twenty-first-century US society indicate that 30% of women were between the ages of 11 and 17 at the time of their first completed rape (Black et al. 2011). When we accept the idea of a complete disjunction between two types of societies—western and Sierra Leone as Wessells seems to depict—with two diametrically opposed common experiences of childhood trauma, it can morally discipline us in falsehood. This understanding of disjunction may nurture a hypocritical US stance. It affirms our recognition of the need to address the sexual victimization of girl children in African societies such as war-torn Sierra Leone while denying the same necessity in western societies such as the United States since, presumably, instead of any abuse US children enjoy "play, outings with their family, summer travels, and going to school." Denial of the widespread problem of child sexual abuse is quite costly for victimized US girls (and boys).

The problem of US-American hypocrisy surfaces repeatedly in the state's formal positions on child soldiers expressed in global forums, policies for recruitment of youth for its own military, and treatment of child soldiers it regards as enemy combatants. The US condemnations of the use of child soldiers in the context of the intense geopolitics of the United Nations may illustrate the most public displays of this hypocrisy. In such international arenas US political leaders appear to articulate their staunch moral opposition to child soldiers. But then they pursue their own perceived national interests at the cost of full participation in global agreements aimed at curbing child soldiers. In one instance in 1999, President Bill Clinton declared:

> Today, the time has come to build on the growing world consensus to ban the most abusive forms of child labour—to join together and to say there are some things we cannot and will not tolerate. We will not tolerate children being used in pornography and prostitution. We will not tolerate children in slavery or bondage. We will not tolerate children being forcibly recruited to serve in armed conflicts. (1999)

President Clinton declared this at the 1999 International Labour Conference where they debated and adopted Convention No. 182, the Convention concerning the Prohibition and Immediate Action for the Elimination of the Worst Forms of Child Labour (Clinton 1999). But in the meetings in which the agreement was debated, the United States had argued against other national groups, including the African groups, on their proposal for an outright ban on the use of children under 18 years old in all kinds of armed conflicts (Dennis 1999; Rosen 2012; Combined News Service, *Newsday* 2000).

The United States refused to sign on to the Convention on the Rights of the Child (1989) and other international treaties that directly oppose the use of child soldiers. It did, however, join the Optional Protocol to the Convention on the Rights of the Child (2000) on the involvement of children in armed conflict, but reserved its right to continue to recruit 17 year olds into its military. In its military recruitment practices the United States steadfastly clings to its tradition of pressuring teenagers into volunteering for the military. They routinely use financial incentives and other inducements just as the youth are completing high school. This aggressive strategy can have a disproportionate impact on low-income 16- and 17-year-old students of color. There is technically an opt-out clause for parents of the children, but often it is made available with inconsistent and ambiguous communication about it (Castro 2015, 9).

Education scholar Erin Castro describes the daily high pressure tactics of military recruiters located within high schools where "low-income students of color in high-poverty schools are labeled as 'not ready for college,' but are at the same time actively recruited into the military" (2015, 16). In the drive to swell the ranks of its soldiers in response to the "war on terror" unscrupulous strategies for the recruitment and deployment of youth in the US military increased in the early twenty-first century (11–12). Also, youth were deployed to conflict zones. During 2003–2004, the US Army deployed approximately sixty 17-year-olds to Afghanistan and Iraq (Rosen 2012, 88). The moral valuing of childhood that is given expression in these recruitment practices seems to sacrifice protection of youth, especially in low-income communities. Protection of these youth from armed conflict situations seems to be sacrificed to the value of safeguarding the nation's political commitment to maintaining a sizable military with no mandatory military draft policy.

A 2017 *Huffington Post* headline announced: "Girls in the DRC Are Choosing to Be Child Soldiers to Escape Poverty" (Chakamba 2017).

The article reported on the Child Soldiers International (CSI) Report "'If I Could Go To School...' Education as a Tool to Prevent the Recruitment of Girls and Assist with Their Recovery and Reintegration in the Democratic Republic of Congo" (Child Soldiers International 2017). The headline and the evidence in the DRC report capture the themes of poverty, education, and supposed choice made by the girls. These same themes are also at issue in the US recruitment of teenage children as soldiers that Castro analyzes in her study. The conditions of poverty and hunger in the United States differ from the context of the Democratic Republic of the Congo where there are more widespread, extreme conditions of hunger, poverty, armed conflict, and instability of basic state functions. Yet, the economic vulnerability of certain children in both contexts played a role in social pressure exerted on them to enter the military. The utility of their economic vulnerability proved useful for the aims of swelling the population of the armed forces at the expense of concern for the children's safety and educational choices.

A different example of US hypocrisy in global negotiations on shared global values centered on US gun culture. It provides another display of how the state's protection of its internal cultural values and political loyalties superseded unambiguous articulation of its international opposition to child soldiers. In 2001 the UN Conference on the Illicit Trade in Small Arms to eliminate illegal trade in light weapons constituted another effort to apply international pressure to create a wide menu of strategies to eliminate the use of child soldiers. Journalist and political scientist P.W. Singer complained that "following intense lobbying by the National Rifle Association (NRA) leadership, the United States worked to counter any efforts to make international small arms sales more transparent (one doubts whether the core members, who are hunters and sportsmen, would be pleased to support the spread of AK-47s to children abducted by warlords)" (2006, 137). In this instance, the primacy of the revered status of guns and ready access to them so entrenched in dominant US mores was reflected in the leadership that the United States offered the international community. Unfortunately it helped to undermine global agreement on certain strategies to end use of child soldiers.

Few practices more directly illustrate how extreme the degree of US disregard can be for respecting international consensus on the rights of children than the government's decisions about how to treat child soldiers in the context of its own armed conflicts. As anthropologist David Rosen has detailed, in the wake of the September 2011 attacks on the United

States, the US government argued that it did not have to follow international law in its treatment of juvenile prisoners captured in Afghanistan and Iraq and then held at Guantanamo Bay prison (2012, 92). The US government officials maintained that the United States was "not obligated to meet the most minimal standards of humane treatment of detainees, stating that it was not bound by the laws of war, nor was it required to provide any of the protections afforded to child soldiers contained in the Optional Protocol" (96). Rosen offers a horrifying account of the torture of brown Muslim children identified as enemy combatants by the US military in Afghanistan (100–103). The moral understandings of the rights of child soldiers embodied in state policies and practices of the US "war on terror" bring attention to the ways in which the identity of the children can mitigate any scruples about what it means for the state to deliberately participate in harming them.

Regardless of the rhetoric of leaders at international forums the actual practices of the state expose the dominant moral standards of the society with regard to child soldiers. The US government practices have been at best ambivalent in their formal support of global prohibitions on child soldiers. At worst, because of their protection of child soldiering among their own military ranks and disregard for the lives and dignity of child soldiers it identifies as its enemies, US-American state practices have evidenced an intransigent stance of hypocrisy with regard to ending this practice. This stance separates its public, international condemnations of others who sanction child soldiers, from the impunity we deserve for our practices that support them.

When the cultural foundations of one's moral approach are riddled with such inconsistent and untrustworthy commitments to stopping the practice of utilizing children as soldiers, it becomes even more pressing to probe the moral purpose driving one's critique of child soldiers in Africa. Our motives shape the conceptualization of the strategic interventions that are deemed necessary to end this practice. For a US perspective, if one's guiding moral purpose rests on a radical differentiation between them and us, it is likely to foster yet another paternalistic imposition of values that augments the longstanding destructive history of European Christian colonization of Africa. International relations scholar Vanessa Pupavac demonstrates how paternalism can emerge in the moralization agenda of international interventions on behalf of child rights. The interventions respond to the crises of armed conflicts that arise in the global south, including child soldiers. Pupavac provides a trenchant critique of the approach by global leaders in advancing what she calls the children's rights regime. When evaluating international strategies based on the UN Convention on the Rights of the Child (1989), she finds problematic linkages to earlier child-salvation approaches of colonial era missionaries.

> While nineteenth-century European missionaries spoke of the need to civilise the natives, today's human rights campaigners and international peace counsellors speak of the need to promote children's rights and create tolerant cultures. The presumption underlying the children's rights paradigm is that the people and their child-rearing and other cultural practices are the problem. As a consequence, international organisations assume that external actors are required to intervene to define social norms and ensure their institutionalisation. (Pupavac 2001, 109)

In accord with Pupavac's critique, the children's rights moral rationale for radical global intervention rests upon a distinction between them (global south) and us (outsider human rights advocates) on support for child soldiers. Their assumed moral deficiency requires a mission to change the entire structuring of their cultural values related to their children. Pupavac challenges this paternalistic logic about the global south by pointing out that because "of economic and social necessity, children in developing countries take on adult roles including work at a much younger age than in Western countries" (2001, 101). But even this defense of developing countries in the global south rests upon drawing distinctions between their societal norms and those of western countries. In contrast to an emphasis on opposing norms and values articulated by Pupavac and those she criticizes, I believe that we must also examine the possibility that highly developed nations such as the United States and the developing nations share some of the cultural values that fuel tolerance for child soldiering.

Alongside of scrutinizing varied forms of hypocrisy in US practices that reflect disagreements with any global consensus on opposing the use of child soldiers, there are internal expressions of national values that may be relevant and need attention too. In some instances of community conflicts that involved violence within the United States, there has been widespread support for certain children "taking on adult roles" because their communities and indeed their nation purportedly needed them to do so, as in the case of the civil rights movement. Any moral mapping of the strategic choices communities make in conflict situations about the use of children for political ends should include the identification of US domestic moral values that have embraced the deployment of girls of African descent as warriors.

WHEN US BLACK GIRL WARRIORS ARE CONSIDERED NECESSARY

For most US-based critics who oppose the recruitment and deployment of African girls as child soldiers no cause can be imagined that could warrant the exploitation and trauma that they endure as soldiers. Yet there have been certain circumstances of community-wide racial conflict in the 1950s and 1960s in the United States when, for civil rights movement supporters, a costly form of child soldiering was virtuous and necessary. The circumstances did not include armed conflict between two warring sides. However, in many of the settings where their campaigns occurred, the non-violent civil rights activists were confronted by considerable violence. They were violently attacked by armed state officials, especially local police sheriffs, as well as by informally organized white supremacists, such as the Ku Klux Klan. White southern racists responded to the movement by bombing black family homes and churches frequently throughout the 1950s and 1960s. The attacks were so frequent in Birmingham that black activists called it "Bombingham" (Eskew 1997; Manis 2001). There were over 50 bombings in Birmingham by white Christians who carried out their terrorism on behalf of their Christian white supremacist beliefs. But in the most well-known Birmingham bombing by white Christians in 1963, a bomb attack on a black church killed four young black girls while they attended Sunday School. For several decades of the mid-twentieth century, African American children and youth marched in civil rights movement mass protests and braved everyday violence and abuse as they desegregated hostile white schools (Franklin 2015). They were jailed and in extreme cases murdered. The contributions of these children are still heralded as heroic and invaluable to that movement's accomplishments by those who oppose white racism and celebrate collective struggle to diminish its influence. Current admirers of the US civil rights movement, therefore, demonstrate a high tolerance for the costs and sacrifices of the children. Admittedly, in the midst of that historical moment debates and disagreements occurred among movement leaders about the children's agency, consent, and vulnerability.

In his study of the role of children and youth in this movement, Christian social ethicist Rufus Burrow cites Thurgood Marshall's concerns about the use of children. Marshall was one of the lead attorneys on the 1954 Brown v. Board of Education Supreme Court school desegregation decision. He responded negatively to Martin Luther King Jr.'s 1956 public comments about the probable need for youth to boycott segregated public schools in order to ensure that the Brown decision was enforced. Marshall said: "I don't approve of using children to do men's work" (as quoted in Burrow 2014, 113). The achievement of the goal of transforming entrenched systems of racist political governance and social mores of the United States did indeed involve difficult and dangerous work. Movement leaders had to decide if children should be recruited to perform that labor. In the context of a heated national conflict over the freedom and equal rights of citizens, how should the criteria be determined for what constitutes abusive forms of child labor deployed within that struggle?

In 1963 adult activists organized thousands of children from third grade to high school to march out of their schools in protest in Birmingham, Alabama. They would then be jailed by one of the most notoriously violent and cruel white supremacist southern sheriffs, "Bull" Connor. Some of the adult activist leaders such as James Bevel argued for the use of children in Birmingham for pragmatic reasons. He explained that the children were willing to take more risks than their parents, were not subject to economic retribution from white employers, and their participation added needed vitality during a lull in the Birmingham campaign (Burrow 2014, 107–111; Halberstam 1998, 438–443).[1] Although he faced some criticism, King persevered in his support for the use of children "on the frontline" in Birmingham (Burrow 2014, 113). When speaking of the jailed children in Birmingham, he likened them to the gospel depiction of Jesus as a leader at the age of 12, reassuring their parents at a mass meeting that "they are doing a job not only for themselves but for all of America and for all mankind" (as quoted in Burrow 2014, 125). Christian faith and rhetoric were persuasive tools for justifying the risks and sacrifices of the children.

---

[1] Many years later, in 2008, after the courageous testimony of his adult daughter recalling her childhood torment, Bevel was convicted of sexually molesting her, starting when she was a teenager (Les Carpenter, "A Father's Shadow," *Washington Post Magazine*, May 25, 2008, 16–21; 29–33).

Soldiering was a particularly useful term for describing the deployment of black children in the civil rights struggle, in part, because it resonated with a righteous sense of obligation familiar to many in the majority of Christian black communities that the leaders sought to mobilize. One anthology, *Hands on the Freedom Plow*, documents the personal testimonies of the young women college students of Student Nonviolent Coordinating Committee (SNCC) and offers a quotation that is emblematic of this commitment. Its opening pages include the words of a freedom song (based on a gospel song): "We are soldiers in the army. We got to fight although we have to cry. We got to hold up the freedom banner. We got to hold it up until we die" (as quoted in Holsaert et al. 2010). Songs such as this one were a staple of spiritual nourishment for the movement that almost always infused the protests led by students. The college student activists were not children, but many were only 18 and 19 years old as they faced the dangers of lynching, rape, and beatings from hostile local whites when protesting and organizing with rural southern blacks on behalf of racial equality.

In *Warriors Don't Cry: A Searing Memoir of the Battle to Integrate Little Rock's Central High*, Melba Patillo Beals recounts the violence she faced when the 1954 Supreme Court school desegregation decision was announced. It started at the age of 12 when she was walking home from school and a white man attempted to rape her. He said "I'll show you niggers the Supreme Court can't run my life" as he pulled down his pants and ripped at her underpants (Beals 1994, 26). Beals and eight other black children were the first to attend a white high school that was forced to racially integrate by the federal government in 1957. She experienced daily emotional torment and physical assaults as she attended the white high school. She was choked, burned, beaten, scalded by other children, and threatened with lynching by adults (1994). Throughout the ordeal, her Christian faith, largely instilled in her by her grandmother, was a resource of support. At one point when Beals breaks down sobbing because she felt overwhelmed by the torment, she receives spiritual advice from her grandmother. Her grandmother responded to her: "You'll make this your last cry. You're a warrior on the battlefield for your Lord. God's warriors don't cry, 'cause they trust that he's always by their side. The women in this family don't break down in the face of trouble" (1994, 57). In this example and many others Beals describes in her memoir, Christian faith and spirituality offered strength and enabled endurance. But Christian faith can also serve as a means for adults to place pressure on a child to sacrifice herself for the community's battle over racial equality. The black children tasked with confronting the onslaught of hatred and violence from white adults and children were required to meet daily with Daisy Bates, the head of the state National Association for the Advancement of Colored People (NAACP) in Arkansas. As Carlotta Walls LaNier later reflected in her memoir, in those meetings Mrs. Bates drilled it into them that "white folks would judge how well integration was working by what the nine of us said and did. So I did what I believed was expected. I played down my suffering" (2009, 109). The expectation of self-sacrifice by black girls deployed in this struggle constituted a moral value often cultivated by their adult black women mentors.

An emphasis on sacrifice can play a pivotal role in the communal moral values and religious commitments that support the use of children on the frontlines of community-wide conflicts, even social movements for racial equality. The suffering that the child warriors endure may be seen as tolerable because it is expected. It may be seen as a mandatory expression of communally valuing sacrifice for: God, justice for their communities, and as King proclaimed about the jailed Birmingham children, "for all of America and for all mankind" (As quoted in Burrow 2014, 125). The children may have been recruited because they were uniquely suited for the risks involved. But their recruitment and deployment raises the question of when this use of children in dangerous situations of communal conflict means that they are being exploited and abused by adults. The safety and well-being of these black girls might have been too easily seen as sacrificeable in the battle against white racism. Even when there is a worthwhile social goal of antiracism, the costs for certain children—black children—of so much danger and trauma can disappear into the realm of necessity rather than "things we cannot and will not tolerate," as President Clinton expressed in his speech against child labor and child soldiers.

Of course, the use of children on "the frontlines" and the Christian rhetoric supporting it in the 1950s and 1960s US civil rights movement is not the same as, for instance, the Christian rhetoric in the abductions and abuse of thousands of children used by Joseph Kony in the Lord's Resistance Army in Uganda starting in the 1980s. The trauma, threats, and violence endured by the black children deployed to the school grounds to desegregate white schools in Little Rock, AK and elsewhere are not the same as those experienced by the child soldiers deployed to loot and terrorize villages in Mozambique, Angola, and Sierra Leone. The incidents of sexual assault of black girls by white racists during the US civil rights era (McGuire 2010) are not the same as those occurring against the thou-

56   T. C. WEST

sands of girls abducted as sex slaves in Mozambique, Congo, and elsewhere, and sometimes shot and killed by their rapist-captors if their babies
made noise during a raid (Honwana 2006, 85–89; Wessells 2006, 94).
The assaults against and exploitation of children on "the frontlines" in
community-wide conflict situations have sociopolitical and historical spec-
ificity. The systematic rape of thousands of girls as part of their recruitment
as soldiers represents a deliberate tactic of war in which some leaders
engaged in certain African contexts. It differs from the terrorism that
white southern racists deliberately inflicted through rapes of more ran-
domly targeted black girls.

    I realize that it is unconventional and perhaps almost impossible for
some to learn of these child soldier crises in Africa without applying a
competitive comparative analysis that judges them to be much worse than
any other example from the United States and other global north nations.
In such a biased and competitive model it is as if there is a moral scale for
weighing the victimization of children and accompanying, requisite condemnation due. And before one even begins to weigh them against each
other, the scale has already been tilted in favor of absolving so-called western, developed nations of culpability in any form of deliberate harm and
risk to vulnerable children. The competitive, comparative mode of
response that separates us from them becomes a handy tool of erasure. In
the US context, concern about the vulnerability and harmful consequences
of soldiering for certain children disappears, especially if they are low-
income high school students, brown Muslim enemy combatants, or even
black girls in the struggle for racial equality. But what if, instead, we cultivated a commitment to transnational solidarity in the need to criticize the
values that perpetuate these forms of exploitation and how they can produce moral indifference to the complex, sociopolitically situated consequences to children. At a minimum, it must begin with scrutinizing the
decisions adults make about whose children are sacrificeable and how religious values justify those decisions as well as the racist biases of
American/western exceptionalism that preempt such considerations. As I
have argued with regard to gender-based violence (West 2019), antiracist
solidarity in opposing exploitation and abuse of children within our varied
global contexts can fuel our commitment to eradicating child soldiering
across our global contexts.

REFERENCES

Beals, Melba Pattillo. 1994. *Warriors Don't Cry: A Searing Memoir of the Battle to Integrate Little Rock's Central High*. New York: Simon and Schuster.

Black, M.C., K.C. Basile, M.J. Breiding, S.G. Smith, M.L. Walters, M.T. Merrick, J. Chen, and M.R. Stevens. 2011. *The National Intimate Partner and Sexual Violence Survey (NISVS): 2010 Summary Report*. Atlanta, GA: National Center for Injury Prevention and Control, Centers for Disease Control and Prevention.

Burrow, Rufus, Jr. 2014. *A Child Shall Lead Them: Martin Luther King, Jr., Young People, and the Movement*. Minneapolis: Fortress Press.

Castro, Erin L. 2015. Not Ready for College, but Ready for the Military: A Policy Challenge for the College- and Career-Readiness Agenda. *Education Policy Analysis Archives* 23: 75. https://doi.org/10.14507/epaa.v23.1887.

Chakamba, Rumbi. 2017. Girls in the DRC Are Choosing to Be Child Soldiers to Escape Poverty. *Huffington Post*, January 9. https://www.huffingtonpost.com/entry/drc-childsoldiers_us_587000cee4b099cdb0fd2de0.

Child Soldiers International Report. 2017. 'If I Could Go to School...' Education As a Tool to Prevent the Recruitment of Girls and Assist with Their Recovery and Reintegration in the Democratic Republic of Congo. https://www.childsoldiers.org/Handlers/Download.ashx?IDMF=81643545-f6f8-49c3-adbe-a202577cfdb2.

Clinton, William J. 1999. *Address at the 87th Session of the International Labor Conference, 16 June 1999*. Geneva, Switzerland: International Labor Organization. https://www.ilo.org/public/english/standards/relm/ilc/ilc87/a-clinto.htm.

Combined News Service. 2000. UN Panel Reaches Accord to Limit Child Soldiers. *Newsday*, 22 January.

Dennis, Michael J. 1999. The ILO Convention on the Worst Forms of Child Labor. *American Journal of International Law* 93 (4): 943–948.

Eskew, Glenn T. 1997. 'Bombingham': Black Protest in Postwar Birmingham, Alabama. *The Historian* 59 (2, December): 371–390.

Finkelhor, D., G. Hotaling, I.A. Lewis, and C. Smith. 1990. Sexual Abuse in a National Survey of Adult Men and Women: Prevalence, Characteristics and Risk Factors. *Child Abuse & Neglect* 14 (1): 19–28. https://doi.org/10.1016/0145-2134(90)90077-7.

Franklin, V.P. 2015. Documenting the Contributions of Children and Teenagers to the Civil Rights Movement. *Journal of African American History* 100 (4, Fall): 663–671.

Halberstam, David. 1998. *The Children*. New York: Ballantine Books.

Holsaert, Faith S., Martha Prescod Norman Noonan, Judy Richardson, Betty Garman Robinson, Jean Smith Young, and Dorothy M. Zellner, eds. 2010.

358   T. C. WEST

Hands on the Freedom Plow: Personal Accounts by Women in SNCC. Champaign: University of Illinois Press.

Honwana, Alcinda. 2006. *Child Soldiers in Africa.* Philadelphia: University of Pennsylvania Press.

LaNier, Carlotta Walls, and Lisa Frazier Page. 2009. *A Mighty Long Way: My Journey to Justice at Little Rock Central High School.* London: One World.

Manis, Andrew M. 2001. *A Fire You Can't Put Out: The Civil Rights Life of Birmingham's Reverend Fred Shuttlesworth.* Tuscaloosa: University of Alabama Press.

McGuire, Danielle L. 2010. *At the Dark End of the Street: Black Women, Rape, and Resistance—A New History of the Civil Rights Movement from Rosa Parks to the Rise of Black Power.* New York: Vintage Books.

Pupavac, Vanessa. 2001. Misanthropy Without Borders: The International Children's Regime. *Disasters* 25 (2): 95–112.

Rosen, David M. 2012. *Child Soldiers: A Reference Handbook.* Santa Barbara, CA: ABC-CLIO.

Singer, Peter Warren. 2006. *Children at War.* Berkeley, CA: University of California Press.

Wessells, Michael. 2006. *Child Soldiers: From Violence to Protection.* Cambridge: Harvard University Press.

West, Traci C. 2019. *Solidarity and Defiant Spirituality: Africana Lessons on Racism, Religion, and Ending Gender Violence.* New York: New York University Press.

CHAPTER 5

"I'd Rather Die than Wrestle": Gender, Spirituality, and Agency Amongst the Luba Mai-Mai

Georgette I. Mulunda Ledgister

She could have passed for my aunt. She wore her hair parted down the middle, with each side braided in fine cornrows from her forehead to the nape of her neck, the ends of which were gathered into a small bun. Her hair was quite thick; and here and there, grey strands peppered the deep black of her hair. She had a few fine wrinkles around small black eyes that seemed to glitter with intensity. I couldn't tell whether the wrinkles were due to age, or whether they were laugh lines. She could have been in her 40s or her 50s. I later found out that she was 52 years old. She wore an oversized black and cream pencil dress, with a matching cream jacket, detailed in black threading. The dress suit would have been at home in any office in the 1980s, but the rhinestones that bedazzled the detailing on the wide black lapels of her jacket placed the ensemble closer to the fashion of the late 1990s and early 2000s (Ledgister 2018).

She was far from the gruesome and unflattering image that many before and after the Congolese Five-Year War of 1997–2002 had painted of her.

G. I. M. Ledgister (✉)
Department of Religious Studies, Agnes Scott College, Atlanta, GA, USA

© The Author(s) 2019
S. Willhauck (ed.), *Female Child Soldiering, Gender Violence, and Feminist Theologies*, https://doi.org/10.1007/978-3-030-21982-6_5

Indeed, as she remarked, "Governor Buta[1] did not recognize me the first time we met." She was referring to a former governor of the Banque Centrale du Congo (Central Bank of Congo) who had been sent to her home district to assess the financial feasibility of a pacification mission. "He was looking for Chatty, the Mai-Mai girl who wore red tights and a red bandana, and hung the remains of the severed sex organs of the victims of her father's fighters attached to her thighs. He could not believe that I—" she pointed to herself with both hands, "—was the Chatty he had heard so much about and had come to fear."

Chatty (Charlotte) Masangu wa Nkulu is the daughter of the infamous Wilson Vwende wa Mutompa Kalunga, simply known as Vwende, leader of the Luba Mai-Mai in Mulongo, a small town in the mineral-rich[2] southeastern district of Malemba-Nkulu in the Democratic Republic of Congo (Congo henceforth). According to the United Nations Organization Stabilization Mission in Congo (MONUSCO), the Luba Mai-Mai were one of several ill-equipped, independent local self-defense militias operating under the name Mai-Mai (*mai* or *maji* in Lingala or Swahili means water) across four provinces in Congo. Whether these militias were based in the provinces of North and South Kivu, Ituri or Upper Lomami, they were uniformly cast as bands of violent men who raped and pillaged the very communities they were unable to protect from neither the ongoing conflict within Congo, nor the conflict between Congo and neighboring Rwanda and Uganda (Ledgister 2018, 7). Chatty was an anomaly. She was a Mai-Mai fighter and leader during the Congolese Five-Year War, second only to her father, who was chief commander of Mai-Mai forces in Mulongo. A divorced mother of adopted children—all orphans of the war—she introduced herself to me as a mother and a father. Hers was a firsthand account of resilience and agency that resisted easy assimilation into narratives of victimhood and acute vulnerability, common in scholarship at the intersection of gender and war in Africa.

Focusing on Chatty's rich and moving account of joining and fighting in the Congolese Five-Year War, this chapter interrogates scholarship on gender and war that portrays African women and girls almost exclusively

---

[1] This name was changed for reasons of anonymity.
[2] According to a 2013 United Geological Survey report, mining accounts for almost 21% of the Congolese GDP, with total exports in 2013 valued at over $10 billion (Thomas R. Yager. *2013 Minerals Yearbook: Congo (Kinshasa) [Advance Release]*. U.S. Geological Survey (U.S. Department of the Interior, U.S. Geological Survey Minerals Yearbook, 2016).

as victims of war, due to uncritical applications of western feminist conceptions of gender in the African context. Chatty's lived experience of the war invites the deconstruction of gender as framed in the West and applied in Africa, while simultaneously inviting the construction of an ontology that can carry the weight and complexity of being a young divorcée turned soldier and warrior, who comes into her own as a mother after the war. Curiously, though Chatty's story reveals the epistemological blind spots of western framings of gender, her lived experience demonstrates the ways in which members of her community paradoxically continue to espouse and cling to western feminist[3] framings of gender that fit their world-sense[4] as poorly as a borrowed, ill-fitting undergarment. This chapter proposes that far from emphasizing the precarity of poor communities such as Chatty's hometown of Mulongo, war compelled Chatty and her people to turn to indigenous epistemologies, and to tap into a mystical power that transcended their material conditions, and—in Chatty's case—her gender. For the Mai-Mai, the context of war invites the decoupling of agency and the body, locating the hope, strength, and survival of women and girls like Chatty in the fullness of personhood—an African indigenous moral ontology rooted in and sustained by the community of the living and the ancestors.

SEARCHING FOR AGENCY IN THE MIDST OF CONTINGENCY

When I met Chatty for the first time, I had predetermined that her role in my research would be peripheral. I was wrong. In the summer of 2017, I traveled to Kinshasa, the capital of Congo, with my then nine-month-old daughter, Zuri, to meet with my mother who would accompany us to Lubumbashi, the provincial capital of Upper Katanga. From there we

---

[3] I use the language of "western feminism" broadly to describe the scholarship of feminist writers from or trained in the western hemisphere. In using the qualifier "western" I am referring to the physical and cultural context in which the scholarship is derived. As Elizabeth Evans points out in *The Politics of Third Wave Feminisms: Neoliberalism, Intersectionality, and the State in Britain and the US* (London: Palgrave Macmillan, 2015, 53) feminisms are multiple and rich in their particularities (and third-wave feminism in particular).

[4] In lieu of employing the term worldview to indicate western conceptions of and apprehension of the world, I am using Oyèrónké Oyěwùmí's concept of world-sense. She critiques the western prioritization of sight as the primary sense operating in social interaction that creates a subject that gazes upon an object (Oyèrónké Oyěwùmí, *The Invention of Women: Making an African Sense of Western Gender Discourses* (Minneapolis: University of Minnesota Press, 1997), 3).

would travel by road for nearly three days to reach Malemba-Nkulu where my father—a pastor and chief mediator of the Global and Inclusive Accord that officially ended the Congolese Five-Year War in 2002—had arranged for us to stay and interview wives of Mai-Mai warlords. However, before leaving for Malemba-Nkulu, I scheduled a single interview with Chatty, who had agreed to travel to Lubumbashi to ease my transition to field-work, and my trip to the less forgiving rural environment of Malemba-Nkulu. My graduate research on agency, gender, and war had brought my mother, my daughter, and myself—three generations of women—together on a journey of academic and self-discovery. Chatty was supposed to serve a peripheral role in the process. As it turned out, she became the center of my research, and continued to have a profound impact on my sense of being long after I returned to the United States.

My choice to conduct fieldwork in Congo was strategic. First, as a Congolese Luba woman, my social location allowed me access to places, persons, and knowledge restricted to outsiders. Second, I was a mom, and I needed all the support I could get to raise my daughter, while research-ing and writing my dissertation. Third, I was pregnant. A month before our scheduled departure from Atlanta, Georgia, my husband and I learned that I was expecting our second child. Rather than postpone my fieldwork, we thought it best to cut the trip back from 12 months to 6 months, and for me to return with Zuri to Atlanta in time for me to deliver our second child. As fate would have it, I lost the baby days after arriving in Kinshasa, just shy of the second trimester. A fourth and final reason for conducting research in Congo quickly became apparent, and that was to be with *my* mother, and to heal.

As soon as I was cleared for travel by doctors in Kinshasa, Zuri, my mother, and I traveled to Lubumbashi to await clearance for travel in-country to Malemba-Nkulu. In yet another twist of fate, violent riots broke out in almost all major city and town centers across Congo, as Congolese citizens protested ongoing delays to presidential elections that had been scheduled for December 2016—eight months earlier. Although Zuri and I were Congolese by origin, we were American by nationality and were confined to Lubumbashi by an orange-level warning from the American embassy. There would be no travel to Malemba-Nkulu in the foreseeable weeks or months, as the embassy could not guarantee the safety of "non-essential personnel" traveling outside of major towns and cities. I was stuck in Lubumbashi. Unwilling to return to Atlanta too early, I embraced the contingent nature of fieldwork, and shifted the focus of my research from studying the agency of women who chose to marry Mai-Mai warlords, to learning from a woman who chose to leave her marriage and to fight as a warrior herself.

Chatty's story upended my theoretical assumptions at the outset. As in much of the scholarship on the role of gender in war in Africa, I assumed that most women and girls involved in armed conflicts such as the Congolese Five-Year War, were the victims of sexual and gender-based violence, and had been coerced into becoming the "bush wives" of Mai-Mai fighters, to use Chris Coulter's (2009) term.[5] While I was curious to discover whether any of these "bush wives" had voluntarily and proactively chosen to marry into the Mai-Mai movement and to remain in the movement after the war, I had not considered that there could be women or girls who were involved in the Mai-Mai movement as a result of choices that did not associate them sexually to male fighters. I had narrowed the range of choices available to women and girls in Malemba-Nkulu to the opportunities that their bodies could purchase them, reducing them to sexual beasts of burdens in service to a war they did not begin.

Yet, western feminist literature on the role of women in war contends that women comprise a highly diverse and differentiated complex social category in wartime as well as in peacetime, and are not faceless objects of war. Rather, women have their own agenda when it comes to war. Carol Cohn (2013) develops a conceptual framework through which she interrogates the seeming immutability of social structures, mores, and institutions that emphasize the biological difference between men and women, and subsequently unequally distribute power and authority between the two, in favor of men. She argues that by locating difference within individuals and not identifying the role that social structures play in constructing difference, the temptation arises to also locate capability (for leadership, management of resources, etc.) within individuals, painting the devastating image of men as biologically more capable, and women as ontologically inferior to men. Cohn affirms Cynthia Cockburn's (2007) stance that war is not an event, and that violence against women should not be viewed as

---

[5] Chris Coulter defines bush wives as women and girls who were abducted during the decade-long war in Sierra Leone that began in 1991 and concluded in 2002, and were taken as wives by ranking militia officers. Coulter distinguishes bush wives from sex slaves, the latter who are women available for rape to any member of a militia at any given moment. While sex slaves were often coerced into combat alongside men, bush wives lived in the household of the militia commander, where they performed household functions under the supervision of favored wives.

merely a weapon or a result of war, but should instead be framed as an unavoidable product of a society that devalues women on the basis of gender; associates subjectivity and agency to maleness, and reduces women to sexual objects or prey through narratives of so-called masculinity and femininity. Cohn makes the fascinating observation that because wars are primarily fought by male combatants, the tasks of cooking, cleaning, and washing—otherwise feminine tasks—are also undertaken by men. Yet, because men engage in these tasks in the hypermasculinized world of war, and in the service of said war, these men are lauded as "real men," who couple the "feminine" tasks of cleaning and cooking, with the "masculine" task of sexual domination over women (and other men).

The sexual domination and aggression of women are key to the work of Meredeth Turshen and Clotilde Twagiramariya (1998), who specifically research gender and conflict in Africa. Turshen and Twagiramariya identify and emphasize the participation of women in armed conflict to counter the masculinized discourse and culture of war, which often portray women as passive victims, denied of their agency. They share accounts of women who are survivors of rape, and particularly accounts of women who exist in the ambiguous and ambivalent world between consent and coercion, and continue to do so in the reconstruction period after the war (particularly when their survival is at stake). For many women in post-war contexts, their community's moral constructions of sexuality often determine whether one should consider a woman a rape survivor, a sex slave, or a colluder. Yet, all of these identity categories are accompanied by the moral burden of guilt, humiliation, and shame, and none offer women moral deniability or the option to claim ignorance of the moral consequences of their actions. Subsequently, many women choose not to report the sexual violence committed against them, and continue to live side by side with the perpetrators of said violence. While Turshen and Twagiramariya make a compelling argument about the role of sexual morality as it is constructed, taught, and enforced by society, their findings reiterate the belief that women's primary modes of being in war are determined by the use of their bodies in conflict.

Mats Utas' (2005) concept of "victimcy" expands feminist discourse on war and gender to allow for another mode of action. Occupying the murky middle ground between victimhood and agency, Utas defines "victimcy" as the tactical agency deployed by young women and girls during the Liberian civil wars of 1990s and early 2000s, who fully embrace the role of the victim to earn particular gains from various stakeholders during the war and the post-war reconstruction period. To an aid worker, Utas' informants report themselves as rape survivors and sex slaves, while to local Liberian politicians, the same informants present themselves as the "girlfriends" of powerful men, to obtain favors from the friends and colleagues of said men. Although "victimcy" does indeed offer a different mode of action in war for women and girls, and one should certainly applaud the courage of Utas' informants to shape social realities to their benefit, the moral ambivalence of the options and choices available to Utas' informants makes it difficult to distance them from charges of manipulation, trickery, and self-debasement for the sake of survival. Still, whether a child soldier is a sex slave, a "bush wife," or uses her victimcy for her own ends, the use of her body is the primary determinant for evaluating her experience of war. Chatty's story paints a startling different picture. She wrestles with the vulnerability and contingency that Luba women and girls experience during war as a result of their gender, and embraces war as the means of transcending the limitations of her gender. Chatty's experience of the Congolese Five-Year war not only resists flat and essentialist narratives of African women and girls' experience of war, but also invites the reader to reconsider constructions of gender that are grounded in the biological and physical. In working with Chatty in Congo, I not only had to contend with the contingency of conducting fieldwork in a post-conflict context, but I had to grapple with the contingency of gender as a research concept in African contexts.

"I'D RATHER DIE THAN WRESTLE": THE WOMAN BECOMES THE WARRIOR

For most of the months that Chatty and I spent together, I was under the impression that she, her mother, and her siblings had joined the Mai-Mai movement because of her father. It was 1998, and Ugandan and Rwandan rebels had crossed the border into the now province of Upper Lomami in search of natural resources to financially sustain their military assaults in Congo, and were making their way through Chatty's home district of Malemba-Nkulu, via the territory of Mulongo. Her home village of Kabumbulu was on their path. The great Luba chiefs of surrounding villages—Great Chiefs Kibenze, Kiyombo, and Mukabo began a campaign in Malemba-Nkulu, visiting each village in the district to recruit young men to join the Mai-Mai movement. Her father, who was a farmer and cattle herder, heeded the call of the great chiefs, and plunged into the *mai*—the ritual waters that transformed one into a Mai-Mai fighter—and completely upended Chatty's life as she knew it at the dawn of her 30s.

Chatty's use of the verb "to plunge" to describe the process of becoming a Mai-Mai was misleading. Given the secretive nature of the ritual, she resisted answering a number of my questions regarding the ritual. However, she did share that contrary to my belief that her father had been immersed in the Congo River, which flowed through her district and skirted around her village, her father had been doused with water prepared and carried in basins from a source known only to the great chiefs. She described the outcome of the ritual as plunging her father into a supernatural realm in which he was in direct contact with the ancestors, who then imbued him with the power to bend and stretch the material world to his will.[6] Although the "plunging" did not physically remove him from the world of the embodied living, the ritual thinned the boundary between the material and immaterial worlds, allowing her father to straddle both. As a consequence, her father was bound by a moral code that forbade physical contact with anyone who had not also "plunged" into the *mai*—including his family, lest he break his connection with the ancestors, and weaken the potency and efficacy of his newfound supernatural capacities. When Chatty's father shared with his family what he had done and who he had become, they were faced with the decision of refusing to join the Mai-Mai—a movement that was derided amongst Christians in Congo as *kindoki*[7] (or *ulozi* in Swahili)—and subsequently losing all physical contact with Vwende, or embracing supernatural powers and facing the atrocity of war. Chatty and her sisters were quick to make their decision. Apparently, the mystical power that the Mai-Mai wielded made Mai-Mai women and girls particularly fearsome, and soldiers were loath to rape a Mai-Mai woman or girl. The decision was therefore simple for Chatty and her

---

[6] In "Warriors of the Water" (2018), I offer a thick description of the metaphysical and ensuing moral implications of the *mai* ritual which transformed Chatty, her sister, her father, and numerous other ordinary people in the village of Kabumbulu into redoubtable fighters.

[7] Simon Bockie (1993, 46–47) uses the Manianga or Lingala term *kindoki* to designate an ambivalent psychic power, or spells and medicine that either protect (*kindoki kia lunda*) or psychically consume one's vitality and fortune (*kindoki kia dia* or eating *kindoki*), The root of *kindoki* is the verb *koloka* or to overpower, which Christian missionaries have erroneously translated to "bewitch," and *kindoki* to "witchcraft." Although the syncretism of the Congolese indigenous lifeworld resists the use of static religious identities, Congolese Christians are careful not to associate themselves with the Mai-Mai.

sisters. They took the plunge and also became Mai-Mai to protect themselves from the risks associated with their gender (Ledgister 2018, 104). However, it wasn't until my final conversation with Chatty that I discovered a deeper—and more painful—justification for her choice to join the Mai-Mai and to fight in the war. Chatty joined the Mai-Mai hoping to die in the war, thus liberating herself from the burden of being a woman who could not bear children.

Chatty left high school in the late 1980s at the tenth-grade level—a decade before the war—to marry. She had begun her secondary education later than most, given the availability of schooling for girls in her village. She was in her early 20s when she got married, and described her spouse at the time—who she never named—as wanting the things that most Luba men wanted out of marriage, namely, children. Unfortunately, Chatty could not conceive.

> I got married and the marriage was not going well. He wanted children. I [did] too. But I wasn't getting pregnant. I don't know why…I wondered why God would let me suffer without children. Every time, he [her husband] would ask me for children, but I couldn't give him any. (Ledgister 2018, 127)

Chatty attributed her pain and her distress not just to her inability to conceive, but to a lack of divine intervention to remedy her situation. When Chatty's husband opted to have children with another woman a decade later, she chose to leave him—and to die. Much of her identity was inextricably linked to the social roles assigned to her gender and dictated by her anatomy. She was a young wife, and therefore expected to fulfill her womanhood (and her husband's desires) by bearing and raising children. Curiously, Chatty did not question her gender, her anatomy, or her reproductive health. In fact, Chatty did not question her husband's reproductive health either. I heard in Chatty's words a theodical response to her pain—a questioning of God who possessed the power to ease her suffering, and chose not to do so.

As a result of her lack of agency—an inability to voluntarily determine outcomes in her life—Chatty decided to choose the one option within her reach. The war had almost reached her village, and news of atrocities perpetrated by Rwandan and Ugandan troops had traveled throughout the region. While others in her village had already begun joining the Mai-Mai movement, her initial decision to join the Mai-Mai had nothing to do with the defense of her people. She rushed headlong into the war hoping to die.

The war came to Malemba-Nkulu. I was tired of wrestling [...] I was wrestling with God. With myself. With the suffering of my body [...] knowing
that I was not even able to give life [...] This [conception] was up to God—
Leza [...] I decided to fight. I was hoping that in the war, I would get killed.
I said to myself that *I'd rather die than wrestle* (emphasis added). I knew I
didn't have much chance to survive [the war]. We [the people of Kabumbulu
village] heard that many people were killed by the [Rwandan and Ugandan]
rebels. So, I decided to become Mai-Mai and to fight in the war. (Ledgister
2018, 129)

To escape the social and psychological constraints under which she was
living—constraints imposed upon her as a result of her gender and the
supposed roles her gender demanded that she serve—Chatty chose to end
her life which she perceived as an inevitable outcome of infertility.
However, Chatty did not experience her intended outcomes when she
plunged into the *mai* to become a Mai-Mai fighter. Chatty the woman
indeed died—a metaphysical death—transcending the constraints of the
life she lived as a result of her gender, and accessing membership into a
community of the embodied and disembodied living, bonded together by
their mission to fight for their land and their people. Consequently, Chatty
the warrior was born. She shared her interpretation of her survival during
the war in her characteristically direct manner:

I guess God had more life for me. It was a sign that there was something I
was supposed to do with my life. I decided to become a mother. And a
father. I decided to take the children that had been abandoned during the
war when their parents were killed. I took them and brought them home
with me. (Ledgister 2018, 129)

Contra dominant narratives of the destructive impact of war on women
and girls—narratives that are indeed well founded—in Chatty's case, the
context of war offered an unlikely invitation to life and agency, through
her access to the mystical power of the ancestors. Yet, Chatty was clear to
distinguish God and the ancestors. Both existed in the same immaterial
and metaphysical plane, but the presence of one did not subsume the presence of the other as Congolese Christians vehemently argued. Chatty
defined the ancestors as intermediaries between God and the embodied
living. The ancestors were the powerful and immaterial presences of
women and men who had crossed from the material to the immaterial
world, and intervened in her community in times of trouble.

The *mai* ritual that Chatty and other fighters underwent symbolized an ethos of continuity extant in African modes of being and knowing. Death and life existed on the same continuum, as did God, the ancestors, and the living. According to Munyaradzi Felix Murove, one of the most destructive vestiges of colonialism in Africa was the disruption of the African ethos of continuity not just between persons, but the disruption of continuity *within* African persons:

> The Westernisation or modernisation of African societies implied an onslaught on African culture and values. This onslaught was done under the guise that Africans were not fully human and the mission of colonialism and the Christian religion was to turn these Africans into human beings by bequeathing to them Western moral values and culture. Up to this day there is an expectation that the African must have completely abandoned his or her traditional values. (2016, 142)

Colonizing missions not only created arbitrary boundaries of difference between communities, dividing one to conquer the other, but it infected the consciousness of African persons to embrace the dualism of colonial Christianity, and to denigrate and subdue the material in favor of the immaterial. The Christianity of colonizing missions that required African converts to prove the so-called authenticity of their conversion, fragilized the continuity of the African world-sense—an ethic of "holding together" from the Latin prefix *con-* and root *tenere*. Colonial Christianity unraveled the fabric that wove the colonized, converted, and therefore "civilized" African into the community of the living and the ancestors, barely holding her together with a theology that put into question the worth and humanity of her culture, values, and even her very person. The resulting outcome for many colonized Africans was a *somatophobia*, to use M. Shawn Copeland's (2009) term, stoked by a hyperawareness and policing of the physical and the material.[8]

Western feminist scholarship has provided a critical corrective of the *somatophobia* and accompanying patriarchy of Christianity and its detrimental impact to women, girls, and non-gender-conforming persons

[8] M. Shawn Copeland (2009) critiques the dualist heritage of Christianity in the West, which swings from a hyperawareness of the body that uplifts a particular image of God (white, male, and heteronormative), to a complete somatophobia that promotes a theology of immolation and surrogacy—usually to the detriment of non-white and non-gender-conforming people.

inside and outside of the Church. However, the very tool that western feminism has used in its attempts to liberate persons from the bondage of *somatophobia* and patriarchy is the tool that white male power used to subjugate persons in the first place: a hyperawareness of the body, or what Oyèrónkẹ́ Oyěwùmí calls *somatocentricity*.

> In pointing out the centrality of the body in the construction of difference in Western culture, one does not necessarily deny that there have been certain traditions in the West that have attempted to explain differences according to criteria other than the presence or absence of certain organs: the possession of a penis, the size of the brain, the shape of a cranium, or the color of the skin.... [T]he establishment of disciplines such as sociology and anthropology, which purport to explain society on the bases of human interactions, seems to suggest the relegation of biological determinism in social thought. On closer examination, however, one finds that the body has hardly been banished from social thought, not to mention its role in the constitution of social status.... [T]o say that bodies have been absent from sociological theories is to discount the fact that the social groups that are the subject matter of the discipline are essentially understood as rooted in biology. (1997, 3)

Oyěwùmí's critique of the somatocentricity of western scholarship points to the detrimental impact of uncritically applying western feminist—body centered—frameworks to the African cultural context, particularly given the problematic history of colonialism on the continent. Rather than liberating African women and girls like Chatty, somatocentric scholarship not only inadvertently emphasizes the physical difference between African women and girls, and their Eurocentric counterparts, but denigrates African women and girls for remaining under the so-called bondage of their post-colonial communities, which continue to embrace the very somatophobic culture that the West bequeathed to them during colonialism. While it is an impossible—and futile—feat to attempt a return to precolonial Africa, Chatty's experience of power and agency as a result of becoming a Mai-Mai warrior invites a reclamation of indigenous epistemologies that transcend the dualist paradigm that haunts western feminist scholarship.

As an individual, Chatty wrestled with the identifiers of a divorcée and infertility—identifiers that were imposed on her and which she internalized in turn. However, as a Mai-Mai warrior, Chatty was no longer a woman, but a *person* who joined a community that reestablished and embodied the continuity between the material and immaterial world. Yet

Chatty's recounting of her initiation into the Mai-Mai movement begs the question of what exactly held together, or restored a sense of continuity between her and the new community she joined, and within herself. What mystical element did the ancestors place in the hands of Mai-Mai warriors to defend civilians during the Congolese Five-Year War, and effectively reverse the invasion of Malemba-Nkulu by Rwandan and Ugandan troops? What exactly was the nature of Mai-Mai power?

THE POWER OF THE WATER

As I reflect on my fieldwork in Congo, the question of the nature of the Mai-Mai's mystical power features prominently in my interviews with Chatty. Notably, Chatty evaded all the questions pertaining to Mai-Mai power, and revealed very little about the mechanism operating behind the extraordinary feats she performed during the war. For instance, when she recounted an occasion during which she disarmed national army soldiers (Forces Armées de la République Démocratique du Congo or FARDC) sent to kill her father and to neutralize the Mai-Mai of Mulongo who refused to answer to the distant government in Kinshasa, Chatty spoke of using a fistful of sand, uttering the words "This is the soil of our ancestors," and throwing the sand in the faces of armed soldiers to immobilize them. The ritual was simple—she declined to offer any details beyond sharing the words she spoke—and murderously effective. Upon contact with the sand, the soldiers were purportedly frozen in space and time, allowing Chatty to single-handedly relieve each of them of their weapons. Chatty did share that not a single shot was fired during the stand-off as a result of the ritual, and that she had performed that particular ritual only three times during the war. She ended the story there, not sharing with me whether or not the FARDC soldiers were allowed to live after regaining their mobility.

When my wonderment at her story faded, I began studying the connection between the ancestors, nature, and community. I researched accounts of supernatural feats performed by mystico-political movements like the Mai-Mai, and discovered that the use of objects existing in nature featured prominently in movements similar to the Mai-Mai.[9] According to Catholic

[9] For example, on May 17, 2017, followers of Bundu Dia Kongo (BDK)—a movement that MONUSCO has labeled a religious sect—staged the largest prison break in Congolese history, freeing thousands of inmates (some local sources say over 4000) from the Makala maximum-security prison in Kinshasa, the nation's capital, reportedly stabbing and beheading prison guards with the use of blunt sticks (see Wembi and de Freytas-Tamura 2017).

moral theologian, Laurenti Magesa (1997), the African lifeworld is formed by and flourishes in the interconnectedness between the Divine (the immaterial), creation (the material), and community. He asserts that there is a spark of the Divine, which he calls *vital force*, emanating from the Divine and present in all of creation—animate and inanimate.[10] The highest concentrations of vital force reside in animate objects and the immaterial world—the world of the ancestors and the Divine—and is the source of vital force. The interconnectedness of the African lifeworld to which Magesa refers echoes the ethos of continuity that informed much of the African world-sense in precolonial times, and, I argue, informs the indigenous ontology of the Mai-Mai.

Chatty and other Mai-Mai warriors, through their reintegration into the continuum of life according to the African world-sense—a continuum that begins with the Divine includes animate and inanimate creation, and returns to the Divine in the form of ancestors—activate the vital force present in them and in nature as embodied living beings, to protect and restore wholeness to their communities during the war. As a safeguard against the misuse of vital force, the Mai-Mai are bound by a moral code intended to check against the propensity of humans to forget and to upset the web of interconnectedness that delicately holds life together in the African lifeworld. Unfortunately, numerous documented accounts of atrocities carried out by the Mai-Mai during and after the war reveal that the movement is far from saintly, and is at its core a movement of fighters engaged in a war (Amnesty International 2003; Autesserre 2010). Nevertheless, the context of war paradoxically presents an invitation to life, community, and agency—a story that remains largely absent or untold in current scholarship on gender and war in Africa.

CONCLUSION

In my search for alternate modes of being that celebrate the agency of African women and girls in war, I happened upon an unexpected narrative of mystical power, community, and personhood that challenged western conceptions of gender, but also revealed the ongoing embrace of such

---

[10] See Magesa (1997) and Murove (2009, 163). Murove resists the use of the concept "vital force" to characterize the essence of interconnectedness in African moral consciousness given the aggressive and predatory nature of force, given Belgian missionary Placide Tempels' essentialist hypothesis that force and violence characterizes African morality.

conceptions—despite their destructive effects. As a Mai-Mai warrior, it no longer mattered to the village of Kabumbulu that Chatty had been a divorcée or that she was unable to conceive. As soon as Chatty was initiated into the mystico-political movement that is the Mai-Mai, all that mattered was the strength of her connection to the community of the disembodied living—the ancestors—and the feats that she performed to protect her people. Indeed, her prowess soon gained her renown in the district of Malemba-Nkulu, earning her the title of *seigneur de guerre* or warlord, due to her rank as second in command of her father's fighters. The community of the disembodied living became a source of power for Chatty—a power that transcended her physical circumstances of poverty, precarity, and vulnerability, which were common to most Luba in rural areas, but particularly acute for women and children who were often victims of sexual violence, and conscripted into warring factions against their will. During the war, Chatty was a warrior, not a woman. However, the end of the war obviated the need for ordinary women and men to access supernatural power. According to Chatty, the Mai-Mai were at their core a self-defense militia, and they not only had to disarm at the end of the Congolese Five-Year War, but they were no longer to be considered Mai-Mai. With the end of the war came the unwelcome return to Chatty's positionality as a woman, the loss of the reverence she earned as a fighter, and a resurgence of social limitations on the basis of her gender. Her story resists overgeneralizations of African women and girls' victimhood and precarity in war, as a result of their gender. Inasmuch as western feminist movements have been liberative for some women in the West, they have not been liberative for other women—namely women of color, and African women—given some western feminists' co-optation of patriarchal themes and lenses when it pertains to women who are not white. Chatty's story disabuses one of the temptations to frame African communities as bastions of gender freedom, yet clearly demonstrates the other-worldly power of African women and girls who embrace their own indigenous spiritual practices and sources of knowledge. Chatty transcends patriarchal limitations imposed on her as a poor Luba woman when she becomes a warrior, and simultaneously rises above feminist gender constructions intended to champion her, but in reality limit her personhood. Chatty's story is complex, multilayered, and in many ways invites a return to the core of ethical inquiry. The story of Chatty the woman and Chatty the warrior summons one—summons us all—to embrace a world in which simplistic answers are exchanged for probing questions.

REFERENCES

Amnesty International. 2003. *On the Precipice: The Deepening Human Rights and Humanitarian Crisis in Ituri.* New York: Amnesty International. https://www.amnesty.org/en/documents/document/?indexNumber=AFR62%2F006%2F2200&language=en.

Autesserre, Severine. 2010. *The Trouble with the Congo: Local Violence and the Failure of International Peacebuilding.* New York: Cambridge University Press.

Bockie, Simon. 1993. *Death and the Invisible Powers: The World of Kongo Belief.* Bloomington: Indiana University Press.

Cockburn, Cynthia. 2007. *From Where We Stand.* London: Zed Books.

Cohn, Carol. 2013. *Women & Wars.* Cambridge: Polity.

Copeland, M. Shawn. 2009. *Enfleshing Freedom: Body, Race and Being.* Minneapolis, MN: Fortress Press.

Coulter, Chris. 2009. *Bush Wives and Girl Soldiers: Women's Lives Through War and Peace in Sierra Leone.* Ithaca, NY: Cornell University Press.

Ledgister, Georgette Ilunga-Nkulu Mulunda. 2018. *Warriors of the Water: A Luba Mai-Mai Story of Agency, Personhood and Ancestral Power.* PhD diss., Emory University.

Magesa, Laurenti. 1997. *African Religion: The Moral Traditions of Abundant Life.* Maryknoll, NY: Orbis Books.

Murove, Munyaradzi Felix. 2009. *African Ethics: An Anthology of Comparative Ethics.* Scottsville: University of KwaZulu-Natal Press.

———. 2016. *African Moral Consciousness: An Inquiry into the Evolution of Perspectives and Prospects.* London: Austin Macauley Publishers Ltd.

Oyěwùmí, Oyèrónké. 1997. *The Invention of Women: Making an African Sense of Western Gender Discourses.* Minneapolis: University of Minnesota Press.

Turshen, Meredeth, and Clotilde Twagiramariya. 1998. *What Women Do in Wartime: Gender and Conflict in Africa.* London: Zed Books.

Utas, Mats. 2005. West-African Warscapes: Victimcy, Girlfriending, Soldiering: Tactic Agency in a Young Woman's Social Navigation of the Liberian War Zone. *Anthropological Quarterly* 78 (2, Spring): 403–430.

Wembi, Steve, and Kimiko de Freytas-Tamura. 2017. An Unfortunate Record for Congo: Thousands Flee Cells in Biggest Jailbreak. *New York Times,* May 19. https://www.nytimes.com/2017/05/19/world/africa/congo-prison-break-kabila.html.

CHAPTER 6

Education in Resistance to Child Soldiering: A Latina Liberation Theology Perspective

Débora B. A. Junker

As access to information spreads on a wide-reaching basis, citizens from around the globe are increasingly aware of the calamities afflicting our brothers and sisters. Among so many issues, one of the most pervasive problems facing our world today, and especially our children, is the growing culture of war and violence that plagues us all. Amidst such a backdrop of deadly forces, the phenomenon of arming young boys and girls under the age of 15 with rifles and other kinds of weapons is probably one of the most visible signs that violence has become normalized worldwide. According to the United Nations' Convention on the Rights of the Child, ratified by the Optional Protocol on the Involvement of Children in Armed Conflict, the minimum age for direct participation in armed conflicts is 18, contrary to the previous minimum age of 15 years. Also, the Optional Protocol prohibits compulsory recruitment by government forces of anyone under 18 years of age (UNICEF 2003, 56).[1]

---

[1] See both documents: the Convention of the Rights of the Child at https://www.unicef.org/protection/57929_58007.html and the Optional Protocol on the Involvement of

---

D. B. A. Junker (✉)
Garrett-Evangelical Theological Seminary, Evanston, IL, USA
e-mail: Debora.junker@garrett.edu

© The Author(s) 2019
S. Willhauck (ed.), *Female Child Soldiering, Gender Violence, and Feminist Theologies*, https://doi.org/10.1007/978-3-030-21982-6_6

The violation of children's rights in armed conflicts is not an exclusive phenomenon of modern history. It needs to be analyzed not as an isolated factor but as part of a macrosystem that comprises economic and geopolitical interests, local and international policies, and production and commercialization of arms, among other issues that do not prioritize the most vulnerable people in our societies: children, followed by adolescents, women, urban and rural poor, as well as black and indigenous populations.

The use of child combatants—a preferable term used by UNICEF to reflect the range of roles in which boys and girls are recruited and used for military purposes—in armed conflicts represents one of the crueler and systematic violations of children's rights. Being a highly defenseless segment of society, children are paradoxically and parallely transformed into perpetrators and victims and suffer continuing abuses of their inherent rights. Not only do they become physically injured in these contexts, but also mentally traumatized. While we try to avoid seeing this reality by pretending that this is not happening—as though it would be possible to detach ourselves from the suffering that these realities impose on us—deep down, we know that these devastating facts of existence continue to emerge in our contexts bringing us a sense of powerlessness and despair.

Reflecting on this troubled picture of war and its consequences, I am reminded of Walter Benjamin's interpretation of Paul Klee's painting *Angelus Novus*, a 1920s-era oil transfer drawing with watercolor. In his essay, "Theses on the Philosophy of History," Benjamin exposes his profound understanding of human history inspired by Klee's artwork (1968). Many critics agree that it was Benjamin's views on the artwork that prompted its notorious recognition. He describes:

> A Klee painting named 'Angelus Novus' shows an angel looking as though he is about to move away from something he is fixedly contemplating. His eyes are staring, his mouth is open, his wings are spread. This is how one pictures the angel of history. His face is turned toward the past. Where we perceive a chain of events, he sees one single catastrophe which keeps piling wreckage upon wreckage and hurls it in front of his feet. The angel would like to stay, awaken the dead, and make whole what has been smashed. But a storm is blowing from Paradise; it has got caught in his wings with such violence that the angel can no longer close them. This storm irresistibly propels him into the future to which his back is turned, while the pile of debris before him grows skyward. This storm is what we call progress. (1968, 257–258)

Children in Armed Conflict at https://www.unicef.org/publications/files/option_proto-col_conflict.pdf.

In Benjamin's vision, Angelus Novus was nothing less than History itself, helplessly turning to the wrong way as it gazes at the wreckage of the past.[2] Perhaps the angel of present-day history, having the eyes fixed on the debris that keeps accumulating would contemplate the bodies of children marked by neglect, indifference, and violence as they carry guns in their hands and deep scars in their souls. At this meeting point, where we acknowledge the wrong done to them and to us—for what affects one, affects us all—we might regain the strength to imagine another possible future for all. This chapter aims to contribute in a very modest way toward an uprising that builds a safer reality for some the most vulnerable bodies around us—our children.

THE TRAUMATIC CONTEXTS OF CHILD SOLDIERING

Despite the idea that child combatants are often ascribed to areas that are currently under the siege of armed combats such as Afghanistan, Syria, Somalia, and the Democratic Republic of Congo, a significant number of Latin American children have their fundamental rights violated when they are forced into participating in guerrilla groups. Nevertheless, there are many accounts of the recruitment of minors in many countries of Latin America, and such operation needs to be considered as an amalgamation of several factors such as socio-economic inequality, high poverty levels, displacement, and gang violence. As a Latina theologian, I have seen firsthand how the poor children in Latin America have become victims of oppression, poverty, and violence in their quotidian life. Thus, my ethical commitment to the suffering experienced by these children grounds me and has helped me to continue in the struggle for justice and liberation.[3]

Driven by the threat of violence and despair caused by scarcity, these children sometimes voluntarily put their lives in danger in exchange for security and as a way of survival. Recruitment of children and adolescents

---

[2] The angel of history, as Benjamin refers to it, not surprisingly, is depicted as male. See the end of this chapter for another perspective on how a female angel reacts before the devastation and the debris before her.

[3] My theological approach is informed by Liberation Theology and Latina theologians such as Elsa Tamez, Ivone Gebara, Nancy Cardoso, Maria Clara Bingemer, Tania Mara Sampaio, Nancy Bedford, Ada Maria Asasi-Diaz, and Wanda Deifelt, among others. In the context of this chapter, I am drawing more specifically on the work of Elsa Tamez (2011) as she discussed the armed conflict in Colombia.

in Latin American countries is not a phenomenon exclusively of paramilitary forces, as in the case of the Revolutionary Armed Forces (FARC) and the National Liberation Army (ELN) in Colombia. Other forms of enlistment exist in other Latin American countries, where gang leaders and drug cartels use minors to smuggle drugs across borders, to extend or secure control of the cities (such as the case in "favelas" in Rio de Janeiro) and as informants. They are commonly known as "narco juniors," "sicaritos," or "urban child soldiers." The presence of children in clandestine armies and their participation in criminal activities is a very present reality in the Latin American territory and not infrequently children are found amid crossfire in areas near schools becoming direct victims of lost bullets. The viciousness to which they are submitted comes out of the notion that children as disposable.

In Colombia, more specifically, the presence of children and minors among the ranks of the paramilitary armies and their participation in criminal activities became more evident after the peace agreements between the Colombian government and the guerrilla of the Revolutionary Armed Forces of Colombia (FARC), which propelled a combined effort of leaders from national and international organizations to help the transition process. For instance, children released from FARC-EP participated in a reintegration program led by UNICEF's Transitional Reception and Care Sites (UNICEF 2017). Although these are necessary and commendable initiatives, they are remediable actions in response to the tragic reality caused by armed conflicts where countless children are harmed physically, emotionally, psychologically, and spiritually as a result of events beyond their control. As stated in the Human Rights Watch report:

> Girls in rebel forces face gender-related pressures. Although rape and overt sexual harassment are usually not tolerated, many male commanders use their power to form sexual liaisons with under age girls... These relationships may not appear to be forced, but they take place in a context in which the commanders may have life-or-death authority over their charges. Girls as young as 12 are required to use contraception and must have abortions if they become pregnant. (UNICEF 2003, 11)

From a developmental point of view, traumatic experiences are hard for adults but even harder for children. Children are more at risk of developing different detrimental consequences since their brains are not fully formed yet, and the impact of disturbing experiences in their lives have lasting effects. According to Bellis and Zisk, children exposed to war and abuse (physical, sexual, and emotional) are more susceptible to develop post-traumatic stress symptoms (2014, 186). Trauma disrupts their state of mind, brain, body, and spirit. As noted psychiatrist Bruce Perry states:

> Indeed the residual emotional, behavioral, cognitive and social sequelae of childhood trauma persist and appear to contribute to a host of neuropsychiatric problems throughout life. Traumatic stress in childhood increases risk for attachment problems, eating disorders, depression, suicidal behavior, anxiety, alcoholism, violent behavior, mood disorders and, of course, PTSD, to name a few. (2007, 8)

Recent neuroscience studies confirm the profound effects of trauma on brain development and its impact on individuals and societies, and how children are vulnerable to this kind of injury because of their rapidly developing brain. Trauma, being a result of single or multiple events, damages a person profoundly impacting the mental, physical, social, emotional, and spiritual dimensions of his or her life. Sara McLean argues that although many assumptions about trauma have not been subject to critical review, the prolonged exposure to traumatic events tremendously impacts brain development in children. The growing number of individuals who have exhibited the damaging effects of trauma on their learning abilities, behavior, and health, in general, is undeniable. McLean asserts that neuropsychological studies show a link between trauma and brain function that leads to cognitive difficulties such as language delays, memory, social/emotional bias, and attention deficit (2016, 4–6).

It is fundamental to understand that children and adolescents living within violent and unsafe environments will need not only physical and psychological assistance but also a careful accompaniment to address their reinsertion into educational and learning spaces that will take seriously the multiple ways in which their development has been impeded. Educators, social workers, and caregivers, who have seen firsthand the impact of war on children, are some of the people who can attest to how their learning abilities are compromised by various learning disorders that lead them to schooling failure and consequently school dropout. Although psychological trauma may not be readily apparent as the consequences of poverty, it does reveal itself through the pronounced development of depression, anxiety, anger, fear, dissociative outbreaks, drug and alcohol abuse, and conduct disorders that significantly impact the ways in which they relate to themselves, to one another, as well as to the learning process. As a result, these warning signs demand a concentrated effort to address the complex interplay of the child's psychological, social, and educational development.

Because war undermines the very foundations of children's lives and shatters their hopes, children experiencing these atrocities need reliable and supportive adults to guide and encourage them to navigate the tangled world of trauma. However, adults must avoid demeaning children's capacities as agents and resilient beings. As in the case indicated earlier, children who voluntarily enlist in armed groups are exercising their agency by deciding, according to their assessment, that such a choice will improve their living conditions and prospects for their future lives. The crux of the matter, in this case, would be for adults—through interactions and dialogue—to guide and support children in their process of decision-making. Understanding the inexorable relational capacity of human beings and recognizing how dependable we are on each other to make sound decisions, adults have the responsibility and the onus to protect children. Moreover, they must support them in the process of recovering from the very traumas inflicted upon them by the systems which adults, direct or indirectly, perpetuate. The joint effort and collaboration among children and adults will nurture children's capacity for recovery with resilience, an essential characteristic they need to strengthen in order to prevail over their traumatic circumstances.

Furthermore, accepting the fundamental role education plays in the lives of children, educators are charged with the responsibility of developing educational practices that consider children's well-being as individuals while taking care of the environment they inhabit. As political theorist Hannah Arendt argued:

> Education is the point at which we decide whether we love the world enough to assume responsibility for it and by the same token save it from the ruin which, except for renewal, except for the coming of the new and young, would be inevitable. And education, too, is where we decide whether we love our children enough not to expel them from our world and leave them to their own devices, nor to strike from their hands their chances of undertaking something new, something unforeseen by us, but to prepare them in advance for the task of renewing a common world. (1993, 196)

Accordingly, education—both in a broad sense and in its more specific schooling dimension—becomes a fundamental component to assist children in overcoming their limit-situations. However, it is important to notice that not all kinds of education will help children who are victims of such structural evil and abuse heal, let alone, advance their resilience and sense of agency. Perhaps only an emancipatory education will allow children to recover and flourish. It is the prominent role of education as liberation that I will discuss in the following section.

ROLE OF LIBERATION EDUCATION

I must also emphasize the understanding of history as possibility implies recognizing or realizing the importance of conscience in the knowledge process, in the process of intervening in the world. History as a time of possibility presupposes human beings' capacity for observing, discovering, comparing, evaluating, deciding, breaking away, and for being responsible. (Freire 2004, 113)

Paulo Freire, patron of Brazilian education and one of the most influential critical educators of our times, has helped to expand the understanding of education in its ethical and utopic dimensions and its endless task in the process of decolonization of minds. According to Freire, there is a kind of educational endeavor that perpetuates oppression and alienates people, which he refers to as the banking model of education. As Freire adverts, the epistemological mistake of the banking model approach is to consider knowledge as a package that can be transferred from one person to another, preventing individuals from taking active participation, critical reflection, and creativity within the learning process (1997). Thus, he advocates for education as a practice of freedom in which people subject to conditions of ruthless oppression become conscious of such unjust conditions so as to overcome these conditions through their agency. Analyzing their reality with critical lenses and not accepting injustices practiced against them, the frail in their fragility—but struggling for their liberation—find the strength to overcome the reality of oppression while contributing to the freedom of those who oppress them. In Freire's words, "only power that springs from the weakness of the oppressed will be sufficiently strong to free both" (1997, 26). In this sense, his pedagogy has a distinctive mark—a historical rupture—which directs his attention specifically to the oppressed people as agents of their liberation.

Freire's educational praxis maintains the necessity of people to recognize themselves as agents of their history and to become conscious of their presence in the world even if evil forces try to silence or annihilate that presence. As capable people, they can "rewrite the world" to transform it. However, this task cannot be accomplished in isolation; instead, it needs to be part of a communal effort in the struggle for agency, justice, and democracy. Accordingly, Freire's pedagogy invites us to discover (with those who suffer and with whom we struggle) what can humanize us all.

Freire's liberating pedagogical praxis presupposes an alternative political project based on the ethical commitment to human existence with equality and dignity for all which implies denouncing the oppression and the oppressors and announcing a vision of a transformed world where all can thrive. This dynamic unity between condemning and announcing is what characterizes the utopian nature of liberating education practice. Thus, education is an eminently political activity taking place in a specific time and history. It is a political act because it reveals institutional or personal priorities and ideologies, which are never neutral. Therefore, the very act of denying the political dimension of education is also a political attitude. One of the first tasks for liberating pedagogy is to clarify the legitimacy of the ethical-political dream of overcoming unjust reality. Considering Freire's premises, we should agree that concerns about the well-being of children cannot be restricted to its psychological and physical dimensions dissociated from its political, economic, and ethical aspects. As Henry Giroux states:

> Educational work is both inseparable from and a participant in cultural politics because it is in the realm of culture that identities are forged, citizenship rights are enacted, and possibilities are developed for translating acts of interpretation into forms of intervention. 'Pedagogy' in this discourse is about linking the construction of knowledge to issues of ethics, politics, and power. Making the political more pedagogical requires that educators address how agency unfolds within power-infused relations; that is, how the very processes of learning constitute the political mechanisms through which identities are produced, desires are mobilized, and experiences take on specific forms and meanings. (2000, 25–26)

Freire's theoretical work is profoundly radical in its anti-colonial stance. As an educator who respects the knowledge of peoples and their cultures, he has never yielded to totalitarian, deterministic, violent, or absolute discourses. Instead, he has always believed in history as a possibility, as a political practice that links human suffering to a project of hope. He asserts, "hopelessness is a form of silence, of denying the world and fleeing from it. The dehumanization resulting from an unjust order is not a cause for despair but for hope, leading to the incessant pursuit of the humanity denied by injustice" (1997, 72). However, he adverts that hope, as an ontological necessity, "needs practice in order to become historical concreteness" (2007, 2). Thus, he underscores the importance of having hope to achieve and sustain what he considers the ontological vocation of humankind: humanization. Through human capacity to hope, it is possible to imagine a world where everybody belongs and can blossom safely. In this perspective, he reflects:

> The matrix of hope is the same as the educability of human beings: the incompleteness of their being, which became conscious. It would be an aggressive contradiction if, unfinished and aware of the incompleteness, the human beings do not participate in an ongoing process of seeking hope. This process is education. But precisely because we find ourselves subjected to an endless number of constraints—obstacles difficult to overcome, dominant influences of fatalistic conceptions of history, the power of neoliberal ideology, whose perverse ethics is based on the logic of the market—never, perhaps, we have had more need to stress through the educational practices, the sense of hope needed today. Hence, among several fundamental practices of educators, whether liberal or conservative, it notes the following: change is difficult but possible. (2004, 100)

Thus, hope is what enables us to confront limit-situations. On Freire's terms, limit-situation refers to anything that prevents a person from experiencing the fullness of their cognitive, social, and emotional development impeding one's pursuit of becoming more fully human, that is, aware of one's "incompleteness" in permanent search of one's humanization and freedom. Thus, the limit-situation is not an irreversible condition, but something that can be overcome through critical reflection and subsequent action. Therefore, the task of educators is to unveil opportunities for hope (1997, 80–83).

Children living under limit-situations need caring adults to educate them in hope so that they can overcome their limit-situations. They need to grow and exercise their ability to think, to question, to decide, to experiment hypotheses for action, as well as to develop strategies for survival or even to imagine ways to escape their limit-situations. Their rights, necessitate that they be educated on how to make sound decisions, not in a self-centered fashion but grounded in collective efforts that will attend to their basic needs but also their dreams. This is possible through another concept Freire uses, "untested feasibility," the hope that can only be attained through liberating praxis (1997, 83). For him, to dream is to imagine horizons of possibility.

LIBERATING CHILDREN'S IMAGINATION

The child is made of one hundred. The child has one hundred languages, one hundred hands, one hundred thoughts, one hundred ways of thinking, of playing, of speaking... The child has a hundred languages (and a hundred hundred hundred more) but they steal ninety-nine. The school and the culture separate the head from the body... The child says: 'No way—The hundred is there' Loris Malaguzzi. (quoted in Edwards et al. 1998, 2–3)

Imagination is a fundamental aspect of the educational process because it releases creativity and expands one's capacity to engage with the world through passageways previously inconceivable. Imagination is a matter of being able to see with inner eyes, breaking down boundaries, and discovering new possibilities for human "survivance" in a sense employed by Anishinaabe literary theorist Gerald Vizenor in his *Manifest Manners: Narratives on Postindian Survivance*. According to him, "Survivance is an active sense of presence, the continuance of native stories, not a mere reaction, or a survivable name. Native survivance stories are renunciations of dominance, tragedy, and victimry" (1999, vii). Moreover, imagination as survivance becomes an active resistance against offensive events and a state of victimization creating a dynamic, resilient presence in the world as it is and imagining how it could be.

As Loris Malaguzzi's poem quoted above recognizes, children are bearers of imaginative capacities and wonder. However, as they grow older, these abilities are inhibited by adults who "steal their hundred languages" and dichotomize their minds and bodies. In this context of educational processes imagination is fundamental because it releases both teachers and students from the shackles of corporate culture that seeks to transform their relationships into mere consumerist transactions and part of the disimagination machine apparatus. According to critical educator, Henry Giroux (2014, 26–28), this "disimagination" undermines social engagements by discrediting community, public values, agency, democracy, and collective resistance. Freire corroborates such claims by saying that overcoming injustices, which requires transforming the unequal structure of society, requires an articulated exercise of imagination to envision a world which is not yet, but which we need to shape into being (2004, 14). Therefore, it is the task of adults and educators to provide children spaces so that they can develop their imagination, understanding it as an artistic pathway and a form of resistance that "will not be readily co-opted or domesticated by hegemonic interpretative power" (Brueggemann 2001, xiv).

In the dance between the forces that try to block imagination and the powers that attempt to resist the "disimagination project" we need to stand in solidarity with "the crucified people" of today's world (Ellacuría 1993, 581) and embrace a "hermeneutic of creative imagination" (Reid 2007, 6). Following the lead of Jesus who inspired the imagination of disciples to find creative ways to resist and break the cycles of violence, we are invited to enter this dance of resistance and liberation with an open mind and an emancipated imagination. Mark's Gospel is full of stories of Jesus healing, exorcizing, forgiving, educating, and restoring people's brokenness and making them whole again. Considering the limit-situations imposed on children combatants in close relation to imagination and resistance, one may ask what insights Mark's Gospel would bring to the life of these children and ours as well.

Although an analysis of Mark's Gospel is beyond the scope of this writing, there are remarkable aspects that place Mark as a narrative of resistance—which confronts the forces of the Roman Empire—and a narrative of embrace—which engages children as equal participants in the *kid-dom* of God.[4] I will explore the perspective of Mark to reflect on children in a context of warfare, guided primarily by the interpretation offered by Latina theologian Elsa Tamez in her chapter, *The Conflict in Mark, a Reading from the Armed Conflict in Colombia* (2011).

After a brief description of the armed conflict in Colombia utilizing the United Nations report as a reference, Tamez presents the content of Mark's narrative from the context of the war. She identifies recurring elements throughout the Gospel narrative, which parallels the situation in Colombia where feelings of anguish, fear, persecution, avarice, and thirst for power affect the lives of all. Under conditions of war, she maintains that the most vulnerable victims are children, women, the elderly, and the poor. However, in her description of the struggle in Colombia, she does not make any explicit reference to the presence of children in that circumstance. Mentioned only broadly when grouped among those most vulnerable members of society, the children remain invisible. This fact is

---

[4] I coined the term "kid-dom" of God in light of Jesus's invitation to all people to receive his message as children do and in recognition of the active role of children as full and equal participants of this new community as it appears in Mark's narrative. I was inspired by *mujerista* theologian, Ada Maria Isasi-Diaz who suggests the word "kin-dom" to describe the community of faith as the family of God in which we are all kin. Her use of this word challenges the traditional interpretation of the scriptural view of a Kingdom of God as hierarchical and elitist (1992, 116).

noteworthy considering that Mark's liberating narrative highlights the presence of children in many significant moments within the ministry of Jesus. Children are present and visible not only as supporting characters but as leading actors in the narrative. They are active agents and beneficiaries of Jesus's grace and his caring actions when teaching and performing cures (see e.g. Mark 5:35–44; 6:30–44; 7:24–30; 9:14–29; 9:33–42; and 10:13–16, among others). By his actions, Jesus rescues children from the margins of society and gives them visibility. This remarkable paradigm shift means a symbolic break with the Empire and its oppressive powers. Jesus shows that the encounter with God does not happen in the rigidity of the law but by embracing children and along with them, the other marginalized people. In the devastating world of poor children, Jesus's attitude represents the subversion of an oppressive order and the revelation of God's dream for humankind where a new set of priorities occupy the center stage, and new kinds of relationships are organized. Jesus, as Mark sees him, invites his disciples to engage their imagination to envision a new community inaugurated under these new parameters established by the Son of God.

Even though there is no consideration regarding the effect of war on children or specific suggestions regarding them, the recommendations Tamez proposes to overcome limit-situations imposed by armed conflicts could be employed to assist children living in such contexts. According to her, Jesus—instead of inciting an armed reaction to do justice—calls for a radical attitude to end the violence cycle. Tamez sustains, "Jesus in Mark rejects war and armed conflict and proposes an alternative of human renewal through the practice of justice, of healing wounds, and cleansing evil spirits" (2011, 120). His unrivaled response to the threat of war encompasses the following: not fleeing from conflict but protecting life without ignoring reality; being attentive and vigilant while speaking truth to power; and resisting persecution without being crushed while seeking to defend life in favor of a new humanity. These are suitable strategies to develop with children experiencing the terror of war, abuse, neglect or displacement. Children having their basic rights violated in war zones acquire deep wounds that circulate their bodies and souls as they experience torture, rape, and sexually transmitted diseases, among other cruelties. Very often, they are tormented by nightmares and recurrent thoughts that provoke anxiety, depression and physical illnesses." Interestingly authors such as Ched Myers (2000) and James Poling (2003) have developed conjectures regarding "evil spirits" that correlate mental illness and demon possession indicating how they are connected to political repression and economic exploitation. According to Poling, the story of a boy possessed by an unclean spirit (Mark (9:14–29) reveals "Jesus's healing of mental illness in a charged political situation" and his compassion and willingness to restore the body and mind of the afflicted boy. He adds, "[T]hose who are mentally ill are members of the community who are living out in their bodies the contradictions of poverty and oppression" (178). For Myers, exorcism—more broadly interpreted—as public symbolic action represents Jesus's inaugural challenge to the powers. He claims that "the demoniac represents collective anxiety over Roman imperialism. What Frantz Fanon called the 'colonization of the mind,' in which the community's anguish over its subjugation is repressed and then turned in on itself" (193). Furthermore, the demon embedded in the imperial culture kept the boy impotent, submissive to his imposed conditions, and voiceless.

Despite evidence of the effects of armed conflict on the mental health of children and adolescents, few interventions have been undertaken to try to minimize the long-term impact on children's mental health. However, the healing performed by Jesus in this account goes beyond the physical dimension of the boy's life. Jesus releases the boy and grants him resources to restore his human dignity. It represents his re-integration and participation in the community life as a child, who now restored in his capacity to hear and to speak, can resist the possession of his body, the subjugation of his mind, and the multiple forms of oppression imposed by his social-cultural context which are inconsistent with the *kid-dom* of God.

These attitudes or insights coincide with some concepts Freire proposes in his liberation educational praxis. He argues that "critical perception" of reality needs to embody two elements, action and hope so that people (children and adults) can develop the confidence to overcome limit-situations. One of the impediments preventing people from overcoming suffering is a fatalistic view of the reality that cannot be changed (1997, 80). Thus, a critical reading of their reality implies a learning process to unveil and guide the actions to eradicate undesirable existential situations. Children in contexts of war may have lost their capacity to dream, to hope, or expect anything good in their lives. They have internalized the message that there is no other way to live beyond the misery and atrocity in which they are submerged. In these contexts, educators need to work intensively to nurture their resilience and help them to reject and expel the voices that insist they do not have a future worth living. Also, children themselves, and adults working with them should identify what is the problem (if physical, psychological, or educational), how it is manifested, and act pro-actively to find appropriate solutions. For instance, children need to understand (read) their reality and learn to name the "monster," so to speak. This unveiling process will "disempower" and "dislodge" the negative voices that keep immobilizing them. Thus, the task of critical educators is to nurture children's resilience not by ignoring the injustices and the traumatic experiences but encouraging them to exercise their agency and participate, with adults, in their healing process. According to Freire, this can take place by the process of conscientization which entails a dialectical relation between action and reflection, leading people to embrace their agency. In this sense, gaining an understanding of the roots, limits, and possibilities of their condition will forge the first steps in surmounting the obstacles.

Osvaldo Vena, in his captivating unpublished essay, "Systemic Violence Against Children As a Catalyst for Cultural Biblical Criticism," reflects on the theological significance of poems written by children from Palestine, Israel, and Argentina. In Vena's account, children express their perspectives on the war in an intimate, confident, and honest style. Their dreams and desires for a peaceful world permeate each poem, and although belonging to different contexts, they share the same vision and hope for a world that is not yet among us. Vena expounds:

> The world these children envision is certainly one that has never been experienced in history and in that sense, it belongs to the realm of eschatology. It shares with biblical eschatology a tenacious, though sometimes skeptical, understanding of God's role in history. It holds in tension both assurance of deliverance and acceptance of the present reality of war, faith and fear, hope and despair. (n.d.)

Like the prophets in the Judeo-Christian tradition, these children intrepidly declare how they see no justification for war and they also announce their hope and dreams for a world of peace. In some ways, they share the same plight of the children in the Gospel of Mark who experienced the unsettled context of wartime complicated by religion and cultural disputes. In Mark's perspective, Jesus's engagement with children displays not only his concern and identification with their socio-economic and cultural vulnerability, but also seeks to reveal that the children, as active participants of the *kid-dom* of God, share with adults in the struggle and resistance. Thus, we are inspired and invited by Mark to emulate Jesus's attitude and to participate in the physical, social, and psychological healing process that those impacted by traumatic experiences will need to engage to recover their ability to hope and to dream.

Concluding Thoughts

In contemporary societies where children continue to be recruited into armed conflicts, are treated as disposable, are separated from their parents, are put into chain-link cages, and are dying from lack of water and food while at the borders, we unquestionably and urgently need a process of humanization to restore our souls and de-stone our hearts. In our diverse and chaotic contexts of inequality, violence, and scarcity of human values, we are also invited to join in this effort through our prophetic imagination to resist the forces that seek to separate us from ourselves and our brothers and sisters. The utopian dimension of education is an attempt to demonstrate that freedom to think, create, live and imagine is not possible as a prepackaged educational model but as an expansive and generous pulsation that affirms through concrete actions that the world can be transformed. Imagining this world into being is a call to embrace every day and every place where the lives of children are under siege. We must commit ourselves to a kind of education that leaves the pages of the academic books and the confinement of our institutions to become incarnated in the brown, black, and red bodies of our communities.

Our commitment to the teachings of Jesus and our greatest teachings must move our hearts beyond facile condolences and sympathy. We must commit to a kind of empathy that is suffused with hope and, above all, determined to change our realities through our actions in the world so that these children can imagine and forge into existence a new kind of living.

In our shared endeavor to imagine another kind of world for our children, I wonder if the Angelus Novus was a special kind of angel, an Angelus Mater, capable of genuinely caring for so many children who are injured in our world today. She certainly would rebuke the attitudes of a "human-kind" that by seeking egoistic pursuits proceeds to exterminate the dreams of children, hijacking their rights to education, to safety and family bonds. Noticing children's lives marked indelibly with the stain of suffering, the stench of death, and the trauma of war, she would invite us to stop our frantic life and allow for a moment our eyes to meet the eyes of these helpless ones, so that we could be in touch with their vulnerability and our limitations. Unsurprisingly, she would not only cry but also feel—in her body—the pain inflicted on each child's body as if they were all her children. Like a mother in labor, she would sense the pain of contractions in watching children combatants. She also would take on the suffering of the kidnapped, the orphans, the refugees, the sexually abused, the rejected, the exploited, the profiled, the neglected.

Angelus Mater, unlike the Angelus Novus, would not be paralyzed by what she was seeing. She would move toward the children in an extraordinary effort to embrace and protect them. Upon realizing her limitation to endure and take in such profound anguish, an exceptional spark of wisdom would befall her as she summons humanity's compassion and responsibility. As though feeling the pain of childbirth, she would invite us all to give birth to new humankind. Perhaps, in this *kid-dom* community, we will pay attention to the voices, the bodies, and the wisdom of our children to learn from them. Challenged by these "poet-prophets" in our midst, we would witness justice, where "love and faithfulness will meet and righteousness and peace will kiss each other" (Psalms 85:10).

REFERENCES

Arendt, Hannah. 1993. *Between Past and Future: Eight Exercises in Political Thought*. New York: Penguin Books.

Bellis, M., and Abigail Zisk. 2014. The Biological Effects of Childhood Trauma. *Child and Adolescent Psychiatric Clinics of North America*. 23 (2): 185–222.

Benjamin, Walter. 1968. Theses on Philosophy of History. In *Illuminations: Essays and Reflections*, ed. Hannah Arendt, 257–258. New York: Schocken Books.

Brueggemann, Walter. 2001. *The Prophetic Imagination*. 2nd ed. Minneapolis: Fortress Press.

Edwards, Carolyn, Lella Gandini, George Forman. 1998. *The Hundred Languages of Children: The Reggio Emilia Approach*. Westport, CT: Ablex Publishing.

Ellacuría, Ignacio. 1993. The Crucified People. In *Mysterium Liberationis: Fundamental Concepts of Liberation Theology*, ed. Ignacio Ellacuría and J. Sobrino, 580–603. Maryknoll, NY: Orbis Books.

Freire, Paulo. 1997. *Pedagogy of the Oppressed*. New York: Continuum.

———. 2004. *Pedagogy of Indignation*. Boulder, CO: Paradigm.

———. 2007. *Pedagogy of Hope*. New York: Continuum.

Giroux, Henry. 2000. *Stealing Innocence: Corporate Culture's War on Children*. New York: Palgrave.

———. 2014. *The Violence of Organized Forgetting. Thinking Beyond America's Disimagination Machine*. San Francisco: City Lights.
Isasi-Dias, Ada Maria, and Yolanda Tarango. 1992. *Hispanic Women: Prophetic Voice in the Church*. Minneapolis: Fortress Press.
McLean, Sara. 2016. The Effect of Trauma on the Brain Development of Children. *Australian Institute of Family Studies CFCA Practice Resource*, June, 1–15. https://aifs.gov.au/cfca/sites/default/files/publication-documents/cfca-practice-brain-development-v6-040618.pdf.
Myers, Ched. 2000. *Biding the Strong Man: A Political Readings of Mark's Story of Jesus*. Maryknoll, NY: Orbis Books.
Perry, Bruce D. 2007. *Stress, Trauma and Post-traumatic Stress Disorders in Children*. http://www.traumaandlearning.org/academic-articles.
Poling, James. 2003. *Render unto God: Economic Vulnerability, Family Violence, and Pastoral Theology*. Saint Louis, MO: Chalice Press.
Reid, Barbara. 2007. *Taking up the Cross: New Testament Interpretations Through Latina and Feminist Eyes*. Minneapolis: Fortress Press.
Tamez, Elsa. 2011. The Conflict in Mark: A Reading from the Armed Conflict in Colombia. In *Mark*, Texts @ Contexts Series, ed. Nicole Duran, Teresa Okure, and Daniel Patte, 101–125. Minneapolis: Fortress Press.
UNICEF. 2003. Guide to the Optional Protocol on the Involvement of Children in Armed Conflict. New York. https://www.unicef.org/publications/files/option_protocol_conflict.pdf.
———. 2017. *Latin America & the Caribbean Regional Office (LACRO)*. Regional Office Annual Report. www.unicef.org/about/annualreport/files/LACRO_ROAR_2017.pdf.
Vena, Osvaldo. n.d. Systemic Violence Against Children As a Catalyst for Cultural Biblical Criticism. Unpublished Essay.
Vizenor, Gerald. 1999. *Manifest Manners: Narratives on Postindian Survivance*. Lincoln and London: University of Nebraska Press.

CHAPTER 7

"Some Girls Are So Vicious that Even the Boys Fear Them": Girls and Gangs in Jamaica

Marjorie Lewis, Dianne McIntosh,
and Anna Kasafi Perkins

"I am particularly troubled by the large number of girls who are displaying antisocial behaviours because this was never the norm."—Calvin G. Brown, Chairman of Anchovy High School

It is an oft-repeated claim that Jamaica has levels of murder akin to countries engaged in civil war. This was acknowledged by the Jamaican Minister of National Security Dr. Horace Chang in his June 2018 Sectoral Presentation in Parliament, entitled, "Restoring Public Order and Safety… Securing the Nation." He identified crime as the most serious challenge

M. Lewis (✉)
Atlantic School of Theology, Halifax, NS, Canada

D. McIntosh
Ministry of National Security, Kingston, Jamaica

A. K. Perkins
The University of the West Indies, Mona, Jamaica
e-mail: Anna.perkins@uwimona.edu.jm

© The Author(s) 2019
S. Willhauck (ed.), *Female Child Soldiering, Gender Violence, and Feminist Theologies*, https://doi.org/10.1007/978-3-030-21982-6_7

93

facing the nation, and violence as the "tool of choice for many" (2018). Murder rates have been high in this country with under three million citizens. In 2015, there were 1208 murders, 1354 in 2016, 1616 in 2017 and between January 1 and 13, 2018, 14 more murders than for the corresponding period in 2017 (2018). In lamenting this "worrying trend" Chang remarked:

> Mr. Speaker, in proportion to our population, crime is claiming as many victims as countries with some high-intensity conflicts. At a rate of 54 per 100,000 we were approaching epidemic homicide proportions. (2018)

A recent phenomenon in countries embroiled in civil war or "high intensity conflicts," as Minister Chang calls them, including Nepal, Colombia, Uganda and the Congo are child soldiers, that is, minors who are recruited or used as fighters, cooks, porters, messengers or sexual servants. The stories of such child soldiers have fuelled books and movies such as *Beasts of No Nation* and *A Long Way Gone: Memoirs of a Boy Soldier*. Forty per cent of the hundreds of thousands of child soldiers across the globe are female (Murray 2013). In the case of Jamaica, while there is no outright declaration of and engagement in civil war, there are significant gang conflicts that contribute to the rising death toll, especially in our inner-city communities, in which children have been caught both as victims and increasingly as perpetrators. A 2017 study undertaken by the Ministry of National Security in Jamaica has identified that there are approximately 274 gangs with 9000 members operating in Jamaica. A growing number of school children have been associated with or involved with gangs (see "Security Forces Going After Gang Leaders," *Jamaica Observer* 2018). It is possible to argue, therefore, as this chapter does, that child gang members in Jamaica may be akin to the child soldiers of other national conflicts. The involvement of young boys in deadly gang warfare in Jamaica is recognized in the designation of "shotta" and "fryers"—terms used to describe boys who are oftentimes cold-blooded in their murderous activities. These boy gangsters are referenced often in the Dancehall popular music genre, which valorizes the bad man and the gangster. Marlon James's Man Booker Prize-winning tome *A Brief History of Seven Killings* fictionalizes the activities of numerous Jamaican gangs and their notorious leaders. Yet, a little-recognized group involved in gang activity in Jamaica consists of young girls and women. Very little research has been done on the existence and persistence of such girls in gang activity, although it has been recognized how adult women support and benefit from gang activity in Jamaica, as is captured in songs like those on Jamaican popular musician Tanya Stephens's *Gangsta Blues* album. These women and girls often receive money and other resources for survival, and protection from victimization, abuse and crime not sanctioned by gang leaders; they also are afforded the prestige bestowed on girlfriends and wives of gang members. This chapter explores the glimpses of such girl gangsters in media and newspaper reports, given that there is a dearth of research on them. It will take account of gun crime statistics reported by the police as well as information from two key informants involved for many years in peace initiatives in volatile inner-city communities in Kingston, Jamaica—"Nathan Brown" from a non-governmental organization (NGO) and "Zara Smith"[1] from the government perspective.

The title of this chapter and the quotation at the beginning reference a fear-filled comment made by a teacher at a prominent co-educational high school in western Jamaica. According to this teacher, "*Some of the girls are so vicious that even the boys fear them... Some of these girls are gangsters ... thugs with criminal intentions*" (Frater 2017, emphasis added). These statements present a framing of girls as gangsters, which highlights their relative propensity to violence vis-à-vis boys, who are expected to be violent (a gendered framing, which paints the girl gang members as exceptionally and excessively violent). At the same time, these girl gang members are described as purposefully violent, acting with criminal intent. The teacher's statement expresses both shock and fear at the behaviour of the girls in question because, generally speaking, girls and women are still considered "the gentler sex"; they excel in educational pursuits and continue to garner success at various levels in the society. Indeed, such successes are marked by the election of the first female Prime Minister in 2006, as well as the first female Chief Justice and Director of Public Prosecutions.

GIRL GANG MEMBERS

There is very little research on female gangs and female gang members in the Caribbean. A chapter, "Girls and Gangs in Trinidad: An Exploratory Study," (Wallace 2013) presents an investigation which surfaces a changing paradigm of women who are affiliated with gangs and gang members.

[1] Nathan Brown and Zara Smith are pseudonyms used to provide anonymity for informants who were interviewed for this chapter.

Over time, women's roles in gangs have changed from merely partners of gang members for parties and hedonistic sexual activities to frontline activities. The modern gang landscape in Trinidad and Tobago has women operating in quasi-gangs as well as pursuing illegal activities with other gang members. Wallace proposes that the changing face of female gang membership in Trinidad is linked with the increased involvement of women in crime and illegal activities. Among the complex and personal reasons women have become increasingly involved in criminality are: financial reward; deprivations, which force them to find non-conventional means of survival; identity and status; the need for money coupled with an easy access to a gun; the void created when their men are killed or arrested. Further study needs to be done in countries like Jamaica to ascertain how these girls and women are operating in the gang environment. This chapter is a first nod in that direction.

Jamaican Girl Gang Type and Activity

From the newspaper reports, there appear to be three kinds of gangs in which girls are found: (1) all girl gangs such as the one reported at a prominent all-girls high school in Kingston; (2) male-led gangs in which girls are co-opted; (3) gangs led by adult females. In the case of the "gangster girls" as outlined in the newspaper story, these girls had a "long history of inappropriate behaviour … unconfirmed allegations that they took part in robberies in the Half-Way Tree Transport Centre" (Jones 2015). A similar story is told of "gangster girls" being on the increase in several high schools in the parish of St. James (Frater 2017). According to the reporting, "so-called 'gangster girls', hell-bent on wreaking havoc, are said to be on the increase in several high schools in St James, creating significant challenges for both school administrators and the police on account of their penchant for violence, which they regularly manifest in brutal fights" (2017). Teachers report fearing these female students, knowing of instances where school officials have been violently attacked and wounded by girls. Said one teacher, "To be honest, I just stay out of their way because when you see them you see trouble" (2017). The police sources referred to in the same article make clear that these young girls are on their radar. Police intelligence maintains that "many of these girls are intimately involved with criminal gangs and are involved in vices such as the illicit lottery scam and gun running" (2017). These student gangs may also be affiliated with other criminal gangs operating in the same community. Gang rivalries and vendettas can therefore play themselves out on the school grounds. In some instances, teachers witness students making gang signs or hear them "bigging up" (i.e. praising) known gang leaders (2017).

It is recognized that Jamaican gangs recruit from among high school students. This is not unusual as a similar pattern exists across the Caribbean and Latin America (Goi 2017). It is recognized also that some students are particularly vulnerable to being recruited by gangs. Working for criminal gangs may provide a higher social status, respect and self-worth as well as physical and material security, which many times their families are unable to provide (2017). Perhaps, unsurprisingly, similar factors are at play among the female child soldiers involved in civil war or "high intensity conflicts" across the globe, as the chapters in this volume outline.

Student gang members, including females, often act as "movers," who carry around illicit items such as guns and ammunition with less fear of being caught or earning more lenient sentences. The Jamaica Constabulary Force Research and Evaluation Unit put out a brief report, *Children and Gun Crimes: 2016–2018* (JCF 2018), in which they showed an increase in the number of children arrested for firearms (homemade rifles, pistols, shot guns and revolvers) between 2016 and 2017 (65% increase). The figures for 2018 were not complete, but already by July 21, 14 children had been arrested for possession. The majority of the children arrested for possession were between 15–17 years of age and hailed from the parishes of Kingston and St. Andrew, where many gangs are said to frequent. The JCF in 2018 further reported numbers arrested for possession of ammunition, which were roughly twice the number for firearms. Fewer children are incarcerated for gun crimes—not possession of firearms or ammunition—but in 2016, there were five; in 2017 this increased by one to six and, troublingly, in the first six months of 2018, six children were incarcerated for gun crimes. Troubling also were the numbers arrested for murder and shooting. The JCF Report noted, specifically with regard to these arrests that they were committed by "children within gangs" directly linking those actions with gang activity. Again, the figures for murder showed an increase between 2016 and 2017, from 6 to 16. Eleven children were arrested for homicide in the first half of 2018. These arrests were of children between 14 and 17 years old, with the majority being between 16 and 17 years with significantly more recorded for 17 year olds. Four 17 year olds were arrested for shooting between 2016 and the first six months of 2018.

Another newspaper story by the *Jamaica Observer*, entitled "Attempts to Avenge Female Gang Leader's Death in East Kingston," reported the death of a female gang leader, a top-tier member of the Top Road Gang in Franklyn Town (2017b). The deceased female had been murdered in Dunkirk, another volatile community in East Kingston, and it is reported that men on their way to avenge her death got into a shoot-out with the police. This story is perhaps a glimpse of a female gang member whose story was prominent because she was female and therefore an outlier, whose behaviour was not in keeping with traditional expectations of femininity.

Key Informant Experiences

Key informants Nathan and Zara, who are experienced in working through civil society and government respectively, provided other glimpses of the gender dynamics evident in women and girls in gangs. Nathan reported that being the intimate partner of a powerful Don (top gang leader) or the mother of sons who become Dons were avenues through which women can exercise power in criminal gangs. That power can be wielded either in support of gang activities or, as has been demonstrated in some instances, in diverting young people away from gangs; the latter is the case when these women have themselves rejected crime and benefitting from its spoils. In Nathan's experience, it was a small number of women who had roles as gang leaders or as gun-toting gangsters. The majority of women involved in criminal gangs were in supporting roles of beneficiaries of proceeds of crime, washing bloody clothes, hiding guns, taking food and clothes to men who are in jail or prison and urging on or cautioning the men. This information was corroborated by Zara, who noted that of women ranging in age from late 20s to late 60s brought before the courts for gang-related charges, the majority were charged for participating in or being part of a criminal organization.

Nathan also gave insight into females' greater involvement in crime as against their involvement in violence. He noted that women had more prominent roles in crimes, such as scamming since this requires skills in which women excel—organizing, managing bank accounts, recalling details of telephone numbers of victims and guarding the ill-gotten gains in bank accounts of female family members. (One wonders if this is related to the higher levels of literacy among women in Jamaica.) Women seem to have less prominent roles in gang activities associated with violence such as extortion from business owners, contract killing and robbery. Nathan noted a growth of family businesses developing around scamming and often initiated by younger members of the family. While violence is not directly involved in these enterprises, if predators threaten, then the young members will act to defend the business.

MALE-FOCUSSED RESEARCH

The preceding discussion points to the need for more research on women and girls. This is consistent with the United Nations Sustainable Development Goals (SDGs) which identified gender as a cross-cutting issue. There has been a greater emphasis placed in Jamaica on targeted attention to diverting and rehabilitating boys and young men away from gang membership. The Sectoral Presentation by Minister Chang, for example, made special mention of a focus of the Ministry of National Security "utilizing our social intervention programmes to intercept the recruitment of our men into gangs" (2018). Scholars working in this area have also focussed on boys and young men, for example, Chevannes (1999) in his lecture "What We Sow, and What We Reap: Problems in the Cultivation of Male Identity in Jamaica" and McIntosh (2004), in her article, "Soft Boys to Bad Men: Expressions of Masculinity in Adolescent Boys from Communities Marginalized by Drugs and Guns," and, more recently, by anthropologist, Herbert Gayle. Gayle's research has been covered in both major newspapers, with *The Jamaica Gleaner* (February 2017) in an editorial captioned, "Who Is Engaging Herbert Gayle?" rehearsing evidence by Gayle and supporting Gayle's stance of emphasizing the needs of boys. The editorial based its stance on Gayle's research findings indicating that boys are more at risk of being recruited and socialized into gangs and are the vast majority of children killed. The *Jamaica Observer*, in its editorial entitled, "Sex, Violence and the Miseducation of Dr. Herbert Gayle" (January 2017a), was critical of Gayle's stance, highlighting and rejecting Gayle's positioning of the vulnerability of boys over-against that of girls, quoting this statement made by Gayle:

I understand everybody has a budget for women, I understand that perfectly. I understand that more than anybody else in this country. I understand the meaning of the word 'gender' with a little word called 'agenda' to the side of it.

Gayle created quite a stir when he appeared to dismiss violence against women by equating it with violence against men. He said that there is no such thing as violence against women just violence. In addition, he claims rape as equally a crime of violence against both men and women. In so doing, Gayle ignored the history of rape against women and the greater propensity for women to be subjected to such a violent dehumanizing act, often by persons known to them.

The debate as to whether boys and men are more marginalized and in need of more attention than girls, demonstrated in the different perspectives of these two Jamaican newspapers, strengthens the case for the mainstreaming of gender analysis in attempts to address the root causes of recruitment of children—both boys and girls—by gangs.

Research based on interviews of current and former women and girls associated with gangs and their family members could be triangulated with gender-disaggregated government statistics to expand knowledge and deepen analysis of girls' paths to involvement in gangs. Chang (2018) identified an emerging trend in organized crime, where traditional criminal activities by organized gangs, for example, trafficking in drugs, still exist, but are being superseded by lotto scamming as the main undertaking by criminal gangs. Indications from key informants like Nathan that women tend to have significantly higher leadership roles in lotto scamming than in other organized criminal activities add urgency to the recommendation that greater attention be paid to girls and women in gangs.

Available research suggests that for both girls and boys there is a coincidence if not a correlation between experience of childhood abuse and the propensity to violence and crime. Psychiatrists and psychologists interviewed in the crafting of a 2015 "Upliftment Programme" by the Ministry of Youth and Culture for girls in a juvenile facility noted case histories of sexual violence experienced by girls who often "acted out," including in violent behaviour and, in some cases, were subsequently found guilty of criminal offences as children (Keating et al. 2013). It may be unsurprising, therefore, that both Herbert Gayle and Nathan pointed to mothers as abusers of boys since many of these women may well have been victims of violence themselves. How does being a victim of childhood abuse and/or intimate partner violence affect the propensity to transition from role of victim to role of perpetrator? How does experience of childhood abuse affect levels of tolerance for violence by both girls and boys who become gangsters? The 2018 Report of a "Community Mapping and Women's Community Safety Profiles" (Ashley 2018), commissioned by the Ministry of National Security and executed by the Citizen Security and Justice Programme (CSJP) and the Violence Prevention Alliance (VPA), provide important data on violence. The data link violence (and responses to violence) to constructions of masculinity (becoming a "real man") and femininity (becoming a "real woman"). The research notes, in part, some cultural tolerance for intimate partner violence with the male as perpetrator; such violence is often perpetrated when men object to the desire for economic independence of women. Such independence threatens ideas of masculinity.

Widespread physical and verbal abuse of children resulting in distress, trauma and intergenerational cycles of violence and abuse were also noted in the Report. There is merit in this and other examples of the MNS intentionally collaborating with Civil Society, the Private Sector and International Development Agencies in seeking to counter crime and violence in the Jamaican society. The challenge of coordination to provide results exists. As Chang noted:

> There have been some successes from varying programmes executed by Government, NGOs and in collaboration with our International Development Partners. The weaknesses, however, have been due to inefficient bureaucracy, minimal integration and lack of sustainability. (2018, 18)

Exploration of strategies identified by the UN and key individuals such as Roméo Dallaire et al. (2016) could provide ideas to be tested with respect to girl gangsters in Jamaica. Dallaire et al. (2016) in an article entitled, "Innovation in the Prevention of the Use of Child Soldiers: Women in the Security Sector," note, for example, the merit of UN ideas such as increasing recruitment of women as members of the security forces and leaders in community programmes; mentoring female trainees for the security forces and empowering women; gender awareness training for the security forces and coming to grips with the specific needs of girls and women who have been gang members. While these are important strategies, as Nathan's responses indicate, there is need for continued security of former female gang members, who are susceptible to retaliation and further harm. Nathan tells the sad story of a former female gang leader who subsequently used her influence to steer young people away from crime; until she was murdered. This highlights the need for safety measures for those who are reintegrated.

THEOLOGICAL/ETHICAL CONSIDERATIONS

There is no doubt that youth is a particularly vulnerable time. Girls are particularly vulnerable to sexual and domestic violence as is so troublingly detailed in the 2016 Women's Health Survey Report (Williams 2016). So, it is not inconceivable, as indicated earlier, that some girls may find a measure of security and protection in gang membership. Furthermore, a 2012 Situational Analysis undertaken by Moncrieffe for the Government of Jamaica noted the vulnerability of Jamaican youth who are found to face a plethora of development challenges including unemployment, gaps in the education sector, poverty and health. The main concerns identified in the 2018 Report by Ashley had previously been identified in 2012. Of significance also are findings with respect to health, especially mental health and HIV infection, with young people being among the cohorts most vulnerable to HIV infection. The need for security of citizens and access to justice were identified as having special implications for young people.

The Situational Analysis of Youth noted, in particular, youth involvement in "the Occult" or *Obeah* as it is called in Jamaica. These young people may acquire guard rings or other amulets for protection and prosperity (Moncrieffe 2012, 9). This is unsurprising as this is perhaps both an indication of the growing secularization of the Jamaican society and the continued role of the transcendence among its citizens (Taylor 1992). Jamaica is a particularly religious society with most persons believing in the presence of a spiritual world that impacts the material world. At the same time, the Situational Analysis identifies a "culture of materialism" and a "quick gains" mentality as significant ethical perspectives among the young people. Ironically, it notes the young people's sense of powerlessness and frustration at widespread corruption, violence and poverty and sense of abandonment by the institutions of society. In response, many young people resort to an ethic of survival by any means necessary, inclusive of recourse to supernatural power. The complexity of the moral circumstances of young people may be similarly reflected in the lives and choices of youthful gang members, especially girls. Lewis (2011), in a Bible Study on the ethics of Tamar, notes the parallel with the ethical principle encompassed in the well-known Jamaican saying, "you have to stand on crooked and cut straight," which means that you have to respond with the appropriate ethics even when the odds are against you. This saying seems to describe the plight of Tamar whom we read about in Genesis 38 (2011, 14). In the story, Tamar is a woman at the mercy of her father-in-law,

Judah, in a patriarchal society where women's fates are decided by authoritarian men. Judah denies Tamar the right to marry her brother-in-law, which was the mechanism to offer a widow social security at that time. With limited options, Tamar disguises herself as a prostitute and becomes pregnant by Judah, thus securing her rights after initial condemnation and threat of execution. Tamar's ethics of survival are perhaps her only option where corruption and patriarchy conspire against her: she has to "stand on crooked and cut straight." Arguably, girl gangsters and fighters may well live by this norm in many societies.

Indeed, Perkins (2013), in diagnosing the moral status of the Jamaican society and individual citizens, postulated the existence of a metaphorical disease of the nation's moral system—Moral Degenerative Syndrome (MDS). Perkins (2013) argues that MDS is caused by a plethora of "germs or pathogens," including weak socialization, inappropriate values and attitudes, lack of personal responsibility, and reduced moral sensitivity, imagination and reasoning. Moral despair or fatalism is a central pathogen that may be more pervasive than is often countenanced. These "germs" affect the character of Jamaicans, including the young, distorting their values, attitudes and habits. Such misshapen character elicits the behaviour that leads to violent gang interactions.

In a country where the majority of citizens identify with religious beliefs, with most being Christian, the potential of religion to contribute to a deepening exploration of moral and ethical perspectives as an integral part of the challenge to crime and violence is also an area worthy of further research. The largest Christian groups in the country are conservative denominations outside of the mainline churches.[2] What insights may there be from the work of the Bible Society of the West Indies which in 2012 translated the New Testament into the Jamaican Language (*Di Jamiekan Nyuu Testiment*, Bible Society of the West Indies 2012) and conducted a series of Bible Studies across congregations in the island? What have been the successes in raising the level of consciousness of women using contextual Bible Study by the Roman Catholic Animation programme fashioned after the Basic Christian Community model of Latin America? How can exploration of experiences of contextual readings of the Bible and liberating approaches to moral reasoning contribute to an integrated multisectoral strategy to keep girls as well as boys out of gangs?

---

[2] In contrast, two of the contributors to this chapter (Lewis and Perkins) are from mainline Christian traditions and are influenced by feminist and Womanist theological perspectives.

STEMMING RECRUITMENT, SUPPORTING REHABILITATION

Strategies to stem recruitment and support rehabilitation of girl gang members; to support moral and ethical development; to reduce economic and psycho-social vulnerabilities; to assess civil society, governmental experience and gender dynamics are glimpses of hope and issues deserving of further research. In seeking to promote peace and divert young people from crime and violence, the Jamaican government has over many decades worked formally and informally to mine the positive elements of religion and culture for the cause. In the Sectoral Presentation, Chang (2018) identified the following current priorities for improving citizen security:

1. Public order and law enforcement,
2. Strong anti-gang strategies,
3. Anti-corruption strategies,
4. Targeted social intervention initiatives in volatile communities, and
5. Transformation of our Police Force into a modern service.

Activities associated with these priorities included organizing a 2017 Workshop on post-traumatic stress, which recognized the value of clergy and supported them working in a community affected by violence. Clergy have previously been appointed to key positions such as the Office of Political Ombudsman and worked in cooperation with the police to diffuse tension in communities. A significant initiative was facilitated by the Roman Catholic Animation programme that worked in select communities with the citizens to build independent community organizations that had the capacity for self-advocacy for peace and development. Linked to this effort at capacity building for community cohesion and self-advocacy are efforts by civil society and the government to address systemic economic and psycho-social vulnerabilities of young people. This will work in tandem with the insights provided by Womanist theories and practice, which address directly the experiences of African-descended women in a world where they are doubly disenfranchised due to intersections of race and gender; as is clear, with the girls and women involved in gangs, the question of class further impacts their disadvantage.

As indicated above, the government and civil society groups have initiated programmes, including those that support youth involvement in uniformed groups like the Cadet Corps, Girls Brigade and Girl Scouts. Such group involvement may directly address the status and identity issues that are at play in gang membership while enhancing their future prospects. Other government initiatives have been one-off events, as well as more extended interventions. The Ministry of National Security organized a Triple C Day Camp ("Chance, Choice, Change") as part of activities for Anti-Gang Week 2018. Another programme targeted unattached youth, offenders in juvenile centres and probationers with a focus on life and entrepreneurial skills and training in conflict resolution (Grant 2018). As significant as these initiatives are, it could be argued that coordinated and sustained gender mainstreaming to provide needed data on girls and gangs would be likely to make the implementation of policy initiatives more effective.

CONCLUSIONS

The chairman of one of the high schools in the parish of St. James plagued by girl gang violence has indicated attempts will be made to get trained psychologists to visit the school "to re-socialise" the students who are considered prone to violence. Attempts to re-socialize young people have also been made in conjunction with various Christian groups. There is, however, a need to deepen the analysis perhaps using a postcolonial and gendered lens that can assess the relevance of the dual heritage of Europeanized Christianity and African spirituality and employ the analytical strategy of intersectionality. The government has recognized the role that faith leaders play in social cohesion in communities and in seeking to promote self-advocacy and development and in facilitating institutional change.

The government claims to be taking gang formation and participation seriously. In that regard, the security forces are targeting gang leaders, organizing anti-gang sensitization sessions and developing interventions for young people who have been involved in gang activities or are at risk of being recruited by gangs. The glimpses provided above of girl gang members indicate intersecting factors of economic and psycho-social conditions, spiritual and cultural beliefs, gender roles and family ties that influence recruitment of girls as well as the rehabilitation of girl gangsters. There is scope for further research to test these glimpses and support more effective strategies to keep girls out of criminal gangs.

REFERENCES

Ashley, Deanna. 2018. *Final Report: Contract Between Citizen Security and Justice Programme (CSPJ) and Violence Prevention Alliance (VPA) to Conduct Community Mapping and Women's Community Safety Profiles*. The Ministry of National Security. Unpublished.

Bible Society of the West Indies. 2012. *Di Jamiekan Nyuu Testiment: The Jamaican New Testament*. Jamaica: Kingston.

Chang, Horace. 2018. *Sectoral Presentation: 'Restoring Public Order and Safety... Securing the Nation'*. Ministry of National Security, Jamaica. https://jis.gov.jm/media/2018/06/Sectoral-Presentation-12-June-2018-Final-00000003-.pdf.

Chevannes, Barry. 1999. *What We Sow and What We Reap: Problems in the Cultivation of Male Identity in Jamaica*. Kingston: The Grace Kennedy Foundation. https://www.gracekennedy.com/images/lecture/GKF1999 Lecture.pdf.

Dallaire, Roméo, Shelly Whitman, and Sam Holland. 2016. Innovation in the Prevention of the Use of Child Soldiers: Women in the Security Sector. *Prism* 6: 1. https://cco.ndu.edu/PRISM/PRISM-volume-6-no1/Article/684610/innovation-in-the-prevention-of-the-use-of-child-soldiers-women-in-the-security/.

Frater, Adrian. 2017. Gangster Girls Wreaking Havoc in St James. *The Jamaica Star*, November 7. http://jamaica-star.com/article/news/20171107/gangster-girls-wreaking-havoc-st-james.

Goi, Leonardo. 2017. Jamaica Gangs Follow Regional Pattern of Recruiting from Schools. *Insightcrime*, April 24. https://www.insightcrime.org/news/brief/jamaican-gangs-follow-regional-patter-recruiting-schools/.

Grant, Rosheika. 2018. 255 Young People Benefit from Anti-Gang Sensitisation Sessions. *JIS News*, November 9. https://jis.gov.jm/225-young-people-benefit-from-anti-gang-sensitisation-sessions/.

The Jamaica Constabulary Force Research and Evaluation Unit. 2018. Children and Gun Crimes: 2016–2018. Unpublished.

The Jamaica Gleaner. 2017. Who's Engaging Herbert Gayle?, February 22. http://jamaica-gleaner.com/article/commentary/20170222/editorial-whos-engaging-herbert-gayle.

The Jamaica Observer. 2017a. Sex, Violence and the Miseducation of Dr. Herbert Gayle, January 10. http://www.jamaicaobserver.com/editorial/Sex%2D%2Dviolence-and-the-miseducation-of-Dr-Herbert-Gayle_86203.

———. 2017b. Attempts to Avenge Female Gang Leader's Death in East Kingston, September 25. http://www.jamaicaobserver.com/news/attempts-to-avenge-female-gang-leader-8217-s-death-in-east-kingston_111916?profile=1373.

———. 2018. Security Forces Going After Gang Leaders, September 20. http://www.jamaicaobserver.com/Security_September_20,_2018?profile=1228.

Jones, Ryon. 2015. Girl Gangsters Booted, May 24. http://jamaicagleaner.com/article/lead-stories/20150524/girl-gangsters-booted.

Keating, Sadie, Judith Leiba, and Marjorie Lewis, eds. 2013. Upliftment Programme 2013: Diamond Crest Juvenile Correctional Facility, Alligator Pond, St. Elizabeth, Ministry of Youth and Culture. Unpublished.

Lewis, Marjorie. 2011. You Have to Stand on Crooked and Cut Straight:' Reflections on Tamar. In *Righting Her-Story: Caribbean Women Encounter the Bible Story*, ed. Patricia Sheerattan-Bisnauth, 13–18. Geneva: World Communion of Reformed Churches. http://wcrc.ch/wp-content/uploads/2015/04/RightingHerStory.pdf.

McIntosh, Dianne. 2004. Soft Boys to Bad Men: Expressions of Masculinity in Adolescent Boys from Communities Marginalized by Drugs and Guns. In *Crime and Its Greater Control in China*. Hong Kong: University of Hong Kong.

Moncrieffe, Joy. 2012. IDB/GOJ Youth Development Programme: Qualitative Survey on the Situation of Youth in Jamaica, Commissioned by the NCYD/Ministry of Youth and Culture: 'A So Di Ting Set' Executive Summary. Unpublished.

Murray, Rebecca. 2013. Girl Child Soldiers Face New Battles in Civilian Life. *IRIN News*, February 12. http://www.irinnews.org/analysis/2013/02/12/girl-child-soldiers-face-new-battles-civilian-life.

Perkins, Anna. 2013. *Is Moral Dis-ease Making Jamaica Ill? Re-engaging the Conversation on Morality*. Kingston: The Grace Kennedy Foundation. https://www.gracekennedy.com/images/lecture/grace_lecture_moral-dis-ease-2013_final.pdf.

Taylor, Burchell. 1992. *Free for All? – A Question of Morality and Community*. Kingston: The Grace Kennedy Foundation. Unpublished.

Wallace, Wendell. 2013. Girls and Gangs in Trinidad: An Exploratory Study. In *Gangs in the Caribbean*, ed. Randy Seepersad and Ann Marie Bissessar, 195–219. Newcastle upon Tyne: Cambridge Scholars Publishing.

Williams, Carol Watson, 2016. *Women's Health Survey Jamaica: Final Report*. http://evaw-global-database.unwomen.org/-/media/files/un%20women/vaw/vaw%20survey/jamaica%20womens%20health%20survey%20report%202016.pdf?vs=5406.

CHAPTER 8

Factory Girls and 'Comfort' Girls: A Feminist Theo-Ethical Reflection on Korean Girl Soldiers in Japanese Empire

Keun-Joo Christine Pae

INTRODUCTION

Jae-rim Kim was 14 years old when she boarded a ship to Japan to work at the Mitsubishi plant in Nagoya. She was from a poor farmer's family in Hwasun of the Jolla Province in Korea, the country occupied by Japan from 1910 to 1945. After having completed elementary school, Kim was recruited by a Japanese military policeman into the Women's Volunteer Labor Corps. He promised that as a labor "volunteer" in Japan, she would have the opportunity to earn money and to study at the same time. Believing his words, Kim arrived at the dormitory of the Mitsubishi Nagoya Plant in 1944 during the most brutal time in the Japanese Empire's Asia Pacific War. At the plant, however, Kim was not offered the opportunity for education but forced to paint warplanes and to perform other forms of hard labor. Until today the memories of violence from Japanese managers, unbearable hunger, deprivation of sleep, and a constant fear of

K.-J. C. Pae (✉)
Denison University, Granville, OH, USA
e-mail: paec@denison.edu

S. Willhauck (ed.), *Female Child Soldiering, Gender Violence, and Feminist Theologies*, https://doi.org/10.1007/978-3-030-21982-6_8

death during U.S. airstrikes haunt Kim, who is now almost 90 years old. After surviving the earthquake that hit the Nagoya region in December 1944, Kim was transported to the Mitsubishi plant in Toyama. When she left Nagoya, the plant was severely damaged by the earthquake and U.S. strategic bombing. On August 15th, 1945, Imperial Japan surrendered to Allied forces. Kim and other Korean girls in the Mitsubishi plant in Toyama could finally come back to Korea, the newly independent country from Japan. Neither the Mitsubishi conglomerate nor Imperial Japan paid Korean girls for their labor during the wartime, although they told the girls that their wages were saved in the bank and would be wired to their families in Korea. When Kim came back to Korea, she was penniless only to learn about Japan's deception.[1]

Among millions of Korean girls and women mobilized for Japanese military industries during World War II, Jae-rim Kim was one of 288 girls who were recruited from Chungcheong and Jeolla providences in Korea for the Women's Volunteer Labor Corps (*Yeoja-Geunro-Jeongshindae*) in Japan. The heightened production demands and labor deficits caused by the Pacific War led the Japanese Empire to deploy colonial Korean girls and women in the countryside to industries designated as important such as iron and steel mining, manufacturing, and ship and aircraft building (Kim 2007). Schools, local patriotic organizations, and recruitment offices throughout Korea actively enlisted female employees for Japan's wars in Asia Pacific (2007).

Kim's story did not end with the fall of the Japanese Empire. For the last two decades, the Korean survivors of the Women's Volunteer Labor Corps have filed a series of lawsuits against the Japanese government and heavy industries whose product lines exploited Korean laborers. They have sought to rectify injustice done to them and educate Korean society about Japan's wartime forced labor. In 2018, Korean forced laborers in Japan's war industries won a lawsuit against Mitsubishi Heavy Industries, Ltd. The Korean Supreme Court ordered Mitsubishi to compensate them for confiscated wages as well as physical and psychological damages done to them. However, Mitsubishi and the Japanese government still denounce their responsibility to compensate the forced wartime laborers, arguing that "all financial or other reparation issues related to their 1910 to 1945

[1] "A Letter from an Elderly Survivor of Korean Women's Volunteer Labor Corps," Hangyeore News Paper 4/7/2017, http://www.hani.co.kr/arti/society/area/789752.html.

rule of Korea should be regarded as settled by a treaty signed between South Korea and Japan in 1965."[2]

For more than 50 years, the survivors of the Korean Women's Volunteer Labor Corps had lived in utter silence about their horrific experience generally for two reasons. First, the politically conservative neo-Confucian Korean society equated these women with those who were forced into sexual slavery by the military of Imperial Japan, known as the "comfort women" system. Since female chastity was highly valued in the neo-Confucian world, politically and culturally conservative Koreans thought that the survivors of the comfort women system brought shame to the country. Not only the survivors of the comfort women system but all the young women who joined the "voluntary corps (*Jeongshindae*)" during World War II were treated as "prostitutes." Second, since girls like Jae-rim Kim were seen as patriotic "volunteers" for Japan's wars against Allied Forces (1941–1945) to protect "the Greater East Asian Co-Prosperity Sphere," their experience of mobilization for military industries has not counted for soldiering or forced wartime labor (Kim 2007). Moreover, uneducated poor girls' experiences of the war and Japanese colonialism have been usually excluded from the public discourse on war, security, and peace. What truth regarding the soldiering of girls can we learn from Jae-rim Kim's story? What kind of feminist theology and ethics of peace would we imagine if we seriously considered Kim's story?

This chapter theo-ethically contemplates the soldiering of girls in late colonial Korea by examining Japan's mobilization of girls during its Asia Pacific War (1931–1945). More specifically, I argue that soldiering girls in Korea is the manifestation of the idea of a sovereignty's right to kill. Through the lens of "necropolitical labor," which means that the extraction of labor from those who are condemned to death happens for the fostering of lives of others (i.e. state), the soldiering of girls in the Korean context reveals the militarized incorporation of girls into the body of the nation. I hope this analysis will further generate a Christian feminist ethic of peace that is strong enough to stop the nation-state from exercising its right to kill the vulnerable for the fostering of the lives of others.

The readers, however, should be aware that the modern Korea has not witnessed stereotypical girl soldiers, who were abducted and kidnapped to fight enemies, to cook and clean for male soldiers, or to be kept for sexual

[2] BBC News, 11/29/2018, Mitsubishi Heavy Ordered Forced S. Korean War Workers https://www.bbc.com/news/business-46381207.

slavery except for the case of Imperial Japan's military comfort women system. Despite the presence of teenage girls and young women in the guerrilla warfare either against the Japanese Empire or during the Korean War (1950–1953), no significant record is available to show girls' involvement in armed activities. Furthermore, for more than six decades, South Korea's mandatory military service reserved for young male adults has maintained the institutionalized military as hyper-masculinized space. As a result, the bodily presence of girls in the South Korean Army has been unthinkable and even unlawful.

Due to the intensity of the term, "girl soldiers," one might argue that my analysis of the state's mobilization of girls for its war would fit more logically in the frame of "militarizing girls' lives" in colonial Korea. However, I intentionally use the term, "soldiering girls" in order to examine the complexity of the process. The practice of soldiering mobilizes every part of society for war and national security. Girls might voluntarily or involuntarily participate in this mobilization, receiving military training at school, and being recruited into military industries to produce weapons or daily goods for soldiers. Examining these various practices of soldiering girls, this chapter understands the militarization of society as a discursively gendered practice.

What Do We Need for War?: Framing Soldiering Girls as Necropolitical Labor

As an African proverb says, "To raise a child, it takes a whole village." What would it take, when a country wages a war against another country? War does not merely require soldiers or weapons. To feed soldiers, the state should extract a large amount of crops from farmers which might result in their own starvation. If male farmers were drafted to the military, raising crops would fall on the shoulders of women and children. To clothe soldiers, the factory workers, who are likely to be girls and women, should produce military uniforms and shoes. Heavy industries, including the defense industry, make lucrative profits during war. Also light industries hire more laborers and make more profits than in the so-called time of peace. If a warring country has a colony, natural and human resources are likely to be extracted from there. War is like a black hole that sucks up all the possible resources for winning.

Although a wise man's proverb such as "there is no winner in war" is believed to be true, there are winners: a small group of capitalists and politicians who do not shed their blood but make profits from the blood of the majority of people, according to America's military hero and Quaker Brigadier General Smedley Butler's antiwar classic, *War is a Racket* (1936, reprint 2004). Namely, war always needs a group of people, usually from among the poor, who are condemned to death and thus, whose labor is extracted from their bodies for the fostering of the lives of others. Korean American cultural theorist Jin-kyung Lee calls this type of labor "necropolitical labor" (2010). Necropolitical labor is conceptualized as consisting of "a fundamental linkage between the extraction of labor and the conditions of condemnation to a 'living death' perpetrated by the state and capital" (2010). As the most disposable labor, necropolitical labor highlights the intermediate stage between life and death: the extraction of labor is related to and premised on the possibility of death, rather than the ultimate event of death itself. Soldiering might be the best example of necropolitical labor as soldiers, especially low-ranking soldiers, carry out the labor of killing the enemy, risking their own lives in battlefields. Through war, sovereignty exercises its right to kill. According to post-colonial theorist Achille Mbembe, "war is as much a means of achieving sovereignty as a way of exercising the right to kill" (2003, 12). Imagining politics as a form of war, Mbembe further urges us to question "what place is given to life, death, and the human body and how they are inscribed *in the order of power*" (2003, 12, emphasis added).

Soldiering girls should be understood in light of the necropolitical nature of war. More specifically, what place is given to girls' lives, deaths, and bodies and how are they inscribed in the order of the complex power structure? For what purpose are the bodies of girls conscripted to a state's war project? How is their labor extracted from their bodies for the sake of fostering the lives of others or more precisely, the life of sovereignty? By raising these questions, a feminist analysis of "soldiering" examines the state's various practices of mobilizing girls for its military projects, including the institutionalized military, militarized prostitution, the proletarianizing of soldiering, and industrializing economy.

FACTORY GIRLS IN IMPERIAL JAPAN'S ASIAN
PACIFIC WAR: PROLETARIANIZED SOLDIERING

The colonies are the exemplary places where sovereignty freely exercises its right to kill. In the colonies, "the sovereign might kill at any time or in any manner"—the colonized are not subject to legal and institutional rules (Mbembe 2003, 25). In this case, "sovereignty means the capacity to define who matters and who does not, who is disposable and who is not" (2003, 27). As Imperial Japan's colony, Korea offered raw materials from natural resources and human beings for Japan's wars in the Asia Pacific. Especially after Japan's attacks on Pearl Harbor in 1941, Korea played the most crucial role in providing necessary means for the Japanese Empire to carry out its wars abroad.

Japan's imperial wars in Asia Pacific, accompanied by the rapid capitalist industrialization of late colonial Korea, are the important contexts to understand the process of soldiering Korean girls. If wars necessitated the recruitment of girls and young women into military industries and military comfort station prostitution, the capitalist industrialization was perceived to open new doors for poor girls and young women. They were eager to escape their abusive fathers, poverty, and arranged marriages, namely, "gendered structural violence in the context of patriarchal colonial capitalism" (Soh 2008, xii). Many people imagine the forceful draft of colonized girls and women at gunpoint, yet many Korean girls like Jae-rim Kim made autonomous decisions to work in Japan. Unfortunately, their agencies were exploited by Japanese colonizers, who deceived and tricked the girls into either forced labor or military sexual slavery. This is why Japanese historian Naitou Hisako argues that the term, "forced recruitment" should be understood more broadly than kidnapping or abduction (2005). The Japanese Empire considered Koreans disposable for the fostering of its prosperity. Through the colonial education system particularly during the 1930s, Japan molded Koreans into patriotic servants, forcing them to adopt the Japanese language, lifestyle, and names, and eventually to follow Japanese rules "of their own free will" (2005, 93). They could not mentally resist pressure to cooperate with Japan's war effort.

Issuing the series of labor laws, Japan systematically recruited Koreans particularly from 1939 to 1945. During this period, seven million Koreans were mobilized for wartime labor, five million of them, including students and women, were placed at worksites in Korea (Park 2007). Roughly, two million were sent overseas: 200,000 soldiers, 200,000 civilian employees of the military, 720,000 forced laborers, 300,000 members of the volunteer labor corps, 80,000–200,000 comfort women, and 500,000 agricultural laborers in Manchuria (2007). Forced recruitment can be divided into three stages: recruitment through private hiring (1932–1942), official arrangement or government-managed recruitment (1942–1944), and coercive enlistment (1944–1945) (Naitou 2005; Park 2007; Kim 2009). Early recruitment usually targeted impoverished rural populations whose agriculture-based economies had been already severely damaged, as Japan aggressively confiscated agricultural products. However, in the last stage of World War II, the literature on the Women's Volunteer Labor Corps stated that school girls from middle-class families voluntarily joined the corps to serve in war-related enterprises (Kim 2009). In reality, the images of literate middle-class girls were rhetorically constructed in order to create a model female worker so that girls in lower classes would aspire to join the corps. The composition of the corps did represent diverse class and education backgrounds, however, the majority of female forced laborers were recruited among the poor (Soh 2008; Kim 2009). As seen in Jae-rim Kim's case, girls' and young women's hard labor in military industries that required advanced skills, training, and knowledge did not translate to their class mobility during and after the war.

The process of soldiering girls through forced recruitment was deliberate. Through the public education system, which had been introduced to Koreans upon Japan's annexation of Korea in 1910, Japanese Empire trained Korean children to be patriotic citizens, soldiers, producers, and reproducers who must be loyal to the emperor (Kim 2009). By 1940, the public school had registered 50 per cent of all Korean school-aged children, because parents were afraid of inviting trouble from Japanese authorities if they failed to enroll their children (2009). The public school system became a fertile ground to extract labor from children. The school assigned children with gender-specific projects: "boys regularly worked in construction projects whereas girls cleaned Shinto shrines and sewed supplies for the military" (2009, 141). From a Japanese perspective, colonial Korean children were readily available free labor. Since they had been groomed to be loyal to the Japanese emperor, the children were mentally unable to resist when they were conscripted for wartime labor or for soldiering in the imperial army.

An exclusively female labor organization did not exist until 1943, when the Department of Public Welfare announced the policy to enlist middle school graduates for the Labor Volunteer Corps (Kim 2009). Due to the dire shortage of labor faced by the Japanese Empire, Korean girls as young as 12 years old were recruited as "volunteers" for the corps. Teachers, school administrators, district leaders, village headmen, policemen, and other authorities participated in recruiting for the corps. Even the lottery systems were used to enlist girls for the corps (Kim 2007; 2009). Public schools in late colonial Korea were not educational institutions but training and recruiting centers for soldiers and militarized producers and reproducers.

Although wartime factory girls did not physically fight in battlefields, their lives in the factories resembled those of soldiers on active duty. For example, the Fujikoshi Steel Company in Toyama, Japan created hierarchical familial relationships among female workers, similar to the military ranking system. Every Korean girl worker was assigned with an older Japanese big sister who was responsible for the girl's meals (Kim 2009). In the factory, girl workers experienced ritualized work routines and lifestyles. They woke up at 5:00 am, attended the morning worship for the emperor at 6:00 am, worked at the factory from 7:00 am to 5:00 pm, and retired to factory dormitories. The evening was filled with routines such as eating, washing, cleaning, and meeting with dormitory parents, who were in their late teens and early twenties (Kim 2009). The lights were turned off at 9:00 pm. Although Korean girl workers felt strongly bonded with Japanese big sisters who commuted to the factory, and Korean dormitory parents, who lived with them, this hierarchical caring relationship plausibly made surveillance on the girls easier.

As the war between the Japanese Empire and Allied forces intensified, for workers and civilians, routines, lifestyles, and even mentalities "became increasingly synchronized and militarized" (Kim 2009, 151). Both Japanese and colonial populations were constantly exposed to the Japanese war propaganda up until the point that they equated their physical labor with an expression of patriotism.

COMFORT GIRLS IN JAPAN'S WARS IN THE ASIAN PACIFIC: SEXUALIZED SOLDIERING OF GIRLS

The military comfort women system might be the most notorious sexualized war crime committed by Imperial Japan during World War II. Among the comfort women who were recruited from Japan and its colonies, Korean girls and women made up the majority. If the recruitment of girls and women into military industries was concentrated in the post-Pearl Harbor Pacific War, then the military comfort women system existed in the beginning of the Asia Pacific War upon Japan's invasion in Manchuria in 1931.

In colonial Korea, public brothel prostitution, installed and systemized by Japan, was the backbone of the military comfort women system and later systemic prostitution for American soldiers stationed in post-colonial Korea. Throughout the colonial period, poverty drove many Korean girls and young women to the prostitution industry. Brothel prostitution filled with licensed prostitutes enabled the Japanese Empire to systematically consume Korean women's bodies during its military expansion between 1930 and 1945. In the early 1930s, private businesses recruited Japanese women from poor rural areas for "military comfort stations" in China and other areas where large numbers of Japanese soldiers were stationed (Tanaka 2002; Moon 2010). After the Sino-Japanese War in 1937, in particular the massive rape of women committed by Japanese soldiers in Nanjing, China, the Japanese military directly managed the comfort stations in order to control the problem of mass rape and the rampant spread of venereal disease (Tanaka 2002). The military drafted a large number of Korean women mostly in their teens and in their twenties because young Korean women in the Confucian society were "chaste enough to be free of venereal disease and young enough to endure disease if it developed" (Moon 2010, 42). The comfort women system was an integral part of Japan's military expansion.

Comfort girls were recruited in the similar way that factory girls were. Private agencies were involved in recruiting girls at the beginning of the Sino-Japanese War. After Pearl Harbor, the government became more directly involved in recruiting and conscripting girls even through kidnapping. Both wartime factory girls and comfort girls had been first called *Jeongshindae* (volunteer corps). "Comfort women" would be later called *Wianbu* in Korean/*ianfu* in Japanese to differentiate them from the wartime forced laborers (Soh 2008). Like Jae-rim Kim and other wartime factory girls, the survivors of the comfort women system testified that they were promised to earn substantial money to support themselves and their families if they joined *Jeongshindae* and worked in Japan's overseas factories. Tokchin Kim and Sunok Yi were among those who were deceived by private hiring agencies. In 1937, 17-year-old Tokchin Kim was approached by a Korean agent, who lived in her village and worked for a Japanese company. He gave her an attractive offer to work at a silk factory in Japan so she could earn money and study. One of five children of a poor peasant family, Kim took the offer but was sent to a military comfort station in China (Tanaka 2002). In 1938, Sunok Yi was recruited in the same way that Tokchin Kim was and was sent to a comfort station in Guangdong, China (2002). These private agents were military sub-contractors, selected by Japanese military authorities. Toward the end of the war, the Japanese military used the local police to procure women, due to the high demand of their bodies. Both Turi Yun and P'ilgi Mun, who were sent to comfort stations in 1943, testified that they had been detained at the police station before being forced to hop in military trucks to be transported to comfort stations (2002).

In August 1944, the Women's Voluntary Labor Service Law, which allowed the colonial government to force any unmarried girl between 12 and 40 years old to engage in war-related labor for 12 months, was enacted. Shortly after that, some girls 'ironically' ended up at Japan's overseas comfort stations by accepting offers of employment made by labor brokers or government agents to avoid being drafted into the Women's Voluntary Labor Service Corps. Japanese historian Yuki Tanaka states that:

> A rumor spread in Korea that all unmarried girls over 14 years old would be forced to become comfort women. Many middle- and upper-class Korean families withdrew their daughters from women's colleges and hurriedly arranged marriages for them to avoid their being drafted. However, some families in lower social strata felt trapped. (2002, 41–42)

In 1944, a poor girl named T'aeson Kim had been hiding in an attic of her uncle's house to avoid conscription. While having lunch downstairs, she was unfortunately met by a Japanese man with a Korean partner, who entered her uncle's house and offered her a job in Japan. Thinking that it would be better to be a factory girl in Japan than a comfort girl, Kim took the offer. However, she ended up in a comfort station in Burma, more than 2100 miles away from her home (2002).

The stories from the survivors of the Japanese military comfort women system demonstrate the complex structures behind the system, the militarized patriarchal culture in both Japan and Korea, and conflicted memories about the system. For instance, a girl whose name was Oksun Kim was sold to brothels several times by her father until she was finally sold to the private manager of the comfort station in south China. Some girls and women fell in love with Japanese soldiers, who showed sympathy toward them. A survivor whose name was Haksun Kim would be later abused by her husband who in fact, rescued her from a comfort station (Soh 2008). Many women said that they had to serve 10 to 30 soldiers daily. Even pregnant women were forced to receive clients (Tanaka 2002). Despite complexities found in what anthropologist Sarah Soh calls "testimonial narratives," all the stories collected from not only the survivors of the comfort women system but also the veterans who used comfort stations agree that condoms and comfort women were considered the emperor's special gifts for the soldiers (Soh 2008). The comfort women system shows that girls could be systematically sexualized by the sovereignty for its war effort. The girls' sexualized labor was extracted until they could not perform the labor any more. Their human value was reduced to their sexuality, as they were condemned to death for fostering of the life of Japanese Empire.

According to Sarah Soh, comfort women reveal the complex political economy of the late colonial Korea marred with hyper-masculine militarism, capitalist industrialization, and patriarchal culture (2008). They also bodily testify how poor girls and young women have been historically forced to answer the needs of public sex, including (forced) military prostitution. While actively seeking out the opportunity for a better life in an oppressive society, these girls were tricked into the comfort women system. Similarly, the girls' lives in wartime forced labor demonstrate that colonialism unequally affects colonial subjects, based on their race, gender, class, sexuality, and age. The lives of girls and young women living in dire poverty in colonial Korea were surely "the wretched of the earth" (Fanon 1963, reprint 2004).

A FEMINIST THEO-ETHICAL REFLECTION: GIRLS IN A PALIMPSEST OF WAR

Although my analysis has focused on Korean girls' necropolitical labor during Japanese colonialism, their physical and sexualized labor continued after Korea's emancipation. Like the Japanese Empire, post-colonial Korea used the tactics of mass mobilization of female labor forces for the economic development of the country and attempted to unify the people under the anti-communist banner. The mobilized teenage girls and young women worked at factories as well as in prostitution industries. Like many other third world countries, South Korea's economy in the 1960s through the early 1980s relied on women's sexualized labor—poor women were recruited into various forms of prostitution to bring foreign currencies for their developing country, including sex tourism for rich Japanese and U.S. military prostitution that has existed in the country since 1945 when the U.S. military officially stepped on Korean soil.

The colonial Korean girls' experiences of the Asia Pacific War urges feminist theo-ethicists like myself to accentuate God's preferential option for poor girls. To imagine God's preferential option for the girls, we should read girls' stories as palimpsests in human history suffered by war and violence. Arguing that "time is neither vertically accumulated nor horizontally teleological," transnational feminist scholar M. Jacqui Alexander proposes the idea of the palimpsest: "the previous text having been imperfectly erased and remaining, therefore, still partly visible" (2005, 190). The palimpsestic time always offers the present as the meeting point between the past and the future, leading one to consciously look at what has been erased and what will leave traces. By framing time as that of a palimpsest of the patriarchal nation-building, heterosexual militarization, and colonialism, we can look at the stories of girl soldiers from multiple angles and through many nameless victims of Japanese colonialism in South Korea, and child soldiers who have existed throughout human history. Christian feminist theo-ethicists who are concerned about the soldiering of girls should develop skills to read past, present, and future stories of girl soldiers together in order to comprehend the complex web of international politics. These stories appear familiar and unfamiliar, historically specific and transcendental, visible and invisible, and after all, ambiguous.

For example, the testimonial narratives from the survivors of the comfort women system resonate with those of bush wives in Sierra Leone. Just as the comfort women survivors were rejected by Korean society and had to live in silence for more than 50 years (some of them lived in silence all their lives), bush wives in Sierra Leone were shunned by their communities when they came back home. During the Sierra Leonean War, many thousands of girls were abducted from their homes when the rebels or other fighters looted. The majority of them were used as forced labor, frequently raped, or forcefully impregnated. They were also subjected to forced marriage and became so-called bush wives (Coulter 2009). Korean comfort women were the past of bush wives, who are the future of the comfort women.

Intentionally reading and remembering the palimpsests of girl soldiers in human history, feminist theo-ethicists can read the signs of soldiering girls in their particular times and work to prevent it. Furthermore, we should intentionally trace how God has acted on behalf of girl soldiers, not through their so-called heroic actions in battlefields but through their resilience and testimonies against injustice and harm done to them. Theologically speaking, the palimpsestic time of war and violence is embraced, healed, and transcended by the palimpsests of God.

When we look at girl soldiers, we do not examine a particular period of human life. Rather, girl soldiers' experiences show what could happen to women from birth to death, if the sovereign power had no desire to protect them. In this case, the educational system and feminist movements that help girls to be discerning moral agents or simply to work for gender equality can be hijacked by the state's war effort. When the social security net for girls malfunctions, their use of agency to escape structural violence or to better their lives may also harm them, as we saw in cases of colonial Korean girls. Furthermore, due to their gender, sexuality, and age, girl soldiers are sexually victimized and morally stigmatized for an indefinite period. Regardless of what they did during the armed conflict, girl soldiers are stigmatized as immoral and their immorality is usually associated with sexual promiscuity (Steinl 2017). Thus, it is harder for girl soldiers to return to the civilian life even long after the armed conflict is over, which was the case for the Korean survivors of the Women's Volunteer Service Corps and the comfort women system. In response to the re-victimization and stigmatization of girl soldiers, Christian feminist theology should critically analyze the political economy behind soldiering girls, complicate girls' use of their agency in militarized society, carefully trace girl soldiers' survival strategies, and accentuate healing and restoration of girl soldiers after a cease fire.

Finally, a theo-ethical discourse on child soldiers should begin with a humble confession that despite the long presence of child soldiers in the global war theater, Christianity has not developed either a proper discourse or practice to protect children from soldiering and violence in general. Their age, background, use of agency, and gender should now be all incorporated into a new way of theological thinking about war before it is too late.

REFERENCES

Alexander, M. Jacqui. 2005. *Pedagogies of Crossing: Meditations on Feminism, Sexual Politics, Memory, and the Sacred.* Durham, NC: Duke University Press.

Butler, Smedley. 2004. *War Is a Racket.* Edited by Dragan Nikolic. New York: Aristeus Books.

Coulter, Chris. 2009. *Bush Wives and Girl Soldiers: Women's Lives through War and Peace in Sierra Leon.* Ithaca, NY: Cornell University Press.

Fanon, Frantz. 2004. *The Wretched of the Earth.* Translated by Richard Philcox. New York: Grove Press.

Kim, Janice. 2007. The Pacific War and Working Women in Late Colonial Korea. *Signs* 33 (1): 81–103.

———. 2009. *To Live to Work: Factory Women in Colonial Korea, 1910–1945.* Palo Alto, CA: Stanford University Press.

Lee, Jin-Kyung. 2010. *Service Economies: Militarism, Sex Work, and Migrant Labor in South Korea.* Minneapolis: University of Minnesota Press.

Mbembe, Achille. 2003. "Necropolitics." Translated by Libby Meintjes. *Public Culture* 15 (1): 11–40.

Moon, Seungsook. 2010. Regulating Desire, Managing the Empire: U.S. Military Prostitution in South Korea, 1945–1970. In *Over There: Living with the U.S. Military Empire from World War to the Present,* ed. Maria Hoehn and Seungsook Moon, 39–77. Durham, NC: Duke University Press.

Naitou, Hisako. 2005. Korean Forced Labor in Japan's Wartime Empire. In *Asian Labor in the Wartime Japanese Empire: Unknown Histories,* ed. Paul H. Kratoska, 90–98. New York: An East Gate Book.

Park, Soon-Won. 2007. The Politics of Remembrance: The Case of Korean Forced Laborers in the Second World War. In *Rethinking Historical Injustice and Reconciliation in Northeast Asia: The Korean Experience,* ed. Gi-Wook Shin, Soon-Won Park, and Daqing Yang, 55–74. New York: Routledge.

Soh, Sarah. 2008. *The Comfort Women: Sexual Violence and Postcolonial Memory in Korea and Japan.* Chicago: The University of Chicago Press.

Steinl, Leonie. 2017. *Child Soldiers as Agents of War and Peace: A Restorative Transitional Justice Approach to Accountability for Crimes under International Law.* Hague, Netherlands: Asser Press.

Tanaka, Yuki. 2002. *Japan's Comfort Women: Sexual Slavery and Prostitution during World War II and the U.S. Occupation.* New York: Routledge.

CHAPTER 9

Battling a 'War within a War': Challenges of Being Female in Africa

Mary Nyangweso

INTRODUCTION

In 2014, Boko Haram[1] abducted 276 girls from a school in a dormitory in Chibok, prompting a campaign led by Michelle Obama amongst other international figures, for their release. Later on, it took 45 more girls from Wagga, Adamawa State and 'married' them off. It is estimated that Boko Haram may have abducted between 500 and 2000 women since 2013. Since its founding, Boko Haram has razed villages and massacred people in several townships in an effort to establish an Islamic Caliphate in the West African region. In addition to bombing dozens of public places, destroying homes and arresting family members, Boko Haram is known for kidnapping thousands of girls and

---

[1] Boko Haram is a jihadist militant organization based in northeastern Nigeria and in other west African countries such as Chad, Niger and northern Cameroon. The word *boko haram* means western education is forbidden. It was formerly known as Jama'at Ahl as-Sunnah lid-Dawah wal-Jihad.

M. Nyangweso (✉)
East Carolina University, Greenville, NC, USA
e-mail: wangilam@ecu.edu

© The Author(s) 2019
S. Willhauck (ed.), *Female Child Soldiering, Gender Violence, and Feminist Theologies*, https://doi.org/10.1007/978-3-030-21982-6_9

women and using them as 'soldiers' or 'wives' by militants. In some cases, they are used as bargaining chips, cooks, as suicide bombers and as future soldiers (Nwaubani 2018). According to Agence France-Press (AFP), and other news organizations, dozens of these women were eventually slaughtered by their 'husbands' before a battle with troops in the northeast town of Bama (AFP 2015; McCoy 2015). Witnesses told AFP that the soldiers "killed the women to prevent them from marrying soldiers or non-believers" arguing that they would not allow their wives to be married to infidels (2015). Just recently, allegations of sexual assault were reported in Zimbabwe where security forces that were deployed to quell a protest ended up raping women. One of the six women who sought refuge at a safe-house after their ordeal during the night time door-to-door raids by the security forces had the following to say, "they slapped me, then they said they wanted to have sex with me. When I refused, they slapped me again. The first soldier had unprotected sex with me. Then the other one said, 'I want to do the same'" (BBC News 2019). Responding to these allegations, Thando Makubaza, a Zimbabwean Women's Human Rights Activist decried the general perception in Zimbabwe that "a woman's body is not considered hers and any man who wants it can have it." To her, it is her role as an activist to remind everyone that women are more than their bodies "they have feelings, brains and aspirations: and need to be taken seriously," she argues (Nyakanyanga 2019).

Meanwhile, Doriane, a 19-year old from Cameroon recounts her struggle with legitimized violence in her home. She explains:

> I was eight when my mother told me: 'Take your top off. Do you have breasts already? When a girl your age has breasts, men look at her.' I didn't understand what she was doing. Every day, sometimes three times a day, she would flatten my chest with a hot spatula. She would just say: 'It's for your own good.' It was a nightmare. I noticed that the more she massaged me, the more my breasts grew. When she realized it wasn't working, she used a rock. That was hell. It felt like my body was on fire. A guidance counselor, who I told everything, tried to talk to my mom and get her to stop. I was happy because I thought it was over. But she did it again—with heated fruit pits this time. She massaged and massaged. I packed my stuff and moved to my aunt's immediately. Sometimes, I try to understand my mother's actions. It hurts so much when I look at myself in the mirror. (Pare and Bidan 2015)

Breast ironing is a cultural practice that is common in Cameroon and some surrounding regions in Africa. It involves the massaging and pounding of young girls' breasts as soon as they develop using heated objects such as rocks, hammers, spatulas, or pestles or tight elastic bandages. The rationale behind breast ironing is that, by removing the breast tissues, the young girls' bodies will be less attractive to men thereby postponing sexual relationships and pregnancy at a young age and preventing shame on their families. One British woman who went through this ritual explains how it works. "They put the spatula on the fire then they press it on the breast, and yes it hurts... then it goes weak, it's like melting, melting fat and you can feel the breast going back" (Bond 2016). Breast ironing originally practiced in African countries is now international as British parents have been reported to be practicing it on their daughters (Pare and Bidan 2015; Bond 2016). While this practice is culturally legitimate, it is a form of gender-based violence. Similar practices also common in various parts of the continent include female circumcision, child marriage, widow inheritance, honor killings, to mention just a few.

Violence is a common phenomenon the world over. It is about power, control, and the domination of the other. As a tool that has been used for centuries to dominate the weak and the vulnerable in society, violence has been used to define gender relations. Just as violence has served as an effective tool of domination of the other during war, gender-based violence is also effective in defining masculinity and femininity. In African societies, gender-based violence is prevalent as both a tool of war and as a norm for defining gender and gender roles. While they may seem different in their purposes, violence during war and gender-based violence are related in their mission of asserting power on the 'other.' This chapter examines how violence has been used to dominate and to exert power in Africa with a special focus on the challenges that the African woman faces due to this violence. The chapter highlights health and human rights violations she is exposed to daily. Drawing from various examples across the continent, the author describes how gender-based violence is socially constructed and legitimized in Africa and shows how such legitimation enables gender-based violence in the daily experiences of the African woman. The chapter employs feminist and intersectionality frameworks toward highlighting complex social dynamics that inform gender-based violence in Africa.

VIOLENCE IN CONFLICT ZONES

Boko Haram insurgency began in 2009 when this Jihadist group started an armed rebellion against the government of Nigeria (Nossiter 2009). In 2013, over 1000 people died as a result of the conflict. The violence escalated dramatically in 2014 claiming 10,849 victims (Mark 2015). Soon the insurgency spread to neighboring countries like Chad, Cameroon, and Niger escalating the conflict into a regional problem. African women are always caught up in a conflict they know nothing about. As civilians in conflict zones, women in Africa are exposed to sexual violence, including rape, mutilations, and sexual slavery. Other countries that have been affected by violence include Burundi, Congo Brazzaville (Republic of Congo), Central African Republic (CAR), Chad, Cote d' Ivoire, Democratic Republic of Congo, Rwanda, Sierra Leone, Somalia, Sudan, Uganda, and Kenya (Arieff 2010) to mention but a few. In Kenya, for instance, sexual violence—including rape, gang rape, and mutilation, was a feature of the violence that erupted in 2008 following the disputed presidential election. Investigations indicate that such violence was carried out by members of the government security forces as well as non-state militias, humanitarian workers, and other individuals who exploited ethnic and political affiliations.

In Zimbabwe, members of the military, police, and pro-government militias have been accused of perpetrating sexual violence for the purpose of political intimidation. In January 2019, 11 women from Harare's Hopley area alleged that they were raped by soldiers during an ongoing crackdown against opposition activists linked to a protest against fuel price hikes. The protest which turned violent resulted in the killing of 12 people by security forces and the sexual assault of women. As one female survivor of sexual assault explained to Cynthia Goba, on that particular day, during the night she arrived at her home where she saw soldiers near her house in the maize plantation. They asked for her children; when she lied to them that they were not at home, the soldier ordered her to have sex with him. She explains; "I didn't refuse because I wanted to save my children. I, however, told him that I am HIV positive, but he said it didn't matter, so I complied" (Goba 2019). Sexual assault during the war in Zimbabwe is aptly depicted in the film "In a Dark Time" in which a 16-year old Sarudzai recalls a similar ordeal. She was alone in the family home with three younger siblings when militiamen surrounded it. Her father was at a funeral and her mother was hiding in the bush from the militia that was looking specifically for her. Fearing that they would set the hut on fire, Sarudzai stepped out of her home. She was raped right there to punish her mother for supporting Zimbabwe's opposition party. According to Sarudzai and other women featured in the documentary, their attackers were militiamen known as the "Green Bombers," a government-created youth brigade often accused of human rights abuse. Sarudzai explains how her experience made her act and feel differently from the other girls. "I am not a virgin anymore. It happened against my will. Maybe I have HIV. I wish I'd die. Then I'd feel no pain," she adds. The Zimbabwe Women's Lawyers Association's report also indicated that about 1000 women were held in militia camps in 2002.

Stories such as this abound in the experiences of the woman across the continent. In Guinea, members of the presidential guard and police have been reported as having committed dozens of rapes and other sexual crimes against women during a crackdown on anti-military demonstrators in late September of 2009 (Nossiter 2009). In Darfur, state security forces and pro-government militia allegedly employed sexual violence repeatedly as a tool of humiliation and exertion of power. In the Democratic Republic of Congo (DRC), rape and other forms of sexual violence have been a feature of conflict going back to the 1998–2003 civil war. During this recurring conflict, state security and combatants from neighboring countries inflicted sexual violence on DRC civilians on a massive scale. This forced John Holmes, a representative of the United Nations under-secretary General for Humanitarian Affairs, to characterize sexual violence in DRC as the worst in the world (Brown 2012). While precise statistics on how many were affected with this violence are inaccurate and often lacking, UNICEF estimated that in 2008, "hundreds of thousands" of women and girls had been raped in DRC since the mid-1990s, with about 1000 rapes occurring every month. Rape and forced concubinage have also been reported in Mozambique, Angola, and South African civil wars.

Broadly speaking, it can be argued that four kinds of rape are identified in a conflict situation. The first, known as genocidal rape, seeks to destroy an ethnic or political group that is perceived to be an enemy as in the case of what happened in Rwanda. The second, known as political rape, is used to punish individuals, families, or communities who hold different political views. The third, often referred to as opportunistic rape, takes place when combatants run amok, assured of impunity in a lawless context. The fourth type, known as forced concubinage, involves the conscription or kidnapping of young girls to wash, cook, porter, and provide sex for soldiers and militiamen, as in the case of Boko Haram. Accurate information on the prevalence of sexual assault is difficult to obtain due to the fact that most victims decline to report their experience due to personal trauma, fear of reprisals, and social stigma associated with such experience. The difficulties are exacerbated in conflict settings due to general chaos and population displacement that often occurs in conflict situations as well as fear for safety and a breakdown or lack of a system to collect and report information.

It is clear from illustrations above that sexual atrocities have been a feature of many African conflict situations over the past two decades. The fact that the African woman continues to confront culturally legitimate and conflict-related violence in the twenty-first century speaks of moral decay on the continent. The social construction of violence sanctions it as the norm. This indirectly sanctions other forms of violence the African woman is exposed to. The normalization of violence is a tool for exerting power and dominating and humiliating the enemy. Where it is used as a tool of war, sexual violence is often referred to as the "collateral damage" of fighting. Perpetrators are motivated by anger, power, objectification of women and the need to retaliate. In many situations, it is employed systematically to intimidate, humiliate, or politically terrorize, in order to extract information, for purposes of ethnic cleansing, or to reward soldiers who have been away from their families, or to destroy thoughts of harboring opposing armed groups. It may also be used as a strategy of revenge for an armed assault carried out by opposing forces. It may be viewed by perpetrators as a way to spread terror among the targeted group—"a step in the process of group destruction" (Arieff 2010). In such cases, sexual assault precedes murder.

SOCIALIZATION OF VIOLENCE

While some have attributed the prevalence of sexual violence in Africa to the eroded status of women over years of conflict, weak authority, a weak justice system and breakdown in community protection mechanisms, this chapter locates all forms of violence in the social construction of values and norms that undermine the humanity of the other. Violence is a social category that can only be appreciated by interrogating the social construction process. Gender-based violence is a product of a larger social system which perpetuates violence and social inequalities such as gender inequality. Gender inequality generated by the gender system gives men power over women through social norms, distribution of resources, and the sanctioning of social interactions and patterns of behavior (Ridgeway and Correll 2004). Socially constructed ideologies about masculinity are implicated in men's perpetuation of violence. Emphasis on qualities such as strength, toughness, control, and sexual dominance that may be demonstrated through violence, indirectly sanction sexual assault (Jewkes et al. 2015). Thinkers such as Kimberlé Crenshaw have articulated how violence can be understood by utilizing intersectionality as a social framework. As an expert in the intersections between social factors such as race and gender in the legal system, Crenshaw is known for coining the term intersectionality to argue for the need to locate experiences in contextual realities that inform them. She argues:

> Recognizing that identity politics takes place at the site where categories intersect thus seems more fruitful than challenging the possibility of talking about categories at all. Through an awareness of intersectionality, we can better acknowledge and ground the differences among us and negotiate the means by which these differences will find expression in constructing group politics. (Crenshaw 1991, 1299)

To Crenshaw, any social reform must ensure that the unique needs of a given group are centered in any discourse about them.

Many cultures in Africa do not only have two gender subcultures, that is, the cultural distinction between two genders, they also endorse male dominance. Culture is a collection of ideas and habits by which members of society learn, share, and transmit values from one generation to another. It includes generally accepted behaviors (Geertz 1973; Linton 1945, 213). The construction and universalization of masculinities and femininities are often based on the common ideology that one gender is better than the other. The application of this ideology often leads to social exclusion, subordination, and marginalization of one gender. This social strategy is often employed consciously or unconsciously and is responsible for the social construction of social inequality and the apportionment of gender roles and social status (Uchechukwu 2017). Social rules governing human experience are intertwined with the basic institutions of society such as the family, economy, and religion, which in turn influence behavior. These institutions operate under clusters of values, norms, and culture that every society embraces over time. They engulf a given community's ideologies and assumptions about what is or ought to be right, appropriate, or inappropriate. Through these ideologies and social goals, society sanctions and rewards appropriate behavior for conformity and punishes deviations from acceptable behaviors. Through socialization, values that shape social behavior are instilled in individuals. Where observed, transition rites or initiations form an integral part of socialization as a way of dramatizing attributes expected of an individual. These culturally specified features of gender, for the properly socialized, are psychological reference points for personal gender identity.

In Africa, acceptable and entrenched cultural practices normalize gender inequality. Due to an embrace of patriarchal ideals and norms, practices such as polygamy, female genital cutting, and child marriages are common place and they often communicate the perception that a woman is not only lesser than a male counterpart, but her role is often limited to reproduction and child rearing responsibilities. In Mozambique, as in several African countries, girls as young as 15 years old are either forced into marriage or encouraged to marry young (Addaney 2018; Torchia 2018). African women experience customary law that marginalizes and denies them opportunities for self-realization. When a married woman is socialized to consider herself a servant to her husband, she is not only marginalized, her self-esteem is undermined. In African traditions, women are not socialized to negotiate sexual advancement from husbands or to have a say in matters of when and whether to use contraception or condoms; women's health is given less priority. A culture that refuses to recognize simple facts such as the non-use of contraceptives exposes women to health concerns such as STIs, HIV, and unwanted pregnancies is a culture that causes great harm to its female members. When gender ideologies are powerful tools for cementing male dominance, the entire social group is made vulnerable to exploitation, marginalization, powerlessness, cultural imperialism, and violence.

Although most societies embrace gender roles because gender role apportioning is often considered a positive way of affirming specific gender strengths and self-worth (Uchechukwu 2017), gender roles are negative when they undermine or discourage full social participation in social development. Since gender roles are often constructed to adhere to a set structural system, even when they seem innocent on the outside, they are often part of a social scheme, a social structure that is intentional and that is embedded within the patriarchal expression of dynamics of power. These roles are often based on the socialized expectations that men should generally work outside the home, do the heavy work, fight the wars, and dominate most if not all spatial ability jobs like Mathematics, Engineering, and Architecture and control the most powerful institutions. It is the expectation that women are to bear and nurse babies, care for the young, and do the family chores such as cooking (2017). Even when women work outside the home, they are expected to still work in the female occupations of child rearing and household care.

Values about gender roles are instilled in children as early as the day they are born. In some communities, the birth of a girl child is received differently from that of a boy. For instance, among the Kikuyu, when a girl is born, the father cuts four sugar canes and places the waste scraps on the left side of the house. If it is a boy, the father cuts five sugar canes as a symbol of his higher role in society. A child belongs to the entire community and is no longer the property of one person, and the sugar cane symbolizes the fact that these children should be treated as expected for their gender. From birth on, the parents and the community at large instill into children the gender expectations of society. In most cases, girls are brought up to embrace household duties such as house care, fetching water and firewood, and treating boys and men as superior entities. Boys, on the other hand, are taught to embrace masculine duties such as hunting, sitting with elderly men to learn leadership wisdom, and to protect their families. At puberty, an individual is considered ready for adulthood and consequent responsibilities. At this time, a sharp distinction between maleness and femaleness is made. While men enter the world of power, the girl is instructed in matters of womanhood such as sexual games, menstruation taboos, and the "secret" of childbirth. Socialization does not value a girl's education because a girl child is not expected to enter the world of power; her education is essentially devalued and considered irrelevant (Mbiti 1969).

As social groups are differentiated during the socialization process, privilege and power are often granted to one group while the other is underprivileged and made powerless. As Iris Young argues, injustice is often a consequence of social differentiation. Power is about privilege and oppression, a structural phenomenon that immobilizes and diminishes a social group. Often privilege, under-privilege, power, and powerlessness are expressed through exploitation, marginalization, powerlessness, cultural imperialism, and violence (1990, 2004). In other words, social differentiation can lead to the suffering of one group as the other is privileged. Gender disparity occurs when power and wealth are transferred from one gender to the other. Gender exploitation is about the transfer of the fruit of material labor to men including other energies such as nurturing and even sexual energies. Exploitation is the transfer of the results of the labor of one social group to benefit another. As Young explains, "Rules about what work is, who does what for whom, how work is compensated, and the social process by which the results of work are appropriated operate to enact relations of power and inequality" (1990, 58). These relations are produced and reproduced through a systematic process to maintain and augment power. Social marginals are those whom the system chooses not to use. Marginalization, as Young explains, is the most dangerous form of injustice since an entire social group is excluded from useful participation in social life. This group's opportunity to exercise their capacities is blocked. The result is material deprivation. When the female gender is rendered powerless, half the resource potential of a social group that is powerless is lost from use. When women produce agricultural products and men take them to market and receive credit for their labor, the woman is denied the credit she deserves. This legitimization of social differentiation often occurs as a cultural enterprise when traditional norms normalize sexual objectification of women. For instance, in the cultural practices of Unyango of the Digo of Tanzania, social differentiation occurs when girls are taught how to take care of their bodies and how to behave when married, especially how to relate to men. In Malawi, for instance, practices such as *Chinamwari* are meant to train teenage girls in techniques that will satisfy a man during a sexual encounter. Important to note, however, is the fact that gender roles have evolved in the twenty-first century as men and women have taken on new demands, expectations, and essentially new roles. For example, men are expected to share roles that were considered feminine such as child rearing and help in household chores (World Bank 2012).

To normalize gender-based violence is to normalize physical, verbal, and sexual assault and harassment of girls and women. In South Africa, for instance, Prinsloo (2006) explains how rape, assault, and sexual harassment are some of the frequently reported forms of gendered practices. Reports of girls being exposed to fondling and rape in school toilets, empty classrooms, and hallways are a common phenomenon. They are subjected to aggressive sexual advances on a daily basis. In Guinea, studies indicate that boys are very aggressive toward girls and they often use force, threat, and teasing to silence the girls. Ombati and Ombati (2012) observe that "sexual violence and harassment in school erect a discriminatory barrier for children especially girls who are seeking an education" (129). It is for this reason that child marriage is condoned, teenage pregnancy is also normalized. Existing data indicate that in countries such as Kenya, Nigeria, Mali, Cote d'Ivoire, Mozambique, and Sudan, which embrace female genital cutting, there are higher rates of teenage pregnancy leading to school dropouts (Kiragu and Zabin 1995; Ombati and Ombati 2012). The reality of child marriage is evident in data that show that one in nine girls from developing countries is married before the age of 15 and that 38 percent of the girls in Sub-Sahara are married off before age 18 (UNICEF 2014). Among the nomadic pastoral communities such as the Samburu, Maasai, Turkana, Pokot, Somali, Rendile Borana and Oromo of Kenya, marriage is common at or shortly after puberty, especially for girls. In some African communities, religious and traditional norms are used to dictate marriage age. Early marriage is considered protection, as parents use this to protect their young daughters from the dangers of sexual assault and pregnancy out of wedlock. According to the beading culture of the Samburu of Kenya, girls are encouraged to engage in sex with a relative in exchange for beaded necklaces. The beaded necklace, which serves as a declaration of engagement, grants a male family relative permission to have sexual intercourse with the girl in question. Because beading is an early promise of marriage to the family, girls may be beaded as early as 6 years old. Although this beading culture is commonly featured as a symbol of Kenyan cultural pride, the violence and abuse that is legitimized in the name of culture, undermine children's and women's pride, integrity, and rights to full social development and societal participation since these girls often have no choice in the matter. The legitimization of gender-based violence such as underage sexual encounters is essentially the legitimization of rape. Unwanted pregnancies in such young girls not only exposes them to reproductive health issues such as child mortality and fistulas, but these girls are exposed to sexually transmitted infections (STIs) and health complications that accompany these practices. The legitimization of gender-based experiences such as female genital cutting, and child marriage scare girls away from attending school. Female genital cutting, a cultural practice that is entrenched in several African communities, is considered a rite of passage which marks a girl's transition into adulthood. This practice, which is linked to proper upbringing, proper sexual behavior, values of virginity, and marital fidelity, is designed in most of these countries as a preparation for a girl to assume adult duties including marriage. The assumption is that female genital cutting makes the girls "clean and beautiful" by ridding them of external vestiges of "maleness" thus making the girls feel grown up, mature, and ready to engage in sexual relations and ultimately marriage.

Social construction is further legitimized by values. While human behavior is not only influenced by culture, values play a significant role in the social construction process. The influence of culture and religion on gender behavior is a dialectical relationship such that it can sometimes be difficult to discern which one of these causes the other. The recognition of how these social facts intersect to influence behavior is central to understanding gender disparity and gender inequality. As a socialization agent, religion is an institutionalized system of symbols, beliefs, and practices. As Peter Berger explains, religion is a world constructor and maintainer. It is the human enterprise by which the sacred cosmos is established (1990, 26). The effectiveness of religion lies in its role in the "ruling relations" as a legitimizing agent of social institutions and the power they possess (Smith 1999). As an agent of social interaction, religion not only influences moral norms and behavior, it legitimizes value patterns thus giving individual members of the society the criteria for accepted and normalized patterns of relationships (Parsons 1964, 81).

The centrality of religion in African cultures is reflected not only in the African religious notoriety as noted by John S. Mbiti (1969), it is also clear in women's experience, a fact that has led Oduyoye to declare African women as religion's chief clients (Oduyoye 1999). Africa is home to three major religions: Indigenous religions, Christianity, and Islam. Central to African religiosity is the holistic approach to life, which makes the expression of religious values in behavior a daily experience. The perceptions of these religions about gender disparity, role, and status are significant. While they have positive values and teachings regarding respect and the treatment of all human beings as children of God and the recognition that human worth transcends all relations, these religions do possess values that justify gender inequality. In some West African countries like Ghana, Togo, Benin, and Southwestern Nigeria, the practices of *Trokosi*, the traditional priestess training sessions, have been used to promote gender inequality and to undermine full social participation of women by keeping enslaved young virgin girls from enrolling or attending school. The word *Trokosi* which literally means "slaves to the gods," involves the sending of young innocent virgin girls to shrines as reparation and sanctity for misdeeds of their family members. Virgin girls, who spend their days collecting water, cooking, cleaning, farming, and caring for livestock, are denied access to education and are essentially banished from their families and exposed to sexual encounters with ritual masters. Some parents remove their daughters from school to enroll them in these traditional priestess training sessions (Tanye 2008).

When examining the values of Africa, it is important to recognize the influence of Judeo-Christian values on gender status, role, and violence specifically. The Jewish creation narrative, subscribed to by these two religions, participates in patriarchal values that describe the woman as having been created from Adam's one rib. This symbolism that is often cited in African churches and Mosques, promotes the perception of a woman as inferior to a man. According to this Genesis account of the Bible, gender inequality is justified by the claim that God created man "in his own image" and that "a man is the image and glory of God, but a woman is the glory of man" (Genesis 3:16). Because the man was not made from woman, but woman from man, she is rendered inferior to man. Teachings of St. Paul, a Christian saint who popularized Christianity and a staunch product of the Jewish culture, reiterates this gender ideology of male dominance in his instructions to the early church when he instructs women to shut up in church (1 Cor. 14:34–35). Paul also teaches about women's submission to their husbands in Ephesians 5:22–33 and Colossians, 4:18. These Christian teachings that reinforce gender disparity are echoed in churches across Africa and the teachings support the social construction and reconstruction of gender disparity and gender inequality.

In Islam, the belief that a woman was created for man is grounded in the *Hadith* and in some Qur'anic passages. Sura 4: 34 and Sura 2: 288 are generally cited in support of the contention that men have a degree of "advantage" over women. Sura 4: 34 translated by A. A. Maududi reads:

> Men are the managers of the affairs of women because Allah has made the one superior to the other and because men spend all of their wealth on women. Virtuous women are, therefore, obedient; they guard their rights carefully in their absence under the care and watch of Allah. As for those women whose defiance you have cause to fear, admonish them and keep them apart from your bed and beat them. Then, if they submit to you, do not look for excuses to punish them: note it well that there is Allah above you, who is Supreme and Great. (Hassan 1991, 110)

This notion describes men as having *qawama* over women because of the advantage that men supposedly have over them and because men spend their property in supporting women (An-Na'im 1996, 214). *Hadith* describes a virtuous woman as one who pleases and obeys her husband at all times. When women are portrayed as being different from men in the amount of *nafs:* (an animal life force), which includes lusts, emotions, and desires and *aqel* (reason, rationality), the ability to control their emotions and to behave in socially appropriate ways, their worth is rendered to be unequal to that of men (Boddy 1989, 53). Consequently, the imposition of strict Purdah—the Muslim practice of secluding girls and women from the public unless accompanied by a male guardian reinforces this ideology. Purdah has been associated with serious hindrance to girls' ability to go to school and to remain in attendance.

Gender-based practices such as female genital cutting and child marriage have found legitimacy in the three religions of Africa. Female genital cutting which is practiced by some Indigenous, Christian, and Muslim followers in Africa is erroneously assumed by some to be a religious injunction. For instance, although the practice is not mentioned in the Torah, the Bible, or the Qur'an, it is often associated with Jewish, Christian, Muslim, and Indigenous values. In Indigenous communities of Africa, where identity formation is central to puberty rituals that embrace female genital cutting, a child is socialized to accept the practice as necessary in defining the femininity of a girl child as male circumcision is perceived to design the masculinity of a boy child. The act of shedding blood during this ritual is considered a binding force that unites the initiates with ancestors for blessings and a healthy life. Re-integration of initiates into society signifies their physical and moral maturity and the approval of their new status by the clan and the ancestors (Wangila 2007; Nyangweso 2014). In the Middle Eastern cultures, where female genital cutting is referred to as *tathir* or *Tahara,* an Arabic word for purification, it is considered as *Khitan al Sunna or al-Sunna,* which means "compliant with the tradition of Muhammad" (Abu-Sahlieh 2001, 11, 143). It is also argued by some Muslims that Ali, the fourth Caliph successor of Prophet Muhammad, recommended it by declaring it a "meritorious act" (Abu-Sahlieh 2001). Based on this claim, advocates of female genital cutting believe that an honorable woman is expected to undergo genital cutting as a meritorious act. In modern society, religious agents continue to advocate against the education of girls, as in the case of Boko Haram in Nigeria and the Taliban in Afghanistan. The message that is communicated to society and to the girl child is that her important role in society is to be a wife and mother.

IMPLICATIONS OF VIOLENCE

Gender violence can lead to long-term physical, mental, and emotional health problems such as hemorrhage, infertility, complications during childbirth, the risk of sexually transmitted infections like HIV, and death being reported in most extreme cases. According to the World Health Organization, women exposed to intimate partners' violence are likely to suffer from mental health issues, sexual and reproductive issues, and serious injury that can lead to death. These women are twice as likely to experience depression, twice as likely to have alcohol use disorders, 16 percent more likely to have a low birth weight baby, one and a half times more likely to acquire sexually transmitted diseases like HIV, syphilis infection, chlamydia, or gonorrhea. Forty-two percent of these women have experienced injuries as a result and 38 percent of them have ended up dead (World Health Organization 2017). Intimate and culturally legitimate violence can be the most fatal and difficult to contain because more often than not, cases of violence go unreported.

The impact of sexual violence on survivors and the community is even more significant since it is coerced. Survivors often suffer short and long-term consequences that are physical, psychological, and social. In addition to physical injuries, potential health consequences include sexually transmitted infections (STIs) including HIV/AIDS, miscarriages, forced pregnancy, and traumatic fistula—debilitating tears in the tissue surrounding the vagina, bladder, and rectum. Further, access to treatment and follow-up medical care is a challenge, especially in conflict zones. Most survivors in Africa are further confronted by the reality of scarce and inadequate facilities, insufficient and lack of trained staff, a situation that often leads to insufficient care. Often, government clinics may not guarantee safety or confidentiality to survivors, a significant factor in the reduced likelihood of victims seeking care. Survivors of assault during conflict or war sometimes face family rejections due to the social stigma often associated with rape. It is devastating when survivors get shunned by their own families and the communities for an act of violence they have no control over. Around the world, sexual violence is routinely directed at females during a conflict situation as a conscious strategy. Rape is used as a weapon to terrorize and degrade a particular community and to achieve a specific political end. The rape of one person is often translated into an assault upon the entire community and the shame of the rape is intended to humiliate the family and all those associated with the survivor. Communities can be destroyed completely by this horrendous act.

Prosecution of perpetrators is rare, as many African countries lack the financial resources for investigation and the expertise to handle sexual assault cases, especially when they happen *en masse*. This is because sexual assault is often perceived as not a big deal. Furthermore, when government security forces, rebel or criminal organizations, militias, and other armed groups or non-state actors are accused of inflicting sexual violence upon the civilian population, it is treated as a 'natural' outcome of the conflict. Sexual violence is often employed by combatant groups as a tool of war that is designed to weaken and damage the entire community. Although the United Nations Security Council recognizes the widespread and systematic sexual violence as constituting a war crime; a crime against humanity, or an act of genocide, and even though international human rights watchdogs like Amnesty International, Human Rights Watch, the International Crisis Group and Physicians for Human Rights have documented systematic rape and sexual torture of women such as during Zimbabwe's political violence since 2000, countries and governments have not been held accountable so they can work at controlling this behavior. For instance, in 2003, Amnesty International warned about the "mounting reports of rape and sexual torture by the militia, continuing the pattern seen before presidential elections in March 2002." Tony Reeler, regional human rights defender with the Institute for Democracy in South Africa, described it as "a new pattern of sexual violence in Zimbabwe." In 2000 and early 2001, human rights watchdogs like Amnesty International, Danish Physicians for Human Rights, and others reported widespread torture of opposition supporters. Most, about 40 percent of them, were women who were beaten up, stripped naked, and humiliated, with some being raped (*the New Humanitarian* 2003; Sayagues 2003). In June of the same month, rape and sexual assault of women became more prevalent and brutal. It allegedly happened in front of family and neighbors, impacting the entire community physically and psychologically. As Reeler explains, "One individual's physical torture becomes a mass psychological torture" (Human Rights Watch 2003).

In spite of this, rape remains the least condemned war crime. For instance, the government of Zimbabwe reacted to the reports by dismissing both local and international human rights groups' reports that documented the use of rape as a political weapon. Belly Dimbi, an official in the Department of Information is reported as saying, "yes, we have seen the allegations, but I don't need to tell you that definitely, these are fabrications." The United Nations Special Rapporteur on Violence against

Women noted in 1996 that during the Rwanda civil wars, women were "individually raped, gang-raped, raped with objects such as sharpened sticks or gun barrels, and held in sexual slavery or sexually mutilated." It was estimated that rapes ranged from 250,000 to 500,000 individuals and pregnancies resulting from rape was approximated at 2000–5000 (Human Rights Watch 1996). In 2001, the International Criminal Tribunal for the former Yugoslavia which began to prosecute rapists declared rape as a war crime. This decision challenged the widespread acceptance that torture of women is an intrinsic part of the war. The Rwanda Tribunal was empowered to prosecute rape as a crime against humanity and a violation of the Geneva conventions. In 1949, the Geneva Convention strengthened Protocol II which extends protection to victims of rape, enforced prostitution, or indecent assault during the conflict. In South Africa, the Truth and Reconciliation Commission "didn't deal with rape as a gross human rights abuse." Instead, as Sheila Mentes, a member of South Africa's Commission on Gender Equality and a lecturer in political studies at Witwatersrand University observed, a great deal of time was devoted to the murder and torture of freedom fighters. Only one day was dedicated to grievances of abused women (IRIN Africa 2003). She argues that efforts are not being made to ensure the social transformation of attitudes that fuel this behavior as this is direly needed in order to protect young girls and women from this epidemic. Governments need to lead these efforts by ensuring that they are not complicit.

All forms of gender-based violence are recognized as a human rights issue, a public concern, and as a barrier to development because any form of violence has been identified as a violation of articles of the Universal Declaration of Human Rights (United Nations 1993). Article 3 clearly stipulates that everyone has the right to life, liberty, and security and article 5 states that "no one shall be subjected to torture or to cruel, inhuman or degrading treatment or punishment." Gender-based violence is specifically condemned in the Convention on the Elimination of Discrimination against Women (CEDAW) which was adopted by the United Nation's General Assembly. Domestic violence against immigrant women is a violation of human rights as per CEDAW General Recommendations No. 19. All countries who are members of the UN are obligated to ensure the protection and support of all women including immigrant women. Hence, practices in the gender-based violence category which include domestic or intimate partners' violence, sexual assault, child marriage, honor killings, and female genital cutting are declared as violations of human rights.

Although early marriage as a practice affects all children, girls are most affected. As stated by UNICEF (2014), most child brides end up in poverty, are less educated, and experience serious health issues, as do their children. Girls younger than 15 years are 5 times more likely to lose their lives during childbirth. According to UNICEF, girls age 15–19 are twice as likely to die during pregnancy or childbirth compared to those over age 20. When a woman is under 18, her child is 60 percent more likely to die in its first year of life than a baby born to a mother over 18 years of age. Countries with the highest child marriage rates have the lowest rates of educated women. While child marriage has been an acceptable practice in many countries, modern societies have tried to protect children by insisting they have opportunities to pursue an education in order to live a better life. It is for this reason that the United Nations, the organization most countries support regarding efforts to promote social justice and welfare, has embraced the *Universal Declaration of Human Rights*, which stipulates basic human rights of all based on "equal and inalienable rights of all members of the human family" (Donnelly 2007). The right to education, shelter, and food are basic to every human being. To deny a child bride an education is to deny her a fundamental right. A country that denies women education not only denies these women a healthy and better livelihood, it also denies the country human ingenuity and human creativity that could go into its development. It is no wonder that countries with the most child marriages happen to be the poorest.

Ultimately, it should be recognized that the social construction of gender inequality robs the society of the potential necessary for general development. It ought to be remembered that the social construct that is aimed at suppressing one gender robs society of useful imprints that some talented men and women would offer society (Uchechukwu 2017, 90). While it can be argued that sex stereotyping that is based on nature or biological structure can be positive where it acknowledges and appreciates specific gender abilities, often gender disparity yields are negative and unjust (82). Undermining or exposing one gender to violence because they are female is an injustice. When religion sanctions behavior by invoking sacred force, it grants such behavior authoritative power that in turn influences and affirms gender inequality. By sanctioning patriarchal inclinations that undermine girls' education, a woman's potential is marginalized and rendered powerless. This persistence of this situation in modern society ought to be taken up for serious reflection.

CONCLUSION

In this chapter, I have examined the challenge of violence in regular and conflict situations in Africa. I have described how violence has been used in conflict situations especially as a tool of gender dominance. I argue that violence has been used as a tool of domination in social experiences. While it is often used as a tool of exerting power on the enemy, as a tool of war in Africa, violence has undermined basic rights of women in Africa. The chapter argues that violence is embedded in the cultural and religious norms that legitimize practices such as female genital cutting, child marriage, rape, and sexual assault. As illustrated from the various case studies cited, culturally legitimate gender-based violence in war has serious consequences. The shame and stigma of being rejected especially by family because one has been raped are the cruelest and most brutal experiences the African woman continues to face in the twenty-first century. Sexual assault in African conflict zones has been acknowledged to be at epidemic levels, and this is a pointer to how serious this problem is.

This chapter recognizes the numerous obstacles that the African faces that should be confronted. For instance, it is important that entire communities begin conversations about violence—all forms of violence and consequences associated with it. It is high time that Africans reflected upon cultural and religious values they hold. There is a need to examine the values that undermine the female child as well. African governments must take their responsibility of protecting women seriously. In addition to condemning these practices, the government's role is to ensure the criminalization of such practices. For instance, the government can establish policies that protect against gender violence in addition to running empowerment projects toward the transformation of attitudes toward violent behavior. For effectiveness, empowerment programs must include education on basic rights, sexual reproductive health, and self-realization. It is good for Africa as a continent to protect women from all forms of violence as they constitute 50 percent of the continent's population. Their health and skill sets are bound to enrich the continent and add to progress. Social transformation in Africa in the twenty-first century must prioritize gender equality and health.

REFERENCES

Abu-Sahlieh, Sami Awad Aldeeb. 2001. *Male and Female Circumcision: Among Jews, Christians and Muslims: Religious, Medical, Social and Legal Debate.* Warren Center, PA: Shangri-La Publications.

Addaney, Michael. 2018. Education can Save African Girls from Early Marriage. *The Herald*, February 19. https://www.herald.co.zw/education-can-save-african-girls-from-early-marriages/.

Agence France-Press (AFP). 2015. Boko Haram 'Slaughter Wives' in Northeast Nigeria, Say, Witness. *NDTV.* https://www.ndtv.com/world-news/boko-haram-slaughter-wives-in-northeast-nigeria-witnesses-748100.

An-Na'im, Abdullahi Ahmed. 1996. Human Rights in the Muslim World. In *International Human Rights in Context: Law, Politics, Morals*, ed. Henry J. Steiner and Philip Alston, 210–220. Oxford: Clarendon Press.

Arieff, Alexis. 2010. *Sexual Violence in African Conflict.* Congressional Research Services. https://fas.org/sgp/crs/row/R40956.pdf.

BBC News. 2019. Zimbabwe Women Urged to Report Rape by Soldiers. *BBC News Africa*, January 29. https://www.bbc.com/news/world-africa-47042101.

Berger, Peter. 1990. *The Sacred Canopy: Elements of a Sociological Theory of Religion.* New York: Anchor Books.

Boddy, Janice. 1989. *Wombs and Alien Spirits: Women, Men and the Zar Cult in Northern Sudan.* Madison: The University of Wisconsin Press.

Bond, Anthony. 2016. Hundreds of British Mums 'Breast-Ironing' Their Daughters Using Red-Hot Rocks, Hammers and Spatulas. *Mirror*, April 10. https://www.mirror.co.uk/news/uk-news/hundreds-british-mums-breast-ironing-7726899.

Brown, Carly. 2012. Rape as a Weapon of War in the Democratic Republic of the Congo. *Torture* 22 (1): 24–37. https://irct.org/assets/uploads/Rape-as-weapon-war-1-2012.pdf.

Crenshaw, Kimberle. 1991. Mapping the Margins: Intersectionality, Identity Politics, and Violence Against Women of Color. *Stanford Law Review* 43 (6, July): 1241–1299.

Donnelly, Jack. 2007. The Relative Universality of Human Rights. *Human Rights Quarterly* 29 (2, May): 281–306.

Geertz, Clifford. 1973. *The Interpretation of Cultures.* New York: Basic Books.

Goba, Cynthia. 2019. Scores of Women Who Were Raped During Crackdown Give Horrifying Experiences at the Hands of Evil Soldiers. *My Zimbabwe News*, January 25. https://www.myzimbabwe.co.zw/news/39536-scores-of-women-who-were-raped-during-crackdown-give-horrifying-experiences-at-the-hands-of-evil-soldiers.html.

Hassan, Riffat. 1991. An Islamic Perspective. In *Women, Religion, and Sexuality: Studies on the Impact of Religious Teachings on Women*, ed. Jeanne Betcher, 93–128. Philadelphia: Trinity Press International.

Human Rights Watch. 1996. https://hrw.org/reports/1996/Rwanda.
———. 2003. Focus on Rape as a Political Weapon. *IRIN.* https://www.irin-news.org/feature/2003/04/08/focus-rape-political-weapon.
IRIN Africa. 2003. Zimbabwe: Focus on Rape as a Political Weapon. *Peace Women: Women's International League for Peace and Freedom.* https://www.peace-women.org/content/zimbabwe-focus-rape-political-weapon.
Jewkes, R., M. Flood, and J. Lang. 2015. From Work with Men and Boys to Changes of Social Norms and Reduction of Inequalities in Gender Relations: A Conceptual Shift in Prevention of Violence against Women and Girls. *The Lancet* 385 (April): 1580–1589.
Kiragu, Karungari, and Laurie S. Zabin. 1995. Contraceptive Use Among High School Students in Kenya. *International Perspectives on Sexual and Reproductive Health* 21 (3): 108–113.
Linton, Ralph. 1945. *The Cultural Background of Personality.* New York: D. Appleton-Century Company Incorporated.
Mark, Monica. 2015. Thousands Flee as Boko Haram Sizes Military Base on Nigeria Border. *The Guardian,* January 6. https://www.theguardian.com/world/2015/jan/05/boko-haram-key-military-base-nigeria-chad-border.
Mbiti, John S. 1969. *African Religions and Philosophy.* London: Heinemann.
McCoy, Terrence. 2015. The Brutal Reason Boko Haram Just Took 500 'Young Women and Children'. *The Washington Post: Morning Mix.* https://www.washingtonpost.com/news/morning-mix/wp/2015/03/25/the-brutal-reason-boko-haram-just-took-500-young-women-and-children/?utm_term=.2c7c319e16f2.
New Humanitarian. 2003. Focus on Rape as a Political Weapon. https://www.thenewhumanitarian.org/feature/2003/04/08/focus-rape-political-weapon.
Nossiter, Adama. 2009. Scores Die as Fighters Battle Nigerian Police. *The New York Times,* July 27. https://www.nytimes.com/2009/07/28/world/africa/28nigeria.html?_r=0.
Nwaubani, Adaobi Tricia. 2018. The Women Rescued from Boko Haram Who are Returning to Their Captors. *Dispatch: The New Yorker,* December 20. https://www.newyorker.com/news/dispatch/the-women-rescued-from-boko-haram-who-are-returning-to-their-captors.
Nyakanyanga, Sally. 2019. Alleged Army Rapes Amidst Zimbabwe Fuel Hike Protests Go Uninvestigated. 50.50, *Gender Sexuality and Social Justice.* https://www.opendemocracy.net/5050/sally-nyakanyanga/alleged-army-rapes-women-protesting-zimbabwe-fuel-hikes.
Nyangweso, Mary. 2014. *Female Genital Cutting in Industrialized Countries: Mutilation or Cultural Tradition?* ABC Clio Praeger.
Oduyoye, Mercy Amba. 1999. *Daughters of Anowa: African Women and Patriarchy.* Maryknoll, NY: Orbis Books.

Ombati, Victor, and Mokua Ombati. 2012. Gender Inequality in Education in Sub-Saharan Africa. *Journal of Women Entrepreneurship and Education* (3–4): 114–136.

Pare, Gildas, and Matthieu Bidan. 2015. The Victims of Cameroon's Horrific Breast-Ironing' Tradition. *VICE France*, August 19. https://www.vice.com/en_us/article/4wbqdj/cameroon-traditionflattening-chests-876.

Parsons, Talcott. 1964. *The Social System*. Glencoe: Free Press.

Prinsloo, S. 2006. Sexual Harassment and Violence in South African Schools. *The South African Journal of Education* 26 (2): 305–318.

Ridgeway, C.L., and Shelly J. Correll. 2004. Unpacking the Gender System: A Theoretical Perspective on Gender Beliefs and Social Relations. *Gender & Society* 18 (4, August): 510–531. https://journals.sagepub.com/doi/10.1177/0891243204265269.

Sayagues, Mercedes. 2003/2019. Rights: Breaking the Silence about Gender Based Abuses in Zimbabwe. Inter Press Service News Agency, www.ipsnews.net/2003/04/rights-breaking-the-silence-about-gender-based-abuses-in-zimbabwe.

Smith, Dorothy. 1999. *Writing the Social Critique: Theory and Investigations*. Toronto: University of Toronto Press.

Tanye, M. 2008. Access and Barriers to Education for Ghanaian Women and Girls. *Interchange* 39 (2): 167–184.

Torchia, Christopher. 2018. In Mozambique, Conservationists Try to Curb Child Marriage. https://apnews.com/f82df4960e314213b4c35cef3b3f6df8.

Uchechukwu, Monica Ejim. 2017. Religion and Gender Roles in Africa: A Case Study of Agricultural Patterns in Nike Primal Community. *UJA Special Edition*. https://www.ajol.info/index.php/ujah/article/view/158930.

UNICEF. 2014. *Ending Child Marriage: Progress and Prospects*. https://www.unicef.org/media/files/Child_Marriage_Report_7_17_LR..pdf.

United Nations. 1993. *Declaration on the Elimination of Violence Against Women*. http://www.un.org/documents/ga/res/48/a48r104.htm.

Wangila, Mary Nyangweso. 2007. *Female Circumcision: The Interplay Religion, Culture, and Gender in Kenya*. Maryknoll, NY: Orbis.

World Bank. 2012. *The Decline of the Breadwinner: Men in the 21st Century*. World Development Report. http://siteresources.worldbank.org/INTWDR2012/Resources/7778105-1299699968583/7786210-1316090663409/Spread-2.pdf.

World Health Organization. 2017. *Violence Against Women*. November 29. https://www.who.int/news-room/fact-sheets/detail/violence-against-women.

Young, Iris Marion. 1990. *Justice and the Politics of Difference*. Princeton: Princeton University Press.

———. 2004. Five Faces of Oppression. In *Oppression, Privilege, and Resistance: Theoretical Perspectives on Racism, Sexism, and Heterosexism*, ed. Lisa Heldke and Peg O'Connor, 37–63. Boston: McGraw Hill.

CHAPTER 10

Pastoral Care in the Trauma of Gender Violence

Mazvita Machinga

I am tired, I do not know what to do, I am just tired of suffering, all I want to do is die. I have come here to ask for help. I do not know what help I need. I have sought help for the past four years and nothing is changing, the situation is worse. My husband acts like he is now possessed with evil spirits.

These are the words of Makasa,[1] a client from Zimbabwe, who had just been referred by her medical doctor for psychotherapy. When she reported for counseling, Makasa was sobbing, suicidal and did not know what to do with her life. She was overwhelmed and seemed to have trouble coping. She feared for her life, health and her children. This client was a victim of gender-based violence. Her husband was abusive, not allowing her to go to work, or even to church. He was not providing enough for the family and yet shouts day in and day out to Makasa, blaming her of being lazy. In another case of ill-treatment, a 30-year-old man lamented:

---

[1] Names have been changed for anonymity.

M. Machinga (✉)
Africa University, Mutare, Zimbabwe

© The Author(s) 2019
S. Willhauck (ed.), *Female Child Soldiering, Gender Violence, and Feminist Theologies*, https://doi.org/10.1007/978-3-030-21982-6_10

I have pain, I am in agony, I am failing to move on with life. I am so much depressed. I have tried my all as a man, but I think I am now convinced that my wife does no longer want to stay in this marriage. I have spent my time apologizing for nothing; I do not feel like a man anymore. I am very unhappy. I am destroyed.

These are the words of Pasi, a man who had come for psychotherapy. He was married for seven years. Pasi was a Christian, a professional person who was active in his church. When he came for counseling, Pasi felt helpless, out of control and just wanted a way out of this marriage. He said that even though there was no physical assault, he claimed that for the past four years he *"was in hell"* and was being abused. He had feelings of emptiness and despair. Upon further questioning, he confided that the emotional turmoil he was going through was deep and painful because his wife had been going out with her high school sweetheart and no longer was interested in him. She had been writing notes with offensive and rude messages to Pasi. Pasi's case is an indication that gender violence can be psychological as well as physical and affects both males and females. Pasi's wife was a domineering force within the relationship. She would just shout at Pasi without even thinking of the impact of her utterances. She made sure that resources which sustained Pasi were removed. For instance, she blocked people from him portraying that it was for his own good. The violence was sometimes subtle but Pasi ended up feeling he was losing control over his life. He had withdrawn and was thinking of killing himself. He was no longer concentrating at work and church. Listening to Pasi, I realized his situation was not just a bad marriage, it was abusive and violent. It was not just a matter of arguments or conflicts that are a normal part of marriage or any committed relationship, but abuse is not normal. This was not only a difficult marital relationship, it was also a violent relationship with one partner systematically seeking to control the other and every aspect of their partner's life. Pasi's wife's behavior demonstrated a total disregard for the well-being of her husband. Her aim was to control and diminish the self-worth of Pasi in order to establish dominance. In gender violence, we observe powerful dominance which leaves the other partner hopeless and helpless. He reports that his wife's actions were disrespectful, disregarding his integrity, and her conduct was tearing him apart psychologically, relationally and spiritually. In this relationship, Pasi asserted that he was objectified and manipulated instead of being related to as a valued husband.

Nevertheless, even though a man like Pasi suffers from gender violence, studies have shown that the vast majority affected by gender violence are women and girls. The dominance that was in Pasi's marriage is a common thing for many women and girls to suffer every day. According to UNAIDS (United Nations Program on HIV/AIDS), at least one in every three women globally has been beaten, coerced into sex or abused in some other way. And according to the United Nations Population Fund (UNFPA 2015), one woman in four has been abused during her pregnancy. Whether it is male or female, most often people are ill-treated by someone they know, or with whom they have interacted. In another gender violence case, Neti was hospitalized after a diagnosis of generalized anxiety disorder and chronic stress. When I visited her in hospital, she appeared confused and had a noticeable sense of hopelessness and desperation as indicated in her utterance:

> I cannot continue to go through this humiliation. I am a learned person, a professional and deserve to be treated better than what my boss is doing. Why is he doing this to me, why does he hate me? I work overtime and my boss does not even acknowledge my hard work. Every day, I must keep my door closed and sometimes even locked because he is always shouting at me for things I do not even know. It is better I leave this job. I am tired, I am drained.

These are the words of an employee who was going through difficult times at work. She reported to the hospital with palpitations, difficulty in breathing, stomach tightness and inability to sleep well, suffering acute stress over the way her boss was treating her. The three cases above are examples of gender-based violence characterized by control and seeking dominance. Gender-based violence can happen to anyone anywhere, in homes, at workplaces and within religious institutions. It destroys self-esteem, sense of worth and hope as indicated in the cases above.

A big part of my work has been with individuals who have suffered or are currently suffering some form of abuse at the hands of others. Since the year 2000, I have been offering pastoral care to survivors of violence from domestic abuse to political terror. As a pastoral counselor and a psychologist, I have worked with abused and abandoned children and youth; and women survivors of violence, some of whom were once incarcerated and are now on parole. The women were once incarcerated since some ended up hurting other people while they were defending themselves from their abusers. From my experiences, I learned that survivors of violence are hurt at various levels: psychologically, emotionally, physically, relationally and spiritually. Violence attacks their beliefs, character and leaves many scars and wounds in such a way that they will never be the same. Each time I sit with survivors, I see myself being invited into their pain, injury and loss. I see myself sometimes standing on messy ground, empathetic and vulnerable, journeying with the struggling survivors. I realize the importance of pastoral care with traumatized people as these individuals need a safe and secure environment to recover. As asserted by Judith Herman, for these people to recover they need help to "recognize a gradual shift from unpredictable danger to reliable safety, from dissociated trauma to acknowledged memory, and from stigmatized isolation to restored social connection" (1997, 155). Effective care integrates various aspects of human realities attending to the spirit and the mental and physical aspects. As a pastoral counselor, I am guided by words of encouragement and strength from the book of Psalms. I have seen that the songs and poems can help survivors find voice for their struggles. Furthermore, use of the Psalms is fitting in that they capture the pain of those overwhelmingly hurt and who have been left struggling to find meaning and purpose. Through narrating their experiences survivors have taught me a lot about recovery. Perhaps the most important lesson, as asserted by Jeff Means, is that the survivors seek help motivated by the drive to connect with another human being who cares and is willing to listen non-judgmentally (2000, 97). This is a very important message: survivors of gender violence do not need isolation; instead, they need reconnection and an opportunity to create and live into a new story/future. I have also known that apart from pastoral care for survivors, I am called also to advocate against all forms of violence in our communities, culture and churches.

As I meet these people who have endured gender violence, I often wonder why human beings treat each other so inhumanely. I realize that, even though gender violence is common, it is a hidden issue. While non-governmental and government agencies have programs in place for reducing gender violence, the Church is not doing much (despite its ethical teachings on love and care). Often there is silence about it in the Church, and yet gender-based violence is something that needs to be discussed openly. Scores of studies and literature have been published but very little comes from the Church. It is high time the Church fully participates in programs to eliminate gender-based violence. It is my hope that perspectives on pastoral care gleaned from this work will be useful to those who reach out to traumatized individuals. The aim of this chapter is to examine the way pastoral care can be extended to the survivors of gender-based violence (GBV).

In many countries, including Zimbabwe, thousands of women and men are being assaulted by intimate partners, ex-partners, bosses at work, family and community members. The prevalence is huge for women. For some, this is an ongoing pattern of coercive control which is usually maintained through physical, psychological and sexual harassment. The sad fact is that cases of reported gender violence are increasing in Zimbabwe and an increase has also been documented in many countries throughout the world. The Zimbabwean Minister of Gender and Women's Affairs, Olivia Muchena, in a UNFPA report (2011) highlighted that cases of violence had alarmingly increased from 1200 reported in 2010 to 2500 recorded from January to April 2012 (see also Muchuchuti 2015). According to *The Zimbabwean* (2012), a local newspaper, domestic violence had been increasing steadily since 2008, which had about 1940 cases reported. In 2011, a total of 10,351 cases were reported while in the first quarter of 2012, there were 3141 cases reported. *The Sunday News*, another local news source, reported in 2017 that at least 22 women are raped daily in Zimbabwe, translating to almost one woman every hour. However, GBV is a global phenomenon and is intertwined with various crimes such as sex work, sex trafficking and drug trafficking. What I am seeing in my therapy rooms are variations of survivors' responses to violence. The various responses mean that there is not one way of helping survivors, there is no one size fits all treatment. Gender-based violence confronts individuals with multi-dimensional havoc in their lives and leaves no corner of one's life unaffected. Even though some people remain silent and never seek help, others seek medical help while some often depend on their spirituality or turn to their spiritual advisors for help. In any case, victims of violence need care and treatment. The message in this chapter is the importance of a pastoral care approach that promotes recovery to guide and motivate church leaders. Pastors and churches will need to better understand what gender violence is, what its consequences are and what can be done to help the recovery of individuals and communities. Before delving into the nature of pastoral care that may assist survivors, it is important to further unpack the issues that lead to gender violence.

UNDERSTANDING GENDER VIOLENCE

The three cases above clearly show what gender violence can look like, though it is a phenomenon that remains vague. Scholars and practitioners have come up with several definitions of gender violence. For instance, according to the 2015 Inter-Agency Sanding Committee Guidelines for Integrating Gender-Based Violence Interventions in Humanitarian Action, gender-based violence is defined as "any harmful act that is perpetrated against a person's will and that is based on socially ascribed (i.e. gender) differences between males and females." It is a result of gender inequality and abuse of power.

As in Pasi, Makasa and Neti's situations, their rights were being violated, harm was perpetrated and pain was inflicted upon them. Unfortunately, gender violence is viewed in a narrow sense of sexual violence or physical abuse by many people. But these cases demonstrate that gender violence comes in different forms. An important factor when dealing with gender-based violence is recognizing these different forms and consequences and acting accordingly.

Gender violence includes but is not limited to sexual violence (rape, sexual assault, sexual harassment and exploitation); physical violence (beating and slapping); emotional violence (psychological abuse); economic violence (denial of resources, services and opportunities) and harmful traditional practices (forced marriages, female genital mutilation); trafficking and forced prostitution. As in the cases of Pasi and Makasa, often victims are denied resources and opportunities. A shared feature in the three cases was emotional and psychological pain and trauma that each was experiencing. Another significant factor to note is that gender violence is not only based on biological differences, being male or female, it is also about how people treat others based on socially constructed differences between roles and responsibilities throughout their life cycles. Gender violence has to do with differences in roles, behaviors, power issues, resource distribution, social constraints and opportunities. So, the question remains why it is important to address gender violence and what effective pastoral care will look like in such cases.

WHY IS IT IMPORTANT FOR THE CHURCH TO ADDRESS GENDER VIOLENCE?

Gender violence can happen among people of all educational, socioeconomic, religious and racial profiles. Its consequences may include but are not limited to short, immediate and long-term impacts on physical and psychological well-being of survivors as indicated in the cases above.

Gender violence destroys human dignity. The Church may promote violence by its failure to address it, as sometimes perpetrators hide behind the protection of the Church. An active church-goer (or clergyperson) looks good to the community and so the violence behind closed doors may go unnoticed longer. I have seen this in my practice where some church members present themselves as good, upright people, but while at home they live a different life altogether. The Church needs to respond because victims of gender violence not only need physical or psychological interventions because the soul and spirit are also affected. The "soul" indicates the essence of life connected to God. For pastoral caregivers, the soul requires care rather than treatment or fixing (Means 2000, 2). Pastoral care will not change what has happened, instead, God's empowering presence is invited to cushion the survivors from more harm and offer comfort. One noted author stated that "God's empowering presence in suffering and recovery is about endurance and survival" (Keshgegian 2000, 172). This means that survivors need strength to reframe their feelings, pain and emotions. They need strength from God who is the fortress of strength and survival (Prov. 18: 10). Their spirit and soul can be transformed by God into a renewed whole. They need renewal of the spirit within so that they continue recreating a new self. This is important since God wants what is best for the souls and spirits of God's people (Jer. 29:11). The Church's involvement is important from human rights perspective and from health and faith perspectives as well. From a rights standpoint, gender-based violence is a serious violation of an individual's human rights. For instance, according to the United Nations Universal Declaration of Human Rights:

- Article 1: "All human beings are born free and equal in dignity and rights…"
- Article 3: "Everyone has the right to life, liberty and security of person."
- Article 5: "No one shall be subjected to torture or to cruel, inhuman or degrading treatment or punishment."

Christian theology asserts the dignity of each person and love of neighbor so that the Church is or ought to be a proponent of human rights. An action related to this stance might be to invite human rights experts to address churches and the community at large. In addition, trauma impacts the health of survivors. It can lead to changes in brain structure and function. These changes can embed long-term vulnerabilities to health problems.

Pastoral caregivers are often called upon to minister to people who suffer these health issues, and getting to their root cause is key. From a faith perspective, both men and women have been created in God's image. The two bear God's image, thus, simply put, there is a need to respect each other instead of hurting each other. In addition, God loves and cares for those who seek after him (Proverbs 8:17). Jesus sought to overcome violence and spoke to those who resorted to violence by modeling love. Hebrews 13:1–3 commands believers to love each other as brothers and sisters. Thus, it is important for churches to carry forward Jesus's message of love and non-aggression by addressing gender violence. One way of doing this is through pastoral care that acknowledges and calls out gender violence and offers help for those who have experienced it.

What Is Pastoral Care?

Various scholars have come up with different definitions of pastoral care. Lartey (1997) describes pastoral care as care of people in their existential situations, as *cura animarum* (cure/care of souls). Pastoral care incudes a wide-range of actions by religious communities for people in need. Another definition views pastoral care as "helping acts, done by representative persons, directed toward the healing, sustaining, guiding, reconciling and nurturing of persons whose troubles and concerns arise in the context of daily interactions and ultimate means and concerns" (Clebsch and Jaekle 1994, 4). From Clebsch and Jaekle's definition, pastoral care will not be effective and helpful if it does not fulfill at least one of these functions, namely healing, sustaining, guiding, reconciling and nurturing. Looking at Pasi, Makasa and Neti, they each needed one of these functions. For instance, Makasa needed healing from the effects of her ill-treatment. Pasi needed affirmation of his value as a child of God and assurance of God's guidance. He needed to make important decisions regarding his marriage. He was confused, and he did not know what to do. Neti needed healing and ways to reconcile with herself and others. In situations like these, a caring and compassionate person is needed to journey with individuals in their distress. Jesus Christ models for us the importance of being available to people in distress and we offer company wherever possible. In pastoral care, Christ can be present through us.

Pastoral care is also viewed as a form of a broader spiritual care. According to Craig S. Cashwell and J. Scott Young, scholars in counseling and psychology, the Latin word for spirit, *spiritus*, means breadth, courage, vigor and life. From the Greek noun *pneuma*, spiritual means "wind, breadth, life and spirit" (2005, 12). When persons face a crisis, they often find help through spiritual resources—their faith and spiritual caregivers. Pastoral care is more than meeting the basic physical, social or emotional needs of a survivor, it is life-giving to those whose hope, courage and strength has been shattered by the traumatic events.

PASTORAL CARE IN THE TRAUMA OF GENDER VIOLENCE

Pastoral care with traumatized people is about honoring the sanctity of life and preserving life through acts of care, love, compassion and empathy. It is integrating various forms of care to meet the holistic needs of the survivors of violence. Caregivers who are informed about the nature and proclivity of gender violence will be better able to address the circumstances of the people who come to them for help. It may mean that we face some hard truths about violence in our communities. Such pastoral care consists of existential and empathic understanding of the survivor's prevailing predicament. It offers acceptance, freedom from shame and empowerment to seek change.

Resources and practices from a community's traditions and religions can be helpful. From the Shona, Ndebele or Zulu tradition, pastoral care would be tapping into a survivor's spiritual and communal resources—the *ubuntu* spirit of care. *Ubuntu* is a southern African philosophy which is essentially about togetherness and caring for each other. This *ubuntu* is an indigenous African concept that promotes a sense of belonging and connection to others in the community. Included in this concept are values that advocate care, compassion, respect, beneficence and fairness. *Ubuntu* spirit views a person from a socio-cultural perspective and considers the importance of collectiveness, being part of a bigger whole (Motsi and Masango 2012). Therefore, doing pastoral care in my context entails working with individuals and having a sense of "togetherness care." The togetherness in times of crisis or trouble has always been part and parcel of the Shona people and is a tool to improved quality of life and coping with difficulties. Through a sense of togetherness there is acknowledgment of a shared responsibility for access to care. In other words, African care is done in the context of community, being guided by the sentiments that to be human is to respect human relations and to recognize the humanity of others. The common principle that undergirds *ubuntu* that is key is the principle of "I am, because we are; and since we are, therefore, I am"

(Ramose 2002, 43). This is expressed in our Zulu language as *umuntu ngumuntu ngabantu* (a person is a person through others). *Ubuntu* speaks about our interconnectedness as people of God. This concept has no room for individualism or living in separation from one another. Survivors will always be surrounded by others. As Ramose points out:

> Ubuntu [sic] understood as be-ing human (humanness); a humane, respect-ful and polite attitude towards others constitutes the core meaning of this aphorism. Ubuntu then not only describes a condition of be-ing, but it is also the recognition of becoming. (2002, 43)

Ramose's assertion affirms the point that we are connected so as to be there for each other. Pastoral care in the trauma of gender violence means being connected to others, utilizing each other, communal resources and shared rituals to bring resolution and comfort. It also means ensuring a sense of belonging, thus strengthening the individual's capacity to cope and attain wholeness. *Ubuntu* is all about caring for those around us. This view is shared by Magezi, when he asserts that "the life of the individual is abundantly lived when it is shared and hidden in the life of his or her community" (2016, 135). The three survivors in the cases above could not manage without the involvement of the other—*ubuntu*.

In the cases of Neti, Pasi and Makasa, rituals and rites are significant components of their treatment processes. As Africans, they use visuals and performing arts to achieve physical and spiritual health, balance and well-being. They can use prayers, music and dance among other arts, to express their feelings. Through the performances, a sense of identity, belonging and sacredness is reclaimed. For example, survivors may use healing scarves or shawls that are made by others for grounding purposes. This is impor-tant in reducing stress hormones while increasing the feel-good hormones such as serotonin. Such will enable one to feel better, stay hopeful and be able to handle crises. They are reminded of their relationship to each other and how that delights God and the inhabitants of the spirit world—the ancestral spirits. Through the rituals survivors attend to that which extends beyond the physical and into the social and spiritual aspects of reality. Rituals have the power to help trauma survivors to process and disengage from the negatives to intentionally focus on the creation of positive emo-tional states. As I claimed in a previous article, performing ritual ceremo-nies brings comfort and ensures a sense of belonging, thus strengthening the individuals and the communities (Machinga 2011).

Pastoral care in the trauma of gender violence is care that is practiced contextually and is need based. It is informed by the affected survivor's prevailing emotional, physical, social, economic or spiritual needs. In the trauma of gender violence, effective pastoral care should assist individuals to move through pain, stalemate and despair toward functional wholeness. It is a pastoral care that honors human worth, enables healing, offers guidance, promotes sustenance and encourages reconciliation. In order to achieve these, I have developed a process of pastoral care for working with victims and survivors of gender violence for different situations, including war and community conflict. I call this process trauma informed pastoral care (TIPC). In my view, this method would be helpful to church leaders and caregivers who find people coming to them for sanctuary from violence, or who come seeking help and support to reintegrate into their communities after experiencing or being involved in violence.

Trauma Informed Pastoral Care (TIPC)

TIPC grew out of listening to the stories and messages that survivors have brought to me about their experiences with violence. It is care that acknowledges the widespread experiences that cause trauma, including gender violence today. TIPC is a non-pharmacological trauma-based intervention that helps individuals understand the impact of trauma on their beliefs, feelings and behavior and capitalizes on an individual's God-given and communal capabilities to recover and move on. It is an integrative approach that seeks to ensure that a survivor's physical, emotional, spiritual and social needs are met. This is a transpersonal approach that integrates African traditional healing concepts, Christian pastoral care practices and social sciences. As asserted by Sundberg and Keutzer, transpersonal literally means across or beyond the individual person or psyche. It refers to an expansion or extension of consciousness beyond the usual ego boundaries and beyond the limitations of time and/or space and is related to "ultimate human capabilities and potentialities" (1994, 547).

To apply transpersonal psychology here means that when addressing trauma, healing is not only confined to rational thinking and sensory experiences but goes beyond individual psyche encompassing wider and deeper aspects of human life. The TIPC approach acknowledges both the personal and the transpersonal realities of human beings and allows survivors to access healing from an expanded viewpoint. Through TIPC, we listen to survivors and offer them opportunities to share their stories and memories. The care goes beyond describing, remembering or retelling their stories but goes on to enable the survivors to feel the pain and suffering of the trauma, to transform suffering into hope for wholeness. When offering pastoral care to survivors it becomes clear that apart from problems that need to be solved, survivors bring messages about the wider world in which they live. TIPC is founded on a hope that is grounded in the belief that positive change and recovery is desirable and possible. There are several factors that make TIPC effective as indicated below:

TIPC Honors Survivors Spiritual and Communal Resources

Trauma informed care honors a survivor's spiritual resources, especially those that enable a survivor to regain and maintain maximum health, well-being and a sense of wholeness. In keeping with the notion of *ubuntu*, TIPC is communal, accessing communal and transpersonal resources. TIPC is informed by the stage of recovery that the survivor is currently in. As asserted by Judith Herman, trauma recovery happens in stages namely; (1) the establishment of safety, (2) remembrance and mourning and (3) reconnection with ordinary life (1997, 133). She views these stages as critical to trauma recovery and failure to move through them continues the suffering. These stages of recovering are consistent with Jaekle's functions of pastoral care. Remembrance and mourning facilitate the healing and sustaining functions of pastoral care while the establishment of safety can be achieved through guidance. Reconnection with ordinary life is achieved through reconciliation and nurturing functions. This means a survivor could be at any stage of recovery and pastoral caregivers need to intentionally acknowledge and normalize the processes.

It is important to normalize because trauma brings about symptoms and reactions that are often devastating and terrifying and it is okay for survivors to experience uncomfortable sensations, painful memories and thoughts. By normalizing, caregivers acknowledge the distressful reactions or worry after exposure to trauma. This knowledge reduces the survivor's concerns that something might be "wrong" with them. It also provides them with assurance that they are not alone in how they are feeling. I assist them to understand that the various feelings and emotions are normal reactions. Normalization is connecting an individual to the whole (society), so that the traumatized person sees him or herself as less disconnected, or as an outlier.

In this worldview, community makes, creates or even produces the individual, who, in turn, depends on the corporate group (Mbiti 1969). Only in terms of others does the individual become conscious of one's own being, duties, privileges and responsibilities toward one's self. Connecting one becomes the beginning of normalizing, recovery and healing.

Dissociation as a Healthy Process Toward Wholeness

In TIPC, the pastoral caregiver journeys with the survivors in the construction of dissociation. Unlike some traditional therapeutic approaches that pathologize dissociation, in TIPC, dissociation is viewed as a protective response to "inescapable" realities (Van der Hart et al. 2004, 906–914). Dissociation is a way traumatized people sort painful and distressful memories in such a way that they can go on living and functioning. It is a way survivors will go about protecting themselves in response to the hurtful experiences and memories. In my experience with the cases mentioned in this chapter, dissociation was common and characterized by flashbacks, re-living and hyper-arousal. Survivors use performance arts and visuals as a way of compartmentalizing the painful experiences and controlling the symptoms. They can make use of rituals such as visiting sacred places in the community and leaving stones, identifying what healing they are seeking. This can include surrendering the painful memories and experiences and leaving them at these sacred places. It is accessing a real resource that addresses the need to compartmentalize the distressing material, in order to be present in the here and now. This is an intentional step of taking oneself out of the distress and moving on with life. Additionally, music can help or repeating a calming mantra to serve to ground them in the present. This means that through healthy dissociation, survivors compartmentalize elements of painful experiences and organize information in a way that propels them forward rather than being stuck. Survivors do not integrate the painful experiences into a unitary whole; instead, the distressful memories are stored in isolated fragments in a way that is growth-promoting.

These memories can be processed and remembered without a survivor losing his or her functioning though effective TIPC. The traumatic memories may still be there but will not be taking control of the life of the survivor. Through TIPC, the compartmentalization allows survivors to live with otherwise irreconcilable conflicts without experiencing any cognitive dissonance. In TIPC, scripture and prayer are used to offer hope and liberty, the dissociated material is submitted to God. Survivors are taught through grounding techniques to be compassionate with themselves and to live in the moment. Spiritual resources are used to transform maladaptive symptoms into adaptive capabilities and renew the survivors' reason to keep living.

When survivors find a place for their distressful feelings and memories, they experience life to its fullest and reclaim their sense of worthiness. When they surrender their pain and hurts to God, they experience release because they are essentially giving their burdens, worries and cares over to God. When Pasi felt helpless and out of control in the relationship, surrendering the pain to God enabled him to stop blaming himself. Instead of thinking that he belonged more to the dead than to the living, his hope for living was rekindled again. The sessions became his source of comfort and protection from the effects of the trauma. Developing a sense of connection with caring people and a caring God became the foundation of his healing. He felt he now had both internal and external resources to ward off the negative effects of gender violence and abuse. Having some place to surrender his painful memories enabled him to overcome the strong and potentially destructive reactions that he was going through. This is the intention of TIPC, which is summarized as including the following aspects:

1. The first aspect is that of breaking the stigma. Religious institutions and pastoral caregivers need to create awareness of what gender violence is. An unknown monster will remain dangerous and continue to cause destruction. When people are aware of gender-based violence, they can identify where it is present, and where intervention is needed. Pastors can ensure that they advocate for zero tolerance of gender-based violence in their sermons and Sunday school classes.

2. Religious institutions must be proactive and have their doors open for any survivors of gender violence. This means that churches need to have people trained in care ministry who can avail time to sit and accompany and offer sanctuary to survivors. Setting aside time to be with survivors helps them to regain a sense of worth. It is also important for churches to be aware of other local resources where survivors can be referred for more help.

3. The safety and protection of victims must be ensured. As indicated above, establishing a sense of safety is central to trauma recovery since trauma affects every aspect of human functioning. There is no healing and progress that can take place if safety and protection issues have not been adequately secured. Survivors' continued feelings of insecurity, out-of-control emotions and confused thinking stifles the healing process. Pastoral caregivers need to ask survivors what safety and protection means to them and discern how they might aid in achieving that.

4. Listening and showing understanding is a vital aspect. Validating the survivors' feelings facilitates healing. TIPC does not problematize the emotions, behaviors or thoughts that the survivor is having; instead, these are normalized and regulated in a positive manner. After talking about the violence, ensuring safety of the survivors and showing understanding, pastoral caregivers identify the needs of the survivors. As previously mentioned, survivors have varying needs basing on the severity and the chronicity of the violence. For example, some survivors maybe suicidal, some anxious, others abusing substances or isolating themselves.

5. TIPC is pastoral care that utilizes traditional healing practices such as visual and performing arts, prayers, music, visiting sacred places and dance.

6. Sustaining is also an important component of TIPC. Pastoral caregivers should ensure that support and ongoing care are available to the hurting person. This is not short-term interaction, but sustainable care. It is pastoral care that encourages resilience and rebuilding trust. Trauma recovery may involve the restoration of damaged relationships including broken relationships with God, self and with other people. Pastors' presence with individuals as they endeavor to reconcile can be important. Pastors can help survivors regain possession of themselves by repudiating those negative self-images imposed by the trauma (Herman 1997, 203). As the victim sheds off her victim identity, a new creature is recreated.

7. Another role of pastoral care is guiding survivors. Survivors need guidance in making wise and prudent choices and will gain confidence in taking their life back. All these are aimed at strengthening survivors so that they live life abundantly.

8. Practical support is necessary, for example, considering what actions should be taken to report to necessary authorities and/or if legal action is warranted.

9. Connectedness with family and community—church community leaders empower communities to establish alternative family support structures to provide an emotional safety net for people ostracized by relatives.

10. Another important aspect of TIPC is family group enrichment. Due to multifaceted challenges experienced by people, pastoral caregivers may establish youth, family, male and female groups to discuss and explore coping strategies. The focus of this approach is to address contemporary challenges experienced on the frontline of life.

11. Self-efficacy and empowerment: In the face of trauma, survivors need to know who they are and to believe in themselves and in their abilities and what they can achieve. The survivors need to feel whole and well. TIPC endeavors to assist survivors to develop a hope for a better future.

In conclusion, in this chapter I have explored pastoral care in the trauma of gender violence. As demonstrated by the cases of Makasa, Neti and Pasi, gender violence has a variety of effects on the victims. Survivors can be assisted to process their painful experiences using a combination of traditional healing practices, Christian practices and caregiving informed by the social sciences. This can be achieved through a long-term care approach, namely the TIPC. I have highlighted various aspects of the trauma informed pastoral care as an intervention to survivors of gender-based violence in a variety of forms, including the aftermath of political terror and children who have been removed from their homes and abused or forced into armed conflict or sex trafficking. I have demonstrated how trauma fractures one's self and impacts one physically, emotionally, psychologically and spiritually. I affirm the importance of communal and shared responsibility for each other, especially within the Church, when it comes to facilitating healing from gender-based violence. I have outlined the importance of *ubuntu*, a southern African philosophy which is significant in trauma informed pastoral care in its emphasis on togetherness in care work. I also indicated how trauma tears apart one's system of self-protection. I highlighted how the Church has an important role to play in assisting survivors to reclaim their sacred identity and help people move on with life. Indeed, TIPC honors survivors' physical, emotional, spiritual and communal resources and proposes that the Church exercises a role in preventing and resisting gender violence as well as caring for those who have experienced it.

REFERENCES

Cashwell, Craig S., and Scott Young. 2005. *Integrating Spirituality and Religion into Counseling: A Guide to Competent Practice*. American Counseling Association.

Clebsch, William, and Charles Jaekle, eds. 1994. *Pastoral Care in Historical Perspective*. Lanham, MD: Jason Aronson.

Herman, Judith. 1997. *Trauma and Recovery*. New York: Basic Books.

Keshgegian, Flora. 2000. *Redeeming Memories*. Nashville: Abingdon Press.

Lartey, E.Y.A. 1997. *Living Colour: An Inter-Cultural Approach to Pastoral Care and Counseling*. London: Cassell.

Machinga, Mazvita. 2011. Religion, Health, and Healing in the Traditional Shona Culture of Zimbabwe. *Journal of Practical Matters* 4: 1–8.

Magezi, Vhumani. 2016. Reflection on Pastoral Care in Africa: Towards Discerning Emerging Pragmatic Pastoral Ministerial Responses. *In die Skriflig*. http://journals.sfu.ca/rpfs/index.php/rpfs/article/viewFile/433/420.

Mbiti, John. 1969. *African Religions and Philosophy*. Ibadan: Heinemann Press.

Means, Jeffrey. 2000. *Trauma and Evil*. New York: Augsburg Fortress.

Motsi, R.G., and M.J. Masango. 2012. Redefining Trauma in an African Context: A Challenge to Pastoral Care. *HTS Teologiese Studies/Theological Studies* 68 (1): 1–8.

Muchuchuti, Ntombiyendaba. 2015. The Psychosocial Divers of Gender Based Violence in Matabeleland South: Zimbabwe. *Journal of Research & Method in Education* 5 (6): 14–22.

Ramose, Mogobe. 2002. *African Philosophy through Ubuntu*. Harare, Zimbabwe: Mond Books.

Sundberg, N., and C. Keutzer. 1994. Transpersonal Psychology I. In *Encyclopedia of Psychology*, ed. Raymond J. Corsini, vol. 3, 2nd ed., 547–548. New York: John Wiley & Sons.

The Zimbabwean. 2012. No to Gender-Based Violence, November 13. https://www.thezimbabwean.co/2012/11/no-to-gender-based-violence/.

United Nations Population Fund (UNFPA). 2015. State of the World's Population. New York.

Van der Hart, Onno, Ellert Nijenhuis, Kathy Steele, and Daniel Brown. 2004. Trauma Related Dissociation: Conceptual Clarity Lost and Found. *Australian and New Zealand Journal of Psychiatry* 38 (11–12): 906–914.

CHAPTER 11

Divine Fortitude: A Reflection on the Incarnation of the Black Female Child Soldier

Evelyn L. Parker

Darling, in NoViolet Bulawayo's novel *We Need New Names*, narrates her experiences of coming of age first among friends and adults in their shantytown in Zimbabwe and eventually in the United States of America. Darling is the embodiment of sassiness, curiosity, and courage as she navigates abject poverty and sociopolitical instability in her shantytown as a ten year old. Stealing guavas with her childhood friends to satisfy their hungry stomachs is a daily task when guavas are in season and almost any other food items in trees and along the streets of the nearby rich neighborhood of Budapest. They risk life and limb just to have something to eat. She is a critical thinker about the God that her grandmother, Mother of Bones, prays to on the Mountain (2013, 104). She is also critically aware of the religious leader, Prophet Revelations Bitchington Mborro, pastor of Mother of Bones's church who rapes the poor of their money and little girls of their virginity. He raped 11-year-old Chipo, Darling's friend

E. L. Parker (✉)
Southern Methodist University, Dallas, TX, USA
e-mail: eparker@mail.smu.edu

© The Author(s) 2019   163
S. Willhauck (ed.), *Female Child Soldiering, Gender Violence, and Feminist Theologies*, https://doi.org/10.1007/978-3-030-21982-6_11

(42–43). Darling, her family, and community have been displaced by the government from their homes and they ended up in the shantytown of Paradise where daily routine and rituals have changed. Darling no longer attends school each day bookended with morning and evening chores. Yet, Darling's young female frame is not daunted by her contextual realities because her divinity comes from the indwelling Spirit of God who empowers African female girls to be sassy, curious, and courageous. Thus, in this chapter I argue the *imago dei*, the image of God, of the female child soldier as the foundation for claims about the fortitude of girl soldiers and the hope that ecclesial leaders and public policymakers will work for the flourishing of former girl soldiers and all girls growing up in conflict areas of Africa.

Who are female child soldiers? While images of little boys come to mind when one mentions child soldiers, this image is a myth. Almost half of all children associated with armed groups in conflict regions of Africa are girls (Save the Children 2005, vi). They are usually abducted by armed groups and "used as active combatants, porters, cleaners, cooks and sexual possessions" (vi). Many girls, as young as eight years old, are raped and sexually abused and thus "injured or permanently disabled and spend the rest of their lives in pain" (vi). How can God dwell in the body of the black female child soldier and reveal to the world the essence of *imago dei*? While this is the central question for this chapter, my social location is the prelude for a response.

My Christian religious belief in the Trinity—a relational Godhead manifest as God known in creation and as the creator, God known in the flesh as Jesus Christ, and God among us as the Holy Spirit—as an African descended woman born and raised in the southern region of the United States informs my argument. I am also a Womanist practical theologian who interrogates theological and cultural theories in light of lived experiences of African descended girls as I look for life-giving practices for the flourishing of girls. A discussion of the *imago dei* and the incarnation of Christ as indicative of the incarnation of black women and girls is relevant to the lives of girl soldiers and serves as the theological starting point for this chapter.

THE BLACK FEMALE CHILD SOLDIER AS *IMAGO DEI*

All human beings, including girls and specifically African descended girls in conflict regions of Africa where there are female soldiers, are the *imago dei*, the image of God. Girl soldiers are created by God "as the essence of moral resistance, redemption, and revelation that is the image of God" (Turman 2013, 15). Their sassiness is resistance, their curiosity/smartness is redemptive, and their beautiful black bodies that are the temple of their goodness reveal who God is. The foundational claim that girl soldiers are *imago dei* is not based on qualitative data on the religious beliefs of girl soldiers who may be Christian, Muslim, African traditionalists, or any other form of religiosity. Rather, the argument that girl soldiers are *imago dei* is rooted in Mercy Amba Oduyoye's biblical and cultural hermeneutics, in her book *Introducing African Women's Theology* (2001, 11). In African worldview, argues Oduyoye, "we find God depicted not only as source of all life, but also, as its sustainer and the controller of human evolution" (45). All humans come from God, live in the material world in the presence of God, and will go back to God when they die. She describes this theocentric belief of African Religion in this manner:

> God occupies a side of the triangle of relations that describes the structure of African Religion. Humans, in the palpable dimension, and spirits, in the 'world in between,' are all derived from, linked to and accountable to God. In the dimension of the spirit are those related to the whole cosmos as of other principles experienced by humans. We also have in this dimension the spirits of humans who once shared our space as humans. The spirits, commonly designated 'ancestors,' continue to interact with us even as they continue to relate to God. It is believed that God sends them back to us as newborn babes. The theology, then, is one that proposes one divine source of all being. (45)

Thus, "the image of God is that of the unique source to which we are bound as humans and to whom we owe the responsibility" to be in relationship with all entities of the cosmos, both natural and supernatural (45). Oduyoye continues:

> That this is God's world, God's realm and sphere of influence has led to women's affirmation of equality before God and in the human community. Equal worth and joint responsibility are presented by women as deriving from God who makes us all human. (45)

African women affirm themselves and African girls as having equal worth to all people, especially men and boys, as derived from God, in the human community and the entire cosmos. African women and girls are the essence of goodness and dignity that is the image of God. The African female child soldier is the essence of equality and worth that is the *imago dei* embodied in their black flesh in the human community. Indeed, as new born baby girls, God uses them to bring our ancestors back into our midst, their responsibility to complete the circle of relationships between God, the ancestors/spirits, and human beings.

The movie *Daughters of the Dust*, written, directed and produced by Julie Dash, is set in 1902 to tell the story of three generations of Gullah women in the Peazant family as some of them prepare to move north to the mainland and away from their ancestral home of St. Helena Island off the cost of the Carolinas.[1] In *Daughters of the Dust*, we catch a glimpse of the role of the African descended baby girl in her mother's womb who enters the world as spirit to negotiate the spirits/ancestors' realm with the human world. The unborn baby girl, who is Eula and Eli Peazant's daughter, as spirit, negotiates the problem that her mother was raped by a white man that her father wants to destroy if only Eula will tell him who the rapist is. The spirit of the unborn baby girl, representing the Peazant ancestors, reminds the Gullah family of their history and important values as they prepare for their daughter's arrival, and as some family members decide to leave home. Julie Dash has the unborn baby girl entering the world as spirit on behalf of the ancestors rather than as a new born babe, which is a slight variation from African religious beliefs that the baby after birth negotiates communion between the ancestors and living Africans. Nevertheless, *Daughters of the Dust* illustrates the belief that the African female child plays a vital role in the circle of relationships between God, spirits/ancestors, and human beings. Thus, the female child soldier, through her role and worth in the circle of relationships, is the image of God as understood in African Religion.

A friend from South Africa told me, as he cuddled his infant granddaughter, that holding her was God's gift of heaven on earth. His declaration echoes what Oduyoye argues is the image of God in African religious beliefs. Indeed, an infant is a gift from God that parents and grandparents can hug and acknowledge as God's sacred gift that we can behold as touchable flesh—"God's tangible grace" (Parker 2009, 136). The same is true as the infant baby girl grows to be a preteen, teenager, and young woman. She is a sacred gift from God that is developing emotionally, physically, intellectually, and spiritually. In her unfolding into a unique sacred

---

[1] See https://www.imdb.com/title/tt0104057/ and https://en.wikipedia.org/wiki/Daughters_of_the_Dust, 1/19/2019).

self, we also acknowledge her vulnerable self as a gendered body that is too often rendered invisible, silenced, objectified, and abused.

The idea of the girl soldier as *imago dei* is also supported by Eboni Marshall Turman's theory of a Womanist ethic of incarnation in her book *Toward A Womanist Ethic of Incarnation: Black Bodies, The Black Church and the Council of Chalcedon*. She posits that what happens to the bodies of black women [and girls] reveals something about how black women [and girls] are as the image of God (2013, 7). Turman argues the theory of a Womanist ethic of incarnation as a mediating ethic to address all forms of injustice in the intracommunal space of the black church (5).

In her detailed discussion of the doctrine of the incarnation in Chapter one, "The Politics of Incarnation: A Theological Perspective," Turman lays the foundation for the identity of Christ as human, divine, and the "hypostatic union of the human and divine natures in the Divine Person of Jesus Christ" (2013, 36). The ecumenical Council of Chalcedon struggled with the "mystery of God enfleshed" and resulted in a statement of faith that affirms the paradox of the body of Christ (37). The doctrine of the incarnation becomes the entry point for Turman's thesis. She argues the Christological unity of the enfleshment of God, *en sarki*,—precedes the experiences of Jesus the human—*kata sarka*. She writes:

> The guiding premise of an *en sarki* confession of Jesus Christ is [an] inexplicable paradox. In other words, it privileges the promise of God that is made manifest in the body of Christ and yet is not subject to the flesh. An *en sarki* perspective therefore concedes that, although inconceivable, the promise of God is not circumscribed by the apparent irreconcilability of human categories. (43)

Turman goes on to argue that an "in the flesh" perspective actually contravenes arguments about what happens to the flesh and makes way "for the potential of what is active in the flesh (*en sarki*) to transpire in the world against normative hegemony" (43). She writes:

> ...what happens in the flesh to Jesus by the work of God precedes what happens to Jesus's flesh in history and what will happen in its future. ... The logic of incarnation asserts that the 'in the flesh' precedes and must be held in tension with the 'according to the flesh' so that future vindication might come to pass. (45)

The incarnation suggests that God is in us *en sarki dei* rather than God with us as Emanu-el (48). With this position, Turman signals her primary thesis about black church women discussed in Chapter five, "Beyond the Veil: Toward a Womanist Ethic of Incarnation." To confront and dismantle the injustice that black women experience in the intracommunal space of African American congregations that are shaped by a white supremacist ideology, a Womanist ethic of incarnation posits the negotiation of *en sarki* or "in the flesh" and *karta sarka* "of the flesh" of black women with their "in the flesh" nature as a priori. She argues the radical subjectivity of black women as agents who have the capacity to seek their own vindication in the face of a white supremacist society and the material evidence of its violence.

This chapter advances *en sarki* or "in the flesh" and the divine activity of God in the flesh of black girl soldiers regardless of their gender and poverty. Just as Turman argues on behalf of black church women, the divine activity in the flesh of black girl soldiers has precedence over the sociohistorical, socioeconomic, and sociocultural contexts that bring black girl soldiers pain and suffering. Black girl soldiers are sacred, *en sarki,* the incarnation of God known in Jesus Christ from infancy to adulthood. Yet, the black girl is vulnerable, *karta sarka,* to patriarchy, sexism, rape, and all other forms of dehumanization. However, their vulnerability to dehumanization and heightened potential for death does not supersede their divinity evident by the incarnate presence of God in their flesh. This chapter also advances the notion of the image of God from African Religion that affirms the important role of African girl babies in the circle of relationships among God, ancestors, and human kind. African Religion thus notes the worth of female child soldiers from birth.

The female child soldier as *imago dei* is also understood as the indwelling of the Holy Spirit in girl soldiers. God is at work in the world as the Holy Spirit. The physician Luke writes in the book of Acts 1: 8 "…you will receive power when the Holy Spirit has come upon you." The Holy Spirit gives power by dwelling within the girl soldier (see John 14:17b) when she co-partners with God through the power of the Spirit to transform unjust situations.

Girl soldiers are from a variety of religious backgrounds that include traditional African Religions, Islam, and Christianity. The above Trinitarian argument about the sacredness of girl soldiers does not suggest all girl soldiers hold a Christian perspective. However, the Trinitarian argument of *imago dei* is a starting point for positing the sacredness, divinity, and worth of girl soldiers. Perhaps there are comparable doctrines in other religions, but this chapter does not explore such doctrines. To be clear, the Trinitarian position of the incarnation of female child soldiers as equal, worthy, sacred, and divine creations of God is the entry point for discussion about their courage before, during, and after servitude as a soldier. What are the contours of courage that God empowers in female child soldiers?

COURAGE TO BE AN AFRICAN GIRL

Darling, the protagonist and narrator in *We Need New Names*, illustrates characteristics of a little African girl created in the image of God. Darling reveals sass, curiosity/smartness, and courage. The qualities of sassiness and being smart, I would argue, are essential for courage. These are characteristics that psychologists and sociologists argue are essential for resiliency of low-income urban adolescent girls confronted with contextual poverty and sexism (Stevens 2002, vii). Sass/sassiness among African descended girls has been misunderstood and misinterpreted as a negative characteristic for a black girl. However, this is an asset for survival and negotiating the terrain of sexism and patriarchy. The attribute of being sassy/sassiness is defined as:

> Willful forthrightness in demeanor that expresses a spirited behavioral expressive style of boldness, independence, and courage, which black adolescent girls learn to deal with everyday hassles. Sassiness can become a form of healthy social resistance that embodies the moral integrity needed to deal with daily confrontations of social and racial inequalities and indignities. During adolescence sassy behavior often emerges as an expressive function of identity exploration. (2002, 189)

When African American girls give a verbal response to racial stereotypes and social devaluation they are categorized as being sassy. Yet, sassiness is a form of resistance that defies the expectation that a black girl will "accommodate their own social devaluation" (2002, 86).

We can infer that sassiness among African girls is like girls in Sierra Leone who emulate the behavior of women's secret societies. In the village of Kamadugu Sokorala the women's society, Segere, commands respect so much so that when they enter a public space "all men, children, and uncircumcised women have to flee indoors, for to be caught by the Segere can entail various sorts of gruesome punishments" (Coulter 2009, 60).

The Segere admonished a husband who had beaten one of their members that he should never again beat her because he would receive a huge hernia on his scrotum if he continued (60). For Sierra Leonean women to demonstrate such willfulness and boldness they must possess the spirit of sassiness cultivated during childhood. In a patriarchal society governed by Muslim and Christian practices about the role of women and girls, the Segere is an important secret society for a Sierra Leonean girl to aspire. While we must note the importance of collective boldness and courage the Segere demonstrated (rather than an individual acting in this way), it suggests the power of collective sassiness that a group of girls can show when they face denigration and dehumanization of their collective personhood. Collective sassiness is more powerful than individual sassiness. Sassiness is an essential ingredient of courage among female child soldiers.

Girls in Kenya are described as *mkakamavu*, a Swahili word that means a girl is not afraid to speak up for herself when mistreated because she knows who she is (unpublished interview with Sketer Makena Riungu, January 25, 2019). Recalling a little girl she once knew who practiced *mkakamavu*, Riungu stated:

> Lacy (a pseudonym) was ten years old when her father married another woman after Lacy's mother passed away. Lacy's stepmother was abusive making her milk ten cows every morning and combine the milk in large containers to deliver to the dairy before going to school. Lacy would always respectfully say, 'Mama, regardless of what you do to me today tomorrow my life will be better. Mama, what you are doing to me is not right.'

Ordinarily, children do not talk back to adults out of respect because adults are their elders, not their peers. However, Lacy persevered, in spite of the abuse she received from her stepmother, and verbally contested the abuse without raising her voice or using foul words. The women of the village, aware of the abuse Lacy received, supported and encouraged her (Riungu, unpublished interview, January 25, 2019). Lacy's acts of *mkakamavu* are synonymous with sassiness, an important component of courage.

Smartness is another essential ingredient of courage among female child soldiers. A critically aware—smart—"black adolescent girl will not collude in their own racial denigration" (Stevens 2002, 86). Smart in African American culture suggests an individual is highly intelligent or "possessing highly developed intellectual capacities" (189). Smart girls are not only intellectually astute they also have the capacity to interpret implicit situations that devalue, dehumanize, and denigrate them. Smart girls are self-aware, and develop self-efficacy and social competence (82). There are theories about the development of smart and sassy identities among North American urban black female adolescents to resist racist definitions of their selfhood (Stevens 2002, 61). Such theories are context specific, yet some parallels can be inferred about East African black female adolescents like Lacy. Attention is given to the theory about the role of the family, more specifically the mother-daughter relationship, plays in developing resistance to racist definitions of black girls. The family is "the primary socialization unit for cultural adaptation" (70). Whether for good or ill social identity development is based on intersubjectivity within the family unit. While adolescents are exposed to other socializing forces outside the family such as peers, school, and church, the family unit is still the primary socializing unit.

> In psychodynamic theory, the significance of parenthood carries enormous weight. The nuclear family is essential to the theory's fundamental postulates of epigenetic psychosexual maturation, in which it is proposed that developmental pathologies are due to failed parental nurturance. New thinking suggests that the family is an ecological unit—a collectivity of kin engaged in transactional processes to ensure its own survival. The family represents a systemic process with its inherent rules, values, and norms. (72)

The family provides the black adolescent girl the connection to other contexts within the ecological system external to the family that include church and school. The family "life course is characterized by the praxes of daily living reflected in the specific cultural norms, roles, and transactional patterns that families use over time to ensure generational survival" (72). This phenomenon, called kinscript, is one of three multigenerational familial praxes. Through kinscripts, the family inculcates skills for survival as well as a sense of worth and self-esteem (73). Families may also expose their children to religious institutions within their nested ecology. Churches are described here as a possible sanctuary from the violence of racism. "Thus, black adolescents who seek safe and suitable locations for identity exploration embrace social institutions that provide solace and communal self-relatedness" (74).

The mother-daughter relationship enhances values and beliefs of the family for the black female adolescent. "The mother models the female identity that the daughter emulates" (Stevens 2002, 75). Early aged adolescent girls and their mothers experience normative contentious relationships because of the mother's need to protect her daughters from dangers in the streets and overt forms of racism and oppression. Daughters push back at their mother's authority and need to protect by talking back or acting *womanish*—a black folk expression popularized by Alice Walker when a mother tells her daughter you are acting like a grown-up woman, older than you are, outrageous, audacious, courageous, or willful (277). The contentious behavior and discord between early adolescent girls and their mothers subsides during middle and late adolescence (79). With maturity, black girls become more attached to their mothers. They emerge as two women bonded in sisterhood (81). The smart and sassy identity— a free-spoken, independent, and spirited behavioral style—is solidified and affirmed by the mother as necessary for resistance and resiliency to racism.

The theory of the mother-daughter relationship is problematic for both North American African American girls and African girls if they don't have mothers or a significant female who acts as mother. Lacy, the Kenyan ten year old is an example. However, Lacy has good relationships with adult women in her village who affirmed her and inculcated values and beliefs that reinforced her self-efficacy and resilience. Her smartness/sassiness was fortified by her relationship with proxy mothers in the village and family outside of her home. Sassiness and smartness in a girl yields courage, a necessary virtue of African descended girls for survival of all forms of oppression. Girl soldiers are especially in need of courage for survival of their horrific situation.

Courage is the spirit of unwavering resolve to stand firm in the midst of violence and danger regardless of the personal toll or cost. Describing a characteristic of moral agency, Katie Geneva Cannon, qualifies courage as unshouted and defines it in this manner:

> [It] is the quality of steadfastness, akin to fortitude, in the face of formidable oppression. The communal attitude is far more than 'grin and bear it.' Rather, it involves the ability to 'hold on to life' against major oppositions. It is the incentive to facilitate change, to chip away the oppressive structures, bit by bit, to celebrate and rename their experiences in empowering ways. 'Unshouted courage' as a virtue is the often unacknowledged inner conviction that keeps one's appetite whet for freedom. The ethical speculation is that courage is the staying power of the Black community wherein individuals act, affirming their humanity, in spite of continued fear of institutionalized aggression. (1988, 144)

While unshouted courage seems to derive from its prominence in the black community, black women bear the historical markings of oppression of the African American community (Cannon 1988, 145–146). They have endured rape as described above in the movie *Daughters of the Dust* and they have made countless sacrifices for the safety and survival of their families, both biological and fictive. Citing Paul Tillich, Cannon states, "courage is an ethical act when humans affirm their own being in spite of those elements in their existence which conflict with their essential self-affirmation" (147). She concludes that unshouted courage can only be lived out in community (151).

Cannon argues that unshouted courage is akin to fortitude and that the urgency of the realities of African Americans require them to develop the virtue of courage, "the ingrown capacity for meeting difficulties with fortitude and resilience" (1988, 145). I argue that Cannon's description of unshouted courage can be captured in the term fortitude, defining it in this manner:

> Fortitude is the intellectual and spiritual strength to persevere even in the midst of seemingly insurmountable odds. It requires courage, patience, and perseverance. Fortitude is 'mental and emotional strength in facing difficulty, adversity, danger, or temptation courageously.' When systemic societal practices veil possibilities for living a wholesome life, women with fortitude press relentlessly toward possibilities for a wholesome life. With unwavering determination and courage, black women with fortitude 'make a way out of no way'. (Parker 2017, 53)

While the virtue of unshouted courage speaks more about the persistent spirit of the African American community to press toward freedom in an oppressive society, fortitude argues the same case for the individual black woman. The object of the aim for unshouted courage and fortitude is both communal and individual; one does not exemplify fortitude without it being for others.

Jesus, the incarnate Christ, revealed the fortitude of God. As a 12-year-old teen his curiosity and *womanish* desire to know more urged him to stay behind in Jerusalem after the Festival of the Passover without the permission of his parents. They assumed he was in the group of travelers. After traveling a full day, they started to look for him among their friends and relatives. After not finding Jesus, they returned to Jerusalem to search for their son. "After three days they found him in the temple, sitting among the teachers, listening to them and asking them questions" (Luke 2:46). All the folks in the temple who heard him were amazed at how smart Jesus was. When his parents saw him they were flabbergasted, and his mother asked him about his actions and expressed how anxious they were to discover he was not among friends and relatives as they sojourned back home to Nazareth. Jesus replied, "Why were you searching for me? Did you not know that I must be in my Father's house?" (Luke 2:49). They didn't understand him. Nevertheless, Jesus returned home with his parents to Nazareth and was obedient to them. Jesus "increased in wisdom and in years and in divine and human favor" (Luke 2:52). These attributes are important for the gift of fortitude.

The body of Jesus held the essence of justice for the marginalized that is the image of God. Acts of justice for the poor, for women, the sick and those incarcerated are indicative of Jesus's ministry that unfolded in his young adult years. Officially announcing his ministry in his hometown, we find Jesus again in the synagogue on the Sabbath day, as was his practice. He unrolled the long scroll to find a certain scripture of the prophet Isaiah for his announcement.

> The Spirit of the Lord is upon me, because he has anointed me to bring good news to the poor. He has sent me to proclaim release to the captives and recovery of sight to the blind, to let the oppressed go free, to proclaim the year of the Lord's favor. (Luke 4:18–19)

After reading the scripture, he rolled up the scroll and handed it back to the attendant and sat down. The gaze of all the people in the synagogue was on him. At that moment he said "Today this scripture has been fulfilled in your hearing" (Luke 4:21). Jesus continued speaking words of wisdom and keen understanding to those assembled. Upon being asked to perform miracles there as they had heard he did in Capernaum he said, "Truly I tell you, no prophet is accepted in the prophet's hometown" (Luke 4:24). Even though they were amazed at the things he said at first, their attitude toward him began to shift until they were filled with rage. They got up and forced him to the edge of town and would have hurled him over a cliff, but he miraculously walked thought the crowd and left his hometown.

Jesus, the incarnate Christ, revealed the essence of the image of God through knowledge and wisdom and a proclivity for the poor, the downtrodden, the widow, the orphan, the sick, and all marginalized people to receive justice. The ultimate expression of love, the sacrifice of his life for the redemption of an unjust world is the defining event of divine fortitude. The totality of the ministry of Jesus reveals fortitude that is the incarnation of the image of God.

Likewise, female child soldiers embody fortitude that is the incarnation of the image of God. The story of abduction, captivity, and release of five teenaged girls in Eastern Democratic Republic of the Congo, told by a pastor working with former child soldiers, illustrates the notion of fortitude described above. Their names, for the sake of confidentiality, are Mary, Elizabeth, Martha, Joanna, and Susanna. All five girls were abducted in conflict regions of Eastern DRC on different occasions while they were going to or coming from school or doing their daily chores. The girls' ages at the time of abduction were 14 and 15 years old. The girls were carried into the bush and were gang raped by their abductors daily as they were held hostage. The five girls bonded and strategized ways they would survive their horrific state. As time went on, they found favor and trust from their abductors. They were given freedom to perform duties for the benefit and support of their abductors that included service as cooks and porters. Mary, Elizabeth, Martha, Joanna, and Susanna eventually learned combat skills and joined the militia in the raiding and pillaging of villages. The girls, over a period of about five years, garnered the trust of the militia leaders and received certain freedoms that allowed them to move about without the gaze of their abductors. The girls plotted a brilliant escape plan and all five fled from their captivity and traveled to western DRC. They found refuge with a religious NGO that helped them rehabilitate and settle into new lives. Mary is currently a leader in the religious NGO securing the release of girls captured by armed groups and supporting their reintegration back to their communities. Elizabeth, Martha, Joanna, and Susanna are all thriving upon reintegration into various communities with jobs and communities that support them. Elizabeth moved to Australia and Joanna to France and both have jobs, husbands, and children. These five young women are the embodiment of fortitude that is the very essence of the incarnation of the *imago dei*. How then might religious leaders and policymakers worldwide address the inhuman problem that creates female child soldiers?

HOPE FOR THE FEMALE CHILD SOLDIER

Affirmation of the incarnation of the image of God in the bodies of female child soldiers must include public and ecclesial policy that recognizes, honors, and protects their human and divine bodies. There have been substantial achievements by the United Nations and the global community to end the practice of using children as soldiers, specifically girls who are forced to become bush wives, sex slaves, spies, cooks, and porters. In 2002, "a treaty to ban the recruitment and use of children in armed conflict" took effect (Zerrougui and Wallström 2019). Members of the United Nations have reached an agreement that children under the age of 18 should never be recruited and used in armed conflict. In 2016, the UN Secretary General identified national military forces using children in armed conflict and is working with those countries to end the practice.

Despite the progress to end the use of child soldiers in conflict regions around the globe there are ten countries that continue to use child soldiers, five of which are Central African Republic, Democratic Republic of the Congo, Nigeria, Somalia, and South Sudan (Briggs 2017). The primary solution to end the use of children as soldiers in conflict regions is to resolve the conflict and sustain peace. Also, strong monitoring by the UN Security Council working group on Children and Armed Conflict has an essential role of informing the UN Security Council about the status of children in conflict regions. However, there is need for an intersectional approach for leveraging conflict and seeking peace in countries that exploit children, specifically girls during conflict.

An intersectional approach gives attention to categories that promote conflict in African countries that include economic, political, and military sectors. Systematic poverty among the masses is an aspect of the problem, even though there are enormous natural resources that could be managed to provide free or affordable education, healthcare, and housing for citizens in African conflict countries. Key to dismantling economic, political, and military oppression in African conflict countries is divestment of European and western interests, of what bell hooks calls an "imperialist, white supremacist, capitalist, patriarchy" (2013, 28). Religious institutions on the world stage, including the World Council of Churches, have the power and capacity to pressure governments that perpetuate conflict in African countries. Religious organizations/institutions as a collective must pool their political and economic power and influence to transform evils in the world, which include the horrific practices associated with female child soldiers. Interreligious dialogues sponsored by the World Council of Churches must engage problems of conflict in Africa and around the globe that are perpetuated by imperialism and economic exploitation of the natural resources on the African Continent. Governments that profit from neo-colonial economic and political practices in Africa have yet to feel the powerful hand of God that demands justice for all God's creation, the least of whom are little black girls. An intersectional approach interrogates factors that include economic, political, and military categories that promote conflict in African countries and addresses these factors through the interfaith community.

An intersectional approach also considers gender, race, religions, sociocultural, and socioeconomic aspects of the problem of female child soldiers. The global problem of patriarchy and sexism as well as race and gender compounded by the pure disregard of the human and divine embodiment of African descended women and girls is the crux of the problem. I posit that religious institutions—churches, synagogues, mosques—are better positioned to address the systemic global problem of an "imperialist, white supremacist, capitalist, patriarchy" (hooks 2013, 28) global society that causes the use of female child soldiers. Gender-related dimensions of internalized racism, sexism, and patriarchy are the root causes for violence against women and girls in conflict regions of Africa (Zerrougui and Wallström 2019). If religious communities would critically assess and live out their theology of *imago dei* and recognize that women and girls embody the goodness of God that is the image of God equally as men and boys, then abhorrent practices related to child soldiering will cease to exist. Here again an interreligious dialogue approach is key to engaging in discourse about human and divine qualities embodied in women and girls. Extensive research on multi-religious beliefs about the theological anthropology of women and girls is necessary for productive interreligious dialogue. Also, research about sites where interreligious dialogue about women and girls is already taking place is important but beyond the scope of this chapter. To be clear, interreligious dialogues are essential for addressing systemic problems related to female child soldiers.

This chapter has focused on the problem of female child soldiers in conflict regions primarily in Eastern Africa. The central argument is female child soldiers are the incarnation of fortitude that is the essence of the *imago dei*. This theological anthropological position is foundational for policy making by public and religious institutions in contexts of power and influence globally.

References

Briggs, Billy. 2017. 10 Countries Where Child Soldiers Are Still Recruited in Armed Conflicts. *Theirworld*, February 28. https://theirworld.org/news/10-countries-where-child-soldiers-are-still-recruited-in-armed-conflicts.

Bulawayo, NoViolet. 2013. *We Need New Names*. New York: Reagan Arthur Brooks/Little Brown and Company.

Cannon, Kate G. 1988. *Black Womanist Ethics*. Atlanta: Scholars Press.

Coulter, Chris. 2009. *Bush Wives and Girl Soldiers: Women's Lives Through War and Peace in Sierra Leone*. Ithaca, NY: Cornell University Press.

hooks, bell. 2013. *Writing Beyond Race: Living Theory and Practice*. New York: Routledge Press.

Oduyoye, Mercy Amba. 2001. *Introducing African Women's Theology*. Cleveland: The Pilgrim Press.

Parker, Evelyn L. 2009. Honoring the Body. In *On Our Way: Christian Practices for Living a Whole Life*, ed. Dorothy Bass and Susan Briehl, 133–148. Nashville: Upper Room Books.

———. 2017. *Between Sisters: Emancipatory Hope Out of Tragic Relationships*. Eugene, OR: Cascade Books.

Save the Children. 2005. Forgotten Casualties of War: Girls in Conflict. https://resourcecentre.savethechildren.net/node/2717/pdf/2717.pdf.

Stevens, Joyce West. 2002. *Smart and Sassy: The Strengths of Inner-City Black Girls*. New York: Oxford University.

Turman, Eboni Marshall. 2013. *Toward a Womanist Ethic of Incarnation: Black Bodies, the Black Church, and the Council of Chalcedon*. New York: Palgrave Macmillan.

Wikipedia, s.v. 2018. Daughters of the Dust. 9:51. https://en.wikipedia.org/wiki/Daughters_of_the_Dust. Accessed 21 October.

Zerrougui, Leila, and Margot Wallström. 2019. *Ending the Use of Child Soldiers*. Swedish Ministry of Foreign Affairs, February 1. http://swemfa.se/2017/02/12/ending-the-use-of-child-soldiers/.

Appendix

Selected Organizations

Amnesty International
https://www.amnestyusa.org/about-us/

The Borgen Project
https://borgenproject.org/about-us/

CARE: Stop Violence Against Women
https://www.care.org/work/womens-empowerment/gender-based-violence

Child Soldiers International
https://www.child-soldiers.org/

Cultures of Resistance Network
https://culturesofresistance.org/end-child-soldiers

Faith Trust Institute
https://www.faithtrustinstitute.org/

Futures Without Violence
https://www.futureswithoutviolence.org/

Global Network of Religions for Children
https://gnrc.net/en/

© The Author(s) 2019   179
S. Willhauck (ed.), *Female Child Soldiering, Gender Violence, and Feminist Theologies*, https://doi.org/10.1007/978-3-030-21982-6

Human Rights Watch
https://www.hrw.org/topic/childrens-rights/child-soldiers

Interagency Gender Working Group
https://www.igwg.org/about-igwg/

Interfaith Coalition Against Domestic and Sexual Violence
https://interfaithagainstdv.org/

Isis: Women's International Cross-Cultural Exchange (Isis: WICCE)
http://isis.or.ug/

National Organization for Women
https://now.org/issues/stopping-violence-against-women/

Polaris Project (Human Trafficking Initiative)
https://polarisproject.org/

Roméo Dallaire Child Soldiers Initiative
https://www.childsoldiers.org/

Save the Children
https://www.savethechildren.org/

Thursdays in Black Campaign: World Council of Churches
https://www.oikoumene.org/en/get-involved/thursdays-in-black

Transforming Masculinities: A Faith-Based Approach to GBV Prevention
https://www.igwg.org/wp-content/uploads/2017/10/TM-for-IGWG-Panel-Sep-2017-PRABU-2.pdf

United Nations Special Representative of the Secretary-General for Children and Armed Conflict
https://childrenandarmedconflict.un.org/children-not-soldiers/

Violence Prevention Alliance (World Health Organization)
https://www.who.int/violenceprevention/en/

War Child
https://www.warchildholland.org/news

3Strands Global: Human Trafficking Prevention
https://www.3strandsglobalfoundation.org/

Index[1]

[1] Note: Page numbers followed by 'n' refer to notes.

© The Author(s) 2019
S. Willhauck (ed.), *Female Child Soldiering, Gender Violence, and Feminist Theologies*, https://doi.org/10.1007/978-3-030-21982-6

Printed by Printforce, the Netherlands